CW00505583

Brecht in Practice

Methuen Drama Engage offers original reflections about key practitioners, movements and genres in the fields of modern theatre and performance. Each volume in the series seeks to challenge mainstream critical thought through original and interdisciplinary perspectives on the body of work under examination. By questioning existing critical paradigms, it is hoped that each volume will open up fresh approaches and suggest avenues for further exploration.

Series Editors
Mark Taylor-Batty
Senior Lecturer in Theatre Studies, Workshop Theatre, University of Leeds, UK

Enoch Brater
Kenneth T. Rowe Collegiate Professor of Dramatic Literature &
Professor of English and Theater University of Michigan, USA

In the same series
*Postdramatic Theatre and the Political: International Perspectives
on Contemporary Performance*
edited by Jerome Carroll, Karen Juers-Munby and Steve Giles
ISBN 978 1 408 18486 8

Theatre in the Expanded Field: Seven Approaches to Performance
Alan Read
ISBN 978 1 408 18495 0

Howard Barker's Theatre: Wrestling with Catastrophe
edited by James Reynolds and Andrew Smith
ISBN 978 1 408 18439 4

Ibsen in Practice: Relational Readings of Performance, Cultural Encounters and Power
Frode Helland
ISBN 978 1 472 51369 4

*Rethinking the Theatre of the Absurd: Ecology, the Environment
and the Greening of the Modern Stage*
edited by Carl Lavery and Clare Finburgh
ISBN 978 1 472 59571 3

Related titles
Bertolt Brecht: A Literary Life
Stephen Parker
ISBN 978 1 408 15562 2

Brecht on Art and Politics
edited by Tom Kuhn and Steve Giles
ISBN 978 0 413 77353 1

Brecht on Film and Radio
edited by Marc Silberman
ISBN 978 0 413 72760 2

Brecht on Performance: Messingkauf and Modelbooks
edited by Tom Kuhn, Steve Giles and Marc Silberman
ISBN 978 1 408 1545 5

Brecht on Theatre
edited by Marc Silberman, Steve Giles and Tom Kuhn
ISBN 978 1 408 14545 6

Brecht in Practice: Theatre, Theory and Performance

David Barnett

Series Editors
Enoch Brater and Mark Taylor-Batty

B L O O M S B U R Y
LONDON · NEW DELHI · NEW YORK · SYDNEY

Bloomsbury Methuen Drama

An imprint of Bloomsbury Publishing Plc

50 Bedford Square
London
WC1B 3DP
UK

1385 Broadway
New York
NY 10018
USA

www.bloomsbury.com

Bloomsbury is a registered trade mark of Bloomsbury Publishing Plc

First published 2015

© David Barnett, 2015

David Barnett has asserted his right under the Copyright, Designs and
Patents Act, 1988, to be identified as author of this work.

All rights reserved. No part of this publication may be reproduced or transmitted
in any form or by any means, electronic or mechanical, including photocopying,
recording, or any information storage or retrieval system, without prior
permission in writing from the publishers.

No responsibility for loss caused to any individual or organization acting on
or refraining from action as a result of the material in this publication can be
accepted by Bloomsbury or the author.

British Library Cataloguing-in-Publication Data
A catalogue record for this book is available from the British Library.

ISBN: HB: 978-1-4081-8366-3
PB: 978-1-4081-8503-2
ePDF: 978-1-4081-8438-7
ePub: 978-1-4081-8602-2

Library of Congress Cataloging-in-Publication Data
Barnett, David, 1968- author.
Brecht in practice : theatre, theory and performance / David Barnett.
pages cm
Summary: "A re-examination of Bertolt Brecht the theatre practitioner in the light
of his theoretical writings and his work in the theatre"– Provided by publisher.
Includes bibliographical references and index.
ISBN 978-1-4081-8503-2 (paperback) – ISBN 978-1-4081-8366-3 (hardback)
1. Brecht, Bertolt, 1898-1956–Criticism and interpretation. I. Title.
PT2603.R397Z55776 2015
832'.912–dc23
2014014152

Typeset by Integra Software Services Pvt. Ltd.
Printed and bound in India

Contents

Acknowledgements

The majority of the research carried out for this book was undertaken while I was in Berlin, supported by a British Academy Research Development Award, and I am most grateful to the British Academy for its generous funding. I also thank Dr Geoff Westgate for his immeasurable time and patience in reading all the chapters, often several times. His observations and suggestions have made a real difference. Thanks also to Tom Kuhn and Steve Giles for providing me with pre-publication manuscripts of the new edition of *Brecht on Theatre* and of *Brecht on Performance*: the new translations now feature in this study. Mark Taylor-Batty has proved a trusty editor, and I have enjoyed working with Mark Dudgeon and Emily Hockley at Bloomsbury.

Introduction

(Re)Introducing Brecht

Bertolt Brecht (1898–1956) is something of a rarity in the field of theatre studies: not only did he gain an international reputation as a playwright, he also developed new ways of understanding theatre and new ways of making theatre as a director. This book focuses on his work as a theorist and practitioner of theatre and aims to introduce students, practitioners and those interested in theatre in general to the principles and nuances of Brecht's thought and its implications for the practice of making theatre.

For all Brecht's familiarity, he still remains remarkably misunderstood. The adjective taken from his name, 'Brechtian', often appears in books and newspaper reviews, but tends to be used to pick out features of a play or production that are more generic than specific. In the following quotations, 'Brechtian' merely means revealing that spectators are made conscious of the fact that they are in a theatre:

> Ramin Gray's Brechtian flourishes – getting members of the choir to read lines from a script down a microphone – might be an alienation too far.[1]
> In a Brechtian coup de théâtre, the director Richard Jones and designer Miriam Buether turn the lights on the audience, casting us as the town's burghers at a rancorous public meeting.[2]

While such features are certainly found in Brecht's theoretical and practical work, theatre history itself is littered with direct address to the audience and acknowledgement of the 'reality' of the theatre, from the Greeks, via the medieval, renaissance and restoration stages, to the anti-illusionist experiments of the last century. Instead of pioneering such effects, it is perhaps more sensible to locate

Brecht in this tradition. However, what is worth noting is that his purposes for exposing the reality of the theatre go unspoken in such references.

Michael Patterson observes a more commercial use of 'Brechtian' and asks, 'can one claim that Brecht's legacy is anything more than a matter of employing a more or less fashionable label to enhance theatre work ranging from performance art to agitprop?'[3] Whether Brecht is indeed 'fashionable' any more is raised by Michael Billington, writing fifteen years after Patterson's essay. Billington contended in 2009 that, in some circles, ' "Brechtian" these days has come to mean "slow, ponderous, didactic". '[4]

Yet while Brecht may be 'misunderstood' on paper, it is in the theatre itself where the most significant problems lie. In her study of Brecht in Britain, Margaret Eddershaw observes that by the 1970s 'Brecht has been appropriated. But the problem with appropriation [...] is that its very purpose is to pull sharp teeth and nullify political bite.'[5] As I will show, especially in Chapters 4, 5 and 6, Brecht's approaches to stagecraft require effort and focus if they are to be effective. Yet in a predominantly commercial theatre system, like that in the UK, where rehearsal periods average four weeks, the time required to interrogate plays and their performance through Brecht's method is difficult to secure. As a result, productions of Brecht's plays often resemble those undertaken in the West Germany of the 1950s and 1960s, as discussed by John Rouse: 'nearly all stylistic elements of Brecht's theatre were adopted [...]', yet 'the [...] theatre neatly separated Brecht's means from his ends'.[6] That is, theatres can use techniques they understand to be 'Brechtian' without necessarily understanding where they come from or why they are being used.

This brief survey reveals that the term 'Brechtian', more often than not, can provide a misleading shorthand for ideas that are both specific and, as will be shown, complex. More importantly, in the examples given above, there is no mention of politics, despite the fact that

Brecht's theories and practices continually grapple with questions of representing the political on stage. If the Brechtian method is to have any meaning, it has to be understood as enabling a radical insight into the way society and its citizens work with a view to changing both of them. This may sound like the 'didacticism' Billington notes above, yet, as Chapter 1 will make clear, Brecht was not trying to teach lessons as such, but rather a new way of viewing the world and its workings. By pointing to instability and impermanence, Brecht wanted to show that the world *could* be changed. As such, Brecht's is a fundamentally political theatre because it asks audiences not to accept the status quo, but to appreciate that oppressive structures can be changed if the will for that exists.

It is worth examining the possible reasons why politics is so frequently lacking from references to the 'Brechtian':

- Brecht was a Marxist, and Marxism, in the wake of the collapse of communism in Eastern Europe in the early 1990s, has in turn been disparaged and dismissed as an unworkable and unrealizably utopian set of ideas. If 'Brechtian' has become a synonym for 'Marxist', then such an association may anchor Brecht in a discredited politics that many believe to have become superfluous or redundant. (Conversely, a successful Brechtian production may well help to redeem Marxism's tenets, for some in the auditorium at least.) In addition, theatre promoters and producers may feel or fear that a connection with Marxism will actually put audiences off a production.
- The 'political' is often understood as concerning political parties, views and policies. It can harangue an audience and be presented in a ham-fisted way, that is, it can be partisan or propagandist. Brecht's understanding of politics in the theatre is, as will be shown in Chapter 1, quite different from and far more subtle than this.

- It is possible to argue that there has not been a 'proper' reception of Brecht's ideas and practices in the UK (and, by extension, the USA), one that connects his method of dramatic analysis with the stagecraft he developed. While his plays have certainly been performed extensively, directors have rarely engaged with his approach to theatre-making. Brecht liked to work with an ensemble to develop the actors' sensitivities to his method over time. It is more difficult to work through Brecht's processes in theatre systems in which there are few ensembles and short rehearsal periods. Thus, the 'political' aspects of Brecht's theories and stagecraft have rarely been palpable in the English-speaking theatre.

- Perhaps the most troubling reason for the refusal to connect Brecht with a particular politics is a wide-ranging de-politicization of Brecht, a phenomenon that has a long history. Only three years after Brecht's death, Martin Esslin wrote a book that attempted to split Brecht's art from his politics.[7] Esslin's sentiments can still be felt decades afterwards, and are present in the following comment from Billington, for example: 'Brecht was a dramatist first and a Marxist second'.[8] Both impulses (p)raise Brecht's art over his politics, and such a shift in emphasis has its consequences. Brecht's plays often end unhappily, for example. If, on the one hand, they are staged as examples of 'great art', they would then accurately and beautifully depict timeless human suffering. If, on the other, productions invite spectators to look on the events with a view to changing them, they would offer insights into the causes of the suffering and suggest that these causes can and should be remedied. Brecht's is a politically interventionist theatre: it encourages spectators to pick out contradictions in society and seek new ways of reconciling them.

This book aims to (re)introduce Brecht the theorist and practitioner to readers and proceeds from his political principles in order to uncover the means he fashioned to achieve them. Brecht will be revealed not as a crude propagandist, but as a shrewd political theorist and practitioner. He continually strove to open up events on stage and expose the social forces acting upon individuals.

A running theme throughout the book is that of 'method over means'. By this I mean that Brecht's innovations for the stage (his 'means') are all products of the way Brecht thought about the world (his 'method'). If practitioners use the innovations without reference to the reasons why Brecht developed them, they will ignore the political starting point and offer performance that no longer provides insights into the workings of the world in favour of mere theatrical effects. Consequently, I will be arguing that what defines Brecht's contribution to theatre-making is his politicized method of approaching dramatic material. This is a key point of departure:

- Brecht's method has a politics: it interprets the world as unstable and consequently changeable. Such a position suggests that what we see on stage is in flux and that even the most awful situations or behaviour need not represent an eternal 'condition', but are subject to human influence.
- Brecht thus charges the theatre with finding suitable means for portraying the world, society and its people as provisional and impermanent.
- However, the means that may be used do not in themselves define the 'Brechtian': Brecht's contribution to theatre-making cannot be restricted to the innovations he introduced into theatre practice. They are a product of his method and are subject to change themselves.
- An emphasis on method also privileges form over content. It is not so much what but *how* something is represented. Brecht's theatre, when understood through the study of his writings and practice, is more concerned with offering interpreted,

contradictory material to an audience for its own deliberation. The theatre is not a pulpit.

I will thus be exploring the different practices Brecht developed in the light of his political ideas; my aim is to set out his politicized positions on theatre-making. The analysis will demonstrate that Brecht as theorist and practitioner is neither outdated nor irrelevant, but waiting to be discovered.

Format and scope

The study examines Brecht in eight chapters. Broadly speaking, the chapters move from theory to practice, although, as readers will note, Brecht could use theory to inform practice and then re-theorize theatre in light of the practice. Theory does not, then, recede into the background as the book progresses, but continues to offer perspectives on the practices Brecht developed. Each chapter can stand alone, but refers readers to other chapters when ideas, terminology, definitions or practices are discussed in greater depth. The following summary surveys the scope of each chapter:

1. Revealing the Radical Theorist
   Introduces the different roles theory played for Brecht and the central position of dialectics, the philosophical methodology he applied to politicize his theatre.
2. *Buying Brass* as Performative Thinking
   Discusses how Brecht takes theory off the page and into the theatre, using performance as a way of engaging with and evaluating the ideas themselves.
3. Brecht and Difference
   Locates the category of 'difference' at the heart of Brecht's theory and practice of theatre, and considers the many ways 'difference' can be felt in Brecht's work.

4. Method Trumps Means

   Sets out Brecht's method for staging drama, and reiterates that the method defines the 'Brechtian', not the theatrical means Brecht employs to bring it onto the stage.

5. Brecht and the Actor

   Extends the ideas of Chapter 4 by arguing that there is no Brechtian 'style' of acting, but an approach to performing based on the dialectical method.

6. Brecht and the Director

   Explores Brecht's understanding of the redefined tasks of the director in a dialectical theatre, and the director's relationship with an ensemble in the rehearsal process.

7. Brecht, Documentation and the Art of Copying

   Examines the special meaning Brecht applies to 'copying' in order to show how readers might set about making use of the ideas and practices of the previous chapters.

8. Brecht's Method in Action

   Offers analysis of and suggestions for staging a play by Brecht (*The Resistible Rise of Arturo Ui*) and a play by a dramatist not associated with the Brechtian tradition (*Closer* by Patrick Marber) as way of showing how Brecht's method can respond to different textual challenges.

   An Epilogue closes the book. It considers Brecht's achievements in the theatre and asks how we might modify and extend some of Brecht's ideas in the light of recent developments in history and society.

Brecht's theories have been much read in English, ever since a representative collection was published as *Brecht on Theatre* in 1964. However, understanding what *Verfremdung* (sometimes translated as 'alienation'), *Gestus* and Brecht's ideas for acting mean in practice has proved more difficult to establish. The chapters present various practical examples of how Brecht worked as a director, and these examples have been taken from the period in which he was most active in that role: when he was artistic director of the Berliner Ensemble theatre company, from 1949 to 1956. In addition, I offer other examples of my own as to how one might apply Brecht's method in practice at various points in the book.

When referring to Brecht's theories, I have mainly chosen to focus on the well-known and well-read essay 'The Short Organon for the Theatre' and material from *Buying Brass* (alternatively known as the *Messingkauf*). Brecht wrote a great deal on the theatre – it is collected in five volumes in German – and most of the important material can be found today in the revised and extended edition of *Brecht on Theatre* and *Brecht on Performance*. On occasion, I have referenced theoretical writings as yet unpublished in English, but only when no viable equivalent was available.

Ultimately, this book aims to address the misconceptions, debunk the myths and, step by step, explain the various components of Brecht's theory and practice, and their interrelationship. I will show how theory can be used to uncover 'the political' in drama in order to produce stimulating, provocative and vibrant performance. The study will not only make readers aware of how subtle and complex Brecht's ideas can be, but also show them how his method can be deployed to generate impressive results. That is, while the theoretical ideas often require a deal of unpacking and explaining, they can translate into elegant solutions in practice.

Revealing the Radical Theorist

Brecht as theorizing practitioner

Stanislavsky did it. Artaud did it. Brecht and a host of others did it and still do it. Some of the most significant makers of theatre also spent much time and effort theorizing theatre. Clearly the two activities are both distinct and closely related to each other. Practice confronts particular problems in the theatre with particular responses: no two plays, scenes or actors are the same, and thus all practice has to focus on the reality of specific issues and contexts as they arise. Theory, on the other hand, is not reality; rather it attempts to construct more generally applicable ideas to drama, theatre and performance as a whole, sometimes in a more systematic way, sometimes in a less organized fashion.

Different practitioners theorize in different ways and for different reasons. This chapter will consider why Brecht devoted so much energy to theorizing theatre and what he hoped to achieve as a theorist. He wrote a great deal in his lifetime: the standard German edition of his complete works runs to thirty volumes. The plays take up ten of these. Perhaps more surprisingly, another five contain his theoretical writings. Theory for Brecht was thus not a hobby or sideline, but an integral part of his engagement with the theatre.

It would be tempting to think that Brecht's biography can offer a perspective on why he wrote so many theoretical essays. He spent fifteen years of his life – from 1933 to 1948 – in exile from his native Germany, having fled the Nazis and moved from country to country

to avoid arrest. In these years he had little access to theatres and
rarely worked as a director. By necessity rather than choice, he found
himself writing rather than making theatre. These were the years in
which he wrote plays such as *Mother Courage and her Children*, *The
Good Person of Szechwan* and *The Caucasian Chalk Circle*. They were
also the years in which Brecht focused on drafting and developing
the ideas for which he is best known today because he was unable
to work with actors on stage. It may, then, be tempting to think
that Brecht theorized theatre as a substitute for the practice that his
circumstances denied him. This notion, however, is not only mistaken,
but misunderstands the role that theory played for Brecht.

If theory were a way of thinking about practice in lieu of practice
itself, then we might expect Brecht's theoretical writing to dry up
around 1949. After all, this was the year when he finally became
the artistic director of his own company, The Berliner Ensemble,
and was able to plan, rehearse and direct until his death in August
1956. He was generously supported in East Berlin with large public
subsidies provided by the government of the German Democratic
Republic (GDR), and it would be difficult to dispute that Brecht's
main creative role in this final period of his life was that of theatre
director. Although the GDR often applied pressure to Brecht, his
output and his commitment to staging his and other people's plays
with the Berliner Ensemble persisted until ill-health led him to
suspend rehearsals of *Life of Galileo* in March 1956. However, while
being very much involved not only in directing, but also organizing
the company and training a new generation of directors and writers,
Brecht did not suddenly stop theorizing. He wrote over 300 pages of
thoughts and ideas, observations and comments between 1949 and
1956 alone.[1] It is clear that while theory for Brecht did indeed help
him think through and envisage a new kind of theatre when in exile,
its function changed, but was in no way diminished when he finally
returned to the theatre full-time in 1949.

The different functions of theory to Brecht

So, why did Brecht value theorizing theatre so highly? There are a number of answers to this question, and I will consider some of the most important ones.

Making theatre is not a self-evident practice or, at least to Brecht, it should not be. One has to step back and ask what one is actually doing when staging a play, particularly with respect to the relationship between the way one represents the world and the effects that may have on an audience. Brecht understood that works of art do not merely reflect the world, but actually help to reinforce and mould our impressions of it. In an essay of 1939, Brecht makes his position clear. He notes that he had seen the film *Gunga Din* in which British soldiers were portrayed in an unwaveringly positive fashion, while the Indians they sought to subjugate were either comical or malign, depending on their actions towards the British. The aesthetics of the film made Brecht feel emotionally manipulated: he detected an affinity with the British even though he appreciated that the Indians were being presented in a flattened, stereotypical manner. He concludes:

> Obviously artistic appreciation of this sort is not without effects. It weakens the good instincts and strengthens the bad, it contradicts true experience and spreads misconceptions, in short, it falsifies our picture of the world.
>
> There is no play and no theatrical performance that does not in some way or other affect the dispositions and conceptions of the audience. Art is never without consequences, and indeed that says something for it.[2]

It is worth lingering on *how* Brecht articulates his ideas here before returning to the substance of the extract. Brecht as theorist can be a careful thinker. He does not generalize, but qualifies the art he is considering ('of this sort') and implicitly suggests that this is not the only way to represent the same story. He also carries out an interesting inversion of the reader's possible expectations. Rather than condemning art for its power to affect the way an audience might think, he latches on to this facet and seeks to rework it to his own advantage. I will return to this approach to thinking about art and reality below when discussing a central term to Brecht's theories: dialectics.

The quotation's content is also important and helps us understand why Brecht wrote so much about the theatre and representation. What we see on a stage has the potential to affect the way we understand and relate to the world beyond it. Representation can shape perception, often in ways that 'contradict true experience'. One need only look to the soap operas that form the backbone of most evenings' scheduling on the major television channels. *Coronation Street* and *Eastenders*, for example, are ostensibly 'realistic', that is, characters and events *seem* to behave as people do in everyday life, and there is no overt stylization to speak of. However, soaps also leave out many aspects that one might associate with everyday life. Not only do the characters refrain from what broadcasters term 'strong language', but elements like casual sexism and racism are also missing unless they form the basis for a particular storyline that will usually show that such attitudes are wrong. These programmes, which are staples of many people's weekly viewing, actively portray a *particular* view of the world that is offered as realistic while actually contradicting 'true experience'. Clearly the aims of such decisions are worthy: the more often (particularly younger) viewers hear expletives, the more likely they are to use them themselves. The more often that discriminatory social attitudes concerning gender, race and sexuality occur, the more difficult it is to challenge and change them. In short, the soaps are trying to influence the way viewers understand 'the normal'. One might, then, acknowledge the good intentions underlying the programme-makers' ethical codes (although it should not be forgotten that there is also a commercial aspect to this as well: by avoiding swearing and offensive behaviours, TV channels can show their programmes to more people and boost ratings). As can be seen from the quotation above, Brecht might have been in favour of aims that strengthen good instincts rather than weaken them. His problem, however, is not with ethical ambitions, but with *how* such ambitions are realized.

In his thoughts on a new kind of theatre, Brecht asks how art in general, and theatre and performance in particular, might *expose* the values they seek to communicate. The soaps do not draw our attention to the absence of swearing, but pass it over. A deliberate decision has been made 'normal' within the fictional world and is therefore invisible to the viewer. The question then arises as to whether other decisions have been taken that are perhaps more questionable. Do more subtle biases concerning gender or race, sexuality or age persist without acknowledgement, too? Do men, for example, tend to play the 'traditional' role of active agent in plotlines while women are only left to respond? Brecht was not so much concerned with *what* art was representing but *how* it was doing so. His theorizing is, in the first instance, a way of asking questions of artistic practice, of peeling off the veneer of what may appear to be 'obvious' and probing the values and interests at work in the many aspects of artistic production.

The problem is that if spectators are presented with representations that pass themselves off as realistic, spectators might mistake fiction for reality. The consequences can be far-reaching, and the so-called '*CSI* effect' is a case in point. The various *CSI* TV series solve crime with forensic medicine. Researchers have observed, however, that 'people who watch such television programs regularly expect better science than what they often are presented with in courts'.[3] A fictional world has the effect of skewing real justice. Brecht is thus seeking ways to remap the relationship between the fictional and the real world, but not because fiction cannot tell us important things about the real world. Rather, spectators need to be in a position in which they can understand that relationship.

Theorizing also allowed Brecht the practitioner to imagine new goals for the theatre. Because theory can speculate on reality, it can draft fresh ambitions for dealing with reality. As such, theory can have a utopian function and imagine new intentions and methods. Brecht has often been reproached for allegedly ignoring the gap between theoretical aspiration and theatrical practice. W. Stuart McDowell, for example, asserts that 'Brecht's theories on acting are more often than not a hindrance for an actor performing Brecht's work'.[4] The problem with this reading is that the author does not acknowledge that reading theory will not in itself lead to successful practice. Stanislavsky strove to achieve believability on stage but did not simply say 'be believable!' to his actors; rather, he spent much of his creative life experimenting with many approaches to achieve this end. Brecht's actors[5] and assistants,[6] as well as his critics who note the divide between the theory and the practice, mostly base their conclusions on the fact that Brecht rarely tried explicitly to realize theoretical positions in rehearsal.

If Brecht wanted to reveal the values that underpin representation in the theatre, for example, he would need to find practical ways of fulfilling that intention. As he wrote himself, 'there is no purely theoretical way of approaching the modern epic theatre'.[7] Instead, the more aspirational aspects of his ideas provided him with goals that were to be achieved through practice, and this would prove difficult, although not impossible. After the Berliner Ensemble's first production in 1949, he asked with palpable frustration, 'but when will the real, radical epic theatre come into being?'.[8] Five years later, he acknowledged that one of his lead actors in *The Caucasian Chalk Circle* could only have mastered the role of Grusha after five years of training at the Berliner Ensemble.[9] Rehearsal by rehearsal, his theoretical plans were becoming realities. Theory could thus provide the launch pad for practical exploration.

For Brecht, theorizing was not only about fashioning ideas that could be tested in practice. This, of course, is a common model for understanding the relationship between the theory and practice as a one-way street. Yet it should be evident that Brecht's production of theory did not always start with the ideas themselves. Particularly in his years with the Berliner Ensemble, Brecht developed a far more dynamic model in which theory and practice informed each other as a two-way street. Here, practice itself can lead to new insights of a more general nature, which in turn may develop new practices. The two sides are in a dialogue with each other, with neither holding the upper hand.

Brecht was a constant reviser of his own work; there are often several versions of the same play, for example, and he did not see the first night of a production as the end of the rehearsal process. The same was true of his theoretical writings. He wrote theoretical texts not only in order to advance his own practices but also to update his own understanding of theatre and its possibilities. It should be of little surprise to find that after five years' work with the Berliner Ensemble, Brecht proposed replacing the key term 'epic theatre' with 'dialectical theatre'.[10] Theory to Brecht was provisional: if it was inaccurate or overtaken by the fruits of practice, it was revised, reformed or rewritten. Brecht's theories of theatre trace paths of discovery rather than the dogmatic retention of terms or ideas.

Finally, it is worth noting that a remarkably small proportion of the essays and notes in the five volumes of theoretical writings was published in Brecht's lifetime. While publishing theoretical texts was an important means of disseminating new ideas for Brecht, one might ask what the point was of leaving the vast majority of the writings out of the public domain. Theorizing without publication reveals how the activity also gave Brecht the space to develop his own self-understanding. He theorized so extensively in order to see what ideas and concepts actually looked like when written down and expressed in language. He could ask himself how useful, how accurate or how applicable they were. This allowed him to return to them, extend them, reconsider them or update them. Theorizing was thus also a way of finding a means to make ideas concrete. Once they were, they could be further interrogated.

Theorizing as a private and public activity

The question then arises as to how Brecht did his theorizing. The virtually complete record of his theoretical musings in German offers some interesting insights. For the most part, the writings themselves are relatively short and sometimes incomplete. They offer a time-lapse record of a mind in motion: getting interested in an idea, thinking about it more and in different ways, then becoming fascinated with another. Over time, ideas are taken up, developed, left to lie, returned to, taken up again and so on, and so on. Brecht said as much in a reflection on his own work, 'my love of clarity comes from my most unclear way of thinking'.[11] While I will return to the love of clarity in Chapter 4, the comment reveals Brecht's lack of systematic thought and the ways in which he often merely explored or articulated a particular idea before stopping and turning to another subject entirely.

On the other hand, Brecht's lengthier essays were often written with an eye on publication. The 'Short Organon for the Theatre', which will form the textual focus for the rest of this chapter, marks a deliberate attempt to marshal and order a complex set of ideas into a readable whole. Brecht's aim was to set out his thoughts on a new theatre in as coherent a way as possible. He described the essay as a 'potted version of the *Messingkauf*.[12] *Buying Brass*, as the *Messingkauf* is also known, will be discussed in more detail in Chapter 2 and is what John J. White has termed a 'monumental superfragment'.[13] In its now collected form, it spans 174 pages and contains documents that range from a single line to several sides.[14] This was a more typical form for Brecht's extended musings. *Buying Brass*'s composition is dated from 1939 to 1955, although this was not steady but sporadic work, undertaken in phases. *Buying Brass* is thus more representative of Brecht's approach to theoretical work than the 'Short Organon' because it flits between different ideas, developing some while leaving others tantalizingly open. However, I will be concentrating on the 'Short Organon' presently because it is both a summary of Brecht's most salient ideas at the end of his exile and is well known and well read. I will not be neglecting the fact that it is a somewhat angular document itself, made up of seventy-seven short, numbered sections that offer a nod to Brecht's more typical modes of theorizing. Brecht did not, however, view the 'Short Organon' as finished; he returned to the essay in 1954 and added ten 'appendices' to the existing sections and an additional extended note.[15] They were never published in what was left of Brecht's lifetime.

So, Brecht the theorist offers the reader not a finished 'theory', but a number of different, evolving threads that run through his work. He not only speculated about the nature of theatre as he found it, he also drafted alternative visions of it, used theory as a way of processing practice and practice as an incitement to new theories. One thus has to proceed carefully when negotiating the relationship between theory and practice in Brecht's work, as theory rarely offers a blueprint or a template for practice as such. Instead it asks readers to be sensitive to what they find in the theatre and to approach Brecht's suggestions for changing practice not with reverence, but with a critical attitude that acknowledges that his thinking was also subject to change. This does not mean that everything was 'up for grabs', as it were, and we will see below that some of Brecht's concepts about the nature of the world were indeed fixed. All the same, Brecht was aware that theory had to meet the test of reality. Yet we should not make the mistake of John

Fuegi, who writes, 'the key test always was: does it work on stage? If not, throw it out. If it does work, and if it conflicts with the theory, throw away the theory.'[16] In this model, theory is one thing, practice is another, and they only meet by lucky hap. Theory and practice, however, are in fact different ways of thinking, one written on the page, the other 'written' by bodies in motion. Each is an experiment and each has its own means of exploring reality. The two are not disconnected from each other, but mutually inform each other, and this is particularly the case in Brecht's own ways of working.

Understanding the assumptions of the 'Short Organon', or: An introduction to dialectics

The 'Short Organon' was written in 1948, on the cusp of the second half of the twentieth century. The Second World War had finished only a couple of years earlier, and the battle lines of the Cold War between the capitalist West and the communist East were already being drawn. Ever since the fall of the Berlin Wall in 1989 and the communist regimes in the East, the ideas and language of Marxism have become increasingly marginalized. However, without a knowledge of either, Brecht's essay can be confusing and unclear.

The 'Short Organon' opens with a prologue that announces that it is concerned with 'theatre for a scientific age',[17] yet this shorthand requires further comment. Brecht wrote a play about what might be called the birth of the modern scientific age, *Life of Galileo*, and it was set, as one would expect, in the seventeenth century. This is not, however, the scientific age to which Brecht is referring in the Organon. Instead there is a reference in the essay to 'a new science' (Organon §19) and this is Brecht's first allusion to Marxism in the text. He is more overt in §45 when associating the 'new social science' with 'materialist dialectics'. Brecht had encountered Marxism in the mid-1920s, had been inspired by its ideas and, more importantly, its way of looking at the world through the philosophical term 'dialectics'.

That Brecht does not mention Marxism by name serves two functions: it does not 'put off' readers who may perhaps be averse to the term, but more importantly, the omission points to the fact that Brecht's Marxism was neither dogmatic nor orthodox. At a time when he was being heavily criticized by left-wing dogmatists and hard-liners, Brecht preferred to use Marxism's *methods* in a variety of ways and not be constrained by one version of the philosophy over the other.

Marxism is a political philosophy with a long history and a complex set of principles. Its most important features for Brecht were:

- Marxism addresses inequalities in society and proposes ways of overcoming them.
- These ways are not based on reforming an already flawed system (capitalism), but fashioning a new and better one (socialism).
- The hope for change is based on the instability of any social system and is brought about by an unchanging methodology: dialectics.

It is the third point that fascinated Brecht and informed his ideas for a new kind of theatre comprehensively. The dialectic is a mechanism that accounts for why things change in history and society. In its most basic form, it can sound hopelessly abstract, but, as I will show, its applicability is eminently concrete. The dialectic is comprised of three parts: a thesis, an antithesis and a synthesis. The thesis exists at a point of space and time, and continues to move forward through time until it is opposed by an antithesis. The relationship between the thesis and the antithesis is one of contradiction, and when the contradiction becomes too great, elements of the thesis and elements of the antithesis form a new entity, the synthesis. The synthesis is now a new thesis, and this, in turn, moves forward through time until a new antithesis emerges, and again their relationship is one of contradiction. Once this contradiction becomes too great, another synthesis comes about and so on in perpetuity throughout history.

A couple of examples might put some flesh on the dialectical bones. The dialectic can be applied to events in history or to the way individuals make their ways through life:

- In history, one could look at a momentous event such as the French Revolution of 1789. The thesis in the run-up to the Revolution is France ruled by an aristocracy. In this form of government, those in control have been in control for centuries because they inherit not only land and wealth, but forms of wielding power that are very much embedded in everyone's day-to-day experience. So, peasants, for example, do not think they have a right to rule and grow up believing their lords and masters are the right people for such a task.
- Over time, however, a new social group emerges, the middle class, and this is the aristocracy's antithesis. This group develops the model of the 'self-made man' and accrues its wealth and influence through its own industry and endeavour. It applies reason to problems (rather than relying on tradition) and exploits the solutions to manufacture new goods, develop new services and new ways of interacting. This is thus the rise of a new merchant class.
- Once the middle class gains sufficient self-confidence, the contradiction between itself and the aristocracy becomes ever greater. There is a clash between those who were born to positions of power and those who have worked their way up, but have very little say in the running of France. The synthesis is the Revolution itself, and the new order that follows.

- Yet history does not stop here because the dialectic never stops: on the eve of the new century, Napoleon stages a *coup d'etat*. The instability of the 1790s created contradictions of its own, and Napoleon later becomes Emperor as a response to that period of upheaval (a strong leader instead of a shaky democracy). However, in due course, he is deposed in 1814, and history continues to move through different, contradictory phases.

On a more individual level, the dialectic also applies to people and their relationships with society. When we think of groups of people as 'children of their time', we are acknowledging that attitudes and behaviours are not generated in isolation, but in dialogue with the dominant ideas and values of any given time. This dialogue, however, often goes unspoken because we respond to stimuli both consciously and unconsciously. That is, we both make decisions *and* absorb ideas. One might ask why men's attitudes to women might be different at the end of the nineteenth century and the beginning of the twenty-first, or why they might be different in today's United States and today's China. To a Marxist, the differences can be accounted for by investigating the different ways in which the respective societies are organized. Each society permits or prevents women from engaging in a variety of activities through law, custom and culture. An understanding of these will help to map differences in attitudes and behaviours.

The dialectical view of human identity suggests that we are in a constant dialogue with our surroundings. People can thus exhibit the contradictions of their times in their own behaviour. Behaving in a contradictory manner already acknowledges that change is possible because people do not simply behave in one way or another, but in different ways according to their circumstances. Thus, if people change their circumstances (society), they will also change themselves. Change is brought about by the dialectical tensions between individual and society. Values and behaviours are not stable:

in the UK, for example, slavery was abolished in 1833, child labour for the under-nines was banned in 1867 and women gained equal voting rights with men in 1928. Each of these *social* changes altered *individual* attitudes and behaviours. It should be noted, however, that the results of such changes are also marked by contradictory responses, to which, in turn, new solutions are to be found. For example, the campaign in 2013 to make Jane Austen's the image on a British ten pound note was successful. This reflects a degree of female self-confidence and an environment accepting of women's achievements that may not have been present a hundred years earlier. On the other hand, the amount of vitriol and sexist abuse aimed at the leaders of the campaign betrays that fact that equal rights have not been greeted positively by everyone and continue to provoke the most unpleasant of responses.

The appeal of dialectics to Brecht

In terms of history or individuals, one might ask what it is that drives change. To a Marxist, it is the material conditions of any given situation. That is, there is nothing mystical or supernatural at work; instead there are real factors in play. *Mother Courage*, for example, is set in the Thirty Years' War, a conflict between Catholic and Protestant armies. Yet Brecht shows time and again that this is not a war of religion, but a war for land, commodities and power. Behind the religious rhetoric is material advantage. To a Marxist, change is always driven by material reality – there are concrete causes that bring about dialectical contradictions.

Brecht was attracted to dialectics for a number of reasons:

- The dialectical account of history and individuals is based on a world of instability. Nothing is ever fixed, and this idea

can become political: if we find ourselves in a society that is oppressive or unjust, there will be ways to change it, despite appearances to the contrary.
- Yet, dialectics do not promise happy endings (indeed, the concept of an ending is itself undialectical), merely more change.
- It is important to remember that the dialectic is not predictable: a particular thesis and a particular antithesis do not necessarily lead to a given synthesis. This is because each side of the dialectic, the thesis and the antithesis, is itself complex and the result of previous dialectical processes.
- But the *prospect* of change is something that offers hope in the face of arguments that suggest change is either not possible or an illusion.

Brecht was very much drawn to a dialectical way of thinking, in which stability and closure are challenged. The passage on *Gunga Din* quoted earlier is an example of dialectical thinking: Brecht does not dismiss art for the power it can exert, but seeks to make use of it to further a different set of ends. Unlike the Greek philosopher Plato, who opposed art for the power it wielded, Brecht wants to rethink the way art works because it is not an undialectical 'thing in itself', but something that can change and be changed.

It is also clear from Brecht's own theatre work that dialectics helped him account for and stage change. For example, in one production, *Battle in Winter*, the protagonist is a young man, Hörder, who begins as a heroic Nazi soldier, but comes to realize the error of his beliefs by the end of the play. The notes on the production describe two different ways the actor Ekkehard Schall approached the character. First, he played Hörder in an unsympathetic fashion, as a Nazi plain and simple. In the second attempt, 'Schall played a likeable young man who, however, talks and acts like a Nazi. It is clear that a young man has been turned into a Nazi. [...] The social insight is greater'.[18]

In this approach, Schall did not represent Hörder as a Nazi, but as someone who has become one, and so the audience could see that the character was not stable as such, but subject to social influence: he is a nice fellow who nonetheless says and does things we find questionable – and this is a dialectical contradiction. This 'nice fellow' re-emerged at the end of the play, and the audience could observe the process that brought about the change. This is because the character was never portrayed as either one thing or another, but as a complex, contradictory mixture of different characteristics and influences.

Dialectics is concerned with unpicking things that appear to be fixed, from the ways society is organized to the ways people think about themselves. What seems solid is undone by its own contradictions. Brecht finds hope for change; this is why dialectics form the basis of the 'Short Organon' and why they run through his ideas for the theatre as a non-negotiable prerequisite. A failure to acknowledge the centrality of dialectics to Brecht's thought makes it virtually impossible to understand Brecht's theories and practice of theatre.

What is Brecht teaching?

In the appendix to §45 of the 'Short Organon', Brecht states, 'the theatre of the scientific age is able to make dialectics enjoyable'.[19] Given the philosophical definition of dialectics provided above, one might well raise an eyebrow regarding this claim, but the 'Short Organon', in its first paragraphs, emphasizes a link between learning and pleasure. Brecht argues that it is enjoyable to learn new things and new ways of understanding things, concluding that 'nothing needs less justification than our pleasures' (§3). While we might want to linger over this pithy claim – pleasure can indeed prove quite costly, for example, and theatres rarely pay for themselves – I will move on to the nature of the learning Brecht seeks to engender in his audience.

Learning can take many forms. One can be taught facts about subjects, and it is clear that learning has taken place successfully if the learner can correctly recall, say, the capital of Tunisia, the boiling point of mercury or the gestation period of a cow. Yet learning, of course, extends far beyond the accumulation of facts. One can also learn lessons about how to behave in difficult situations or towards other people. Brecht has often been accused of using his theatre as a pulpit for such lessons, something often equated with an idea of art having a 'message'. Yet this proposition, that a complex work of art can produce a clear and unambiguous message, seems like a somewhat perverse end for any artist. If art is about exploring questions that resist simple answers, like 'what is justice?' or 'how do I right a wrong?', then how does one reach a simple conclusion? Brecht's may well be a critical theatre, but it rarely offers answers to the questions it poses.

In *The Good Person of Szechwan*, the central character, Shen-Te, has to ask herself how she can be good in a society that exploits goodness. After a couple of scenes she has to invent a 'bad' cousin, Shui-Ta, whom she plays in disguise and who makes decisions that she is unable to make as a 'good' person. Shui-Ta, however, is still Shen-Te, and so she shows the price she has to pay to retain an amount of goodness in her life. By the end of the play, no answer is given to Shen-Te's question, but the suggestion arises that the society in which she lives is configured in such a way that it stifles goodness. Brecht does not offer an alternative society as an answer to the play's central question.

To take a second example, *Mother Courage and her Children* is another play with a divided hero. Mother Courage is a tradeswoman who sells her wares to the two sides fighting the Thirty Years' War while struggling to protect her three children. She is both businesswoman and mother, yet her business activities lead to the deaths of her two sons, and by the end of the play she has lost her daughter to the war, too. One could perhaps blame her for caring more about business than her children, *but* she engages in commercial activity in order to support the children in the first place. By the end of the play, one sees that Mother Courage's decisions are all made in a social context that is hostile to her, but Brecht does not depict a society in which she can flourish.

In both examples, the concept of dialectical contradiction is clear and present. In *The Good Person*, the wish to do good is resisted by a society that permits goodness only in short measures. In *Mother Courage*, the wish to preserve a family is resisted by the social circumstances that demand ruthless business practice for survival. In both examples, the dialectical tension involves questions that go far beyond the wishes of individuals because these individuals are continually constrained by social structures. The lack of resolution at the end of these, and indeed all the rest of Brecht's plays, means that the dialectics at their heart remain open, unsynthesized, and we, as readers or audience members, are invited to speculate on how such contradictions might be overcome. It is thus clear that Brecht is not trying to teach moral lessons, but is inviting us to think beyond the individual and to consider the individual's place in the greater social scheme of things.

So, what is Brecht trying to teach us if it is not moral lessons? A clue is given when he talks of a 'new kind of entertainment' (Organon §23). Brecht does not want to teach simple answers to complex questions, but a *method* of thinking about the questions themselves. Brecht as a Marxist might have been expected to promote the cause of a new socialist society through his theatre. Instead, he views the production of new attitudes to and perceptions of reality as an end in itself. In short, he wants to teach the audience to think dialectically, and this is a radical proposition because it asks us to rethink some fairly fundamental issues concerning plays, how they work, and how they are performed.

Defining 'the Brechtian'

Dramas tend to focus their attention on characters, their desires, their struggles, their triumphs and their defeats. We may think of Antigone, Hamlet, Chekhov's three sisters or Miller's doomed salesman. We may see aspects of ourselves in these figures from the past and thus believe that human beings have not changed that much over time. Brecht, on the contrary, asks us to focus on situations and on how situations inform, affect and transform characters. After all, in a dialectical world, characters do not exist outside society, but are very much a part of it. Brecht limits what characters can do and makes their actions dependent on their material context. Here, characters from the past are different from us because they live under different conditions and consequently have different attitudes and exhibit different behaviours. We can compare ourselves with them and note the differences as well as any similarities.

If we take the example of *Hamlet*, we can perhaps understand this shift in the understanding of character more clearly. In a character-based reading of the play, an intelligent son is charged with the task of avenging his murdered father, Old Hamlet. Over the course of the play, he tussles with the rightness or wrongness of the deed, and in the last scene he finally exacts revenge in an orgy of violence that leads not only to the death of Old Hamlet's murderer, Claudius, but that of his mother Gertrude, his one-time potential brother-in-law Laertes and himself. His girlfriend Ophelia has already taken her own life, having been spurned by Hamlet, who was pretending to be mad. In this reading, Hamlet might be a ditherer, uncertain of carrying out the bloody retribution, a man of principle repulsed by his dead father's commission, or someone quite different. In each interpretation, Hamlet is presented as a type of character facing a difficult decision.

Brecht, on the other hand, views Hamlet's dilemma as one produced by history and social context. In this reading, Old Hamlet represents the old feudal order that had its own moral code based on social hierarchy. Claudius is the representative of a new social order that values individual deeds over collective ones and is a 'self-made man' (he has become king not through tradition, but his own criminal activity). Here both Hamlet and Claudius stand for the new emphasis on an individual's reason, but in different ways. Claudius violates the old order by murdering his brother for personal gain; Hamlet applies reason by resisting his father's call for revenge and the old way of doing things. Brecht concludes that Hamlet suffers a 'relapse' in the final scene by letting the old cry for blood cloud his judgement because he finds himself between the old and the new orders.[20] *Hamlet* is thus no longer only a personal tragedy, but one brought about by Hamlet's place in history because he is confronted by two very different ways of dealing with revenge.

If the individual is more clearly subject to circumstance and situation, then these have a greater role to play in Brecht's theatre, too. This is because a dialectical individual will respond differently in different situations, and so a suitable theatrical form must be found to emphasize situation over character. As a result, the organization of the action is also affected. The old model, taken from the Greeks, of an organically developing plot gives way to episodic action: interconnected acts are replaced by free-standing scenes. The lack of plotted connections between the scenes allows them to show different aspects of a character in order to call the very idea of a unified self into doubt. Thus, at the end of one scene, Mother Courage curses the war for the misery it has brought. Yet at the beginning of the very next one, she is singing its praises because her business is doing well again. Is this the same Mother Courage? Of course it is, yet the structure of the play draws our attention to the ways in which her character is affected by her situation and how contradictory situations provoke contradictory responses.

Brecht notes that 'nowadays humanity adopts the same attitude to its own undertakings as it displayed in the face of unpredictable natural catastrophes in days gone by' (Organon §19). That is, there is a sense of inevitability, that things will not change and that one simply has to put up with things as they are. Indeed, in a world in which globalized capitalism seems to have seen off rival economic systems, we may recognize such an attitude today, too. Brecht, in his dialectically re-thought theatre, does not accept this position, even though characters like Shen-Te and Mother Courage end up in despair rather than hope. His theatre has not taught *them* how to better themselves by bettering their society, but he has given spectators insights into the complex interrelationships between the personal and the social, and has shown how a change in conditions can lead to a change in the characters.

Brecht's wish to teach the audience to think dialectically does not entail a philosophical lesson in theses, antitheses and syntheses. Instead, spectators are encouraged to make connections for themselves. At the end of a dialectical performance, the audience may not have the philosophical vocabulary or even a notion of how a thesis is in a contradictory relationship with an antithesis before a synthesis of the two is brought about. But this is not important. Teaching the dialectical view of the world is far more about getting the audience to recognize a new way of understanding society, human beings and their capacities for change. Teaching is thus not about lessons as such, but is a process of sensitizing an audience to recognize the relationships between the characters and their social contexts. The insights gained in the theatre can then be applied to the spectators' own lives. Thinkers like Brecht may use terms like 'dialectics' and 'antitheses', but spectators are charged with the more concrete tasks of spotting patterns, tracing causes and effects, and constructing relationships between individuals and society.

To summarize: the audience is invited to see the world in a profoundly different way from that which is often presented in the theatre, where individuals may appear to have little connection with society or history (both of which may only provide a backdrop). Brecht asks us to widen the lens to understand the individual as a part of a social system and to identify the dialectical tensions inherent to such relationships. Just as *Gunga Din* can refashion an audience's consciousness to reinforce ethnic stereotypes and perpetuate patriotic allegiances, Brecht wants to refashion consciousness, but in an entirely different way.

In *Gunga Din*, in soaps or in *CSI*, audiences learn passively: opinions and values are developed and reinforced through repetition and unconscious acceptance. In Brecht's theatre, the audience plays an altogether different role because Brecht's interest as a theatre theorist is not actually on the stage, but the auditorium. While he is clearly focused on what is happening on stage, he is ultimately concerned with the effect it has on the audience. Brecht wants his spectators to be surprised by what they see on stage and actively to construct their own accounts of the characters' actions and behaviours, based on their connections with the play's social contexts. This 'surprise' is generated by making that which spectators thought they already knew strange or peculiar. Brecht calls this process *Verfremdung*, and it is dealt with in greater detail in Chapter 3.

Characters are no longer prisoners of their personalities and unchangeable, but part of a bigger, social picture. The action on stage is no longer inevitable, but the result of processes, pressures and contradictions. The audience can stand back from this and consider what could have happened, had things been different. This is an important discrepancy, born of Brecht's desire to bring dialectics into the theatre. Thus, spectators do not learn lessons about how to behave; instead they observe examples of how people behave and are encouraged to ask 'why?'. Learning takes place when the audience develops a new way of understanding the world as dialectical.

The philosophical framework Brecht employs is based on contradictions and is designed to provoke an unequivocal response in the audience, as he puts it: the 'attitude is a critical one' (Organon §22). Spectators are expected to be active when they process the material on stage because the stage does not offer answers to dialectically posed questions. Yet although Brecht is concerned with constructing a dialectical world on stage, either as playwright or practitioner, he does not shape the response of his audience which he hopes will be peopled by 'those who are productive' (Organon §24). By this he means people who are active, who can produce new ideas or new approaches to problems. Activity is thus more important than any particular course of action.

When one thinks of the term 'Brechtian', there is a temptation to identify it with vocabulary taken from Brecht's theoretical writing or particular features of his stagecraft. But such an approach connects the Brechtian with questions of style when it is evident that Brecht was more concerned with underlying philosophical issues: dramatizing and performing a dialectical view of the world. There is certainly nothing novel in claiming that Brecht's approach to theatre is a method and not a style: he says it himself in the 'Short Organon' (see Organon §36, for example), and those who worked closely with him and his work at the Berliner Ensemble very much agree.[21] However, it is worth emphasizing here that it is this dialectical method, not the ways in which Brecht sought to realize it in the theatre, which defines Brechtian theatre.

Making theatre politically

Brecht's aim is not to dramatize human beings as such but 'the *field* of human relations' (Organon §31, my emphasis). By expanding drama's scope, he is interested in treating individuals as parts of a potentially changeable, unstable system rather than as independent units. This has a major influence on Brecht's understanding of theatre and politics. Often, 'political theatre' is taken to mean 'theatre with political content', and includes plays like David Hare's *Stuff Happens* on the run-up to the Iraq War or Caryl Churchill's *Far Away* set in an imagined dictatorship. Brecht proposed a different way of understanding the political on stage: he was not making political theatre but *making theatre politically*.

In order to make sense of this term, it will be necessary to understand what is meant by the key word 'politics'. Lenin, the Marxist revolutionary, defined politics with two simple questions that nonetheless cover a great many issues: 'who? to whom?' Or to expand: he is asking who does what to whom. The question is consequently about power, law, ethics, economics, and politics is the overarching term that runs through them all. Brecht thus wants to craft forms of drama and theatre that can point to the political in the most apparently unpolitical of situations in order to alert the spectator that even these things could change in a changed society.

In Brecht's theatre, two lovers kissing becomes political because their behaviour towards each other will be influenced by their social class and the role of gender within it. A middle-class man's relationship with a middle-class woman will be different from a working-class man's relationship with a middle-class woman or a middle-class man, for that matter. Social class influences attitudes, behaviours and perceptions. These are, of course, different for different people. A middle-class person might want to bridge the social divide by starting a relationship with a working-class person, or merely use the lower-class person to shore up a sense of social superiority. The reasons why the working-class person might initiate the relationship will clearly be different. Brecht is not, however, denying that people have desires. The important thing here is that in any of the examples, desire exists *together with* other factors, whether one is aware of them or not. Making theatre politically is about exposing the aspects of our social make-up that go unspoken or unacknowledged in everyday life.

Our personal lives and our emotions might appear to be our own business, untouched by parliaments, legislators or dialectics. Yet Brecht notes:

> We need a theatre that not only facilitates the sensations, insights and motivations permitted by the particular historical field of human relations on which the action happens to take place, but also employs and produces those thoughts and feelings which help transform the field itself.
>
> (Organon §35)

Here he directly connects our private emotional lives with the conditions of any given society (the 'historical field of human relations'). The comment in turn suggests that feelings of resignation or despair, for example, may *not* in fact be purely personal, but responses to oppressive social relations that give the impression that they are not changeable. We may thus find in Brecht's vision of a new theatre a desire to show how almost everything portrayed is connected with larger social formations and is thus political. Yet the end of the quotation points to how feelings themselves need to be transformed, from, say, resignation into anger so that change might take place after all.

Making theatre politically is concerned with understanding how action on stage is not general but specific: what one does at a particular time in a particular place is, *in part*, a product of that time and that place. Again, Brecht is very clear on this point: 'we must be able to characterize the field in historically relative terms' (Organon §36). In a dialectical world, as in that of the ancient philosopher Heraclitus, one can never put one's foot into the same stream twice. It is always flowing and so even if it seems that one has returned to the same place, it will never be carrying the same water. The dialectic moves through time as a dynamic process, and so the assassination of civil rights leader Martin Luther King on 4 April 1968 might remind us of the assassination of civil rights leader Malcolm X on 21 February 1965. However, a closer examination would reveal that different social factors played their part in both events, despite their similarities and their proximity in history. All the same, a study of the assassinations in drama could tell us important things about civil rights and the forces that oppose them, and so an event's historical specificity is no bar to it being useful in the present.

One final theoretical aspect of the 'Short Organon' that requires consideration is another challenge to something that might be taken for granted in a more conventional theatre: *how* one represents people, actions and things on stage. To Brecht, nothing on stage is value-free. Representation itself can never be neutral: it is always supporting one interest or another. Brecht maintains, 'without opinions and intentions one cannot represent anything' (Organon §55). This is an important observation because it links representing characters and actions with agendas. It asks directors and actors to be conscious, thinking artists. If one does not have an opinion or an objective when representing a character or an action, one could be merely be reproducing the opinions and objectives of someone with a different agenda altogether. What happens when *The Merchant of Venice* is staged? The director clearly has to understand how he or she represents the Jewish moneylender Shylock. This is because this play has been used to comment on the role of Jewish people in general, for better or for worse, at various moments in its production history. However, does this sensitivity not apply to every play? They all include characters that have a gender, an age, a sexuality and an ethnicity, and each of these aspects is charged with meaning in any given society at any given time. When making theatre politically, directors and actors are aware of this fact and approach the business of staging and performing consciously rather than blindly.

'Making theatre politically' is thus concerned with understanding that everything on stage is affected by the question 'who does what to whom?' because it includes the question, 'and for what reasons?' In a dialectical theatre, these reasons are connected to social context – what is permitted and what is not. Nothing is taken for granted, and factors that playwrights might ignore can be brought out by directors and actors who appreciate that a character is not 'just' a nurse, a lover, a refugee or a pensioner, but is in dialogue with a host of contexts that will have an effect on how that character behaves and interacts with others. An acknowledgement of such connections helps both actors and audiences draft a *political* picture of the world on stage that exposes how that world might work and how it might be changed.

The radicalism of the 'Short Organon'

Much of the rest of the 'Short Organon' concerns the ideas and staging methods Brecht wanted to introduce into the very business of making theatre dialectically, and I will return to these in subsequent chapters. His theoretical points, quoted and discussed above, set out a new way of approaching theatre and are a clarion call for its active realization. The 'Short Organon' is concerned with reviewing central aspects of modern theatre and suffusing them with Brecht's dialectical ideas. This stance is radical in a literal sense – the adjective is taken from the Latin for 'root' ('radix'). While radical can also mean 'extreme', Brecht's theories aim to rethink the theatre from the ground, from the roots, up. In Brecht's theatre, little on stage is as it seems because it is always the result of dialectical processes. Brecht proposes that the theatre reveals these processes and stops taking them for granted. And because processes are transactions between people or between people and institutions (like schools, businesses or law courts), representations of processes have to be subjected to a fundamental rethink. Characters can no longer exist as if they were in some way wholly natural and independent, but betray their debt to their relationships with their society. Events, too, do not simply 'happen', but represent forces that may not be visible.

A dialectical theatre is one in which awareness is raised, in both the theatre-makers and the spectators. But it is important to acknowledge what Brecht is and is not teaching. He designed his dialectical theatre in order to generate critical spectators, who would then take their insights into the workings of individuals and society on stage back into their everyday lives. This aim is, again, a radical one that seeks to allow spectators to see the world anew and to change it. The dialectic never reaches a point of rest, and so change will either be managed by the minority in positions of power and privilege or perhaps by new voices that might influence the course of events in their favour. Such an ambition is not as utopian as it may sound: few would have predicted the uprisings known collectively as the Arab Spring even a year before they took place, yet political dynasties have been toppled and new systems introduced. It is true that the outcome of several of the uprisings has not yet brought about what protesters had demanded, but this, as Brecht would tell us, is the nature of the dialectical process: one cannot predict its outcome. And this is perhaps why Brecht cleverly avoided making predictions about a rosy future himself in his drama or his theatre productions. Instead, he put his faith in dialectical theory and its promise of change. Yet theory, however radical, would not deliver results by itself, and so Brecht started to ask how theory might be made more active.

Buying Brass as Performative Thinking

Theorizing with more than one voice

Brecht, as shown in the previous chapter, did not merely understand theory as a set of ideas to be tested in practice. On the one hand, theory provided the germ for practical experiment; on the other, it responded to the findings of those experiments and was developed further in their light. In addition, Brecht, the copious reviser, was rarely content to let his theories lie and continually sought to address issues that might arise from a certain formulation, direction or speculation. In this chapter, I will consider how he developed forms that allowed his theories to open up a dialogue with themselves. Such approaches to theorizing can emphasize its provisional and exploratory status for Brecht and expose it to more dynamic analysis and assessment.

His most ambitious attempt at introducing counter-opinions and -positions is represented by the *Buying Brass* project, which Brecht began in Danish exile in 1939 and continued in fits and starts until 1955, a year before his death in East Berlin. The project remained open as a collection of fragments. It is unlikely that he considered it 'finished', but it is difficult to say whether he planned to return to it with a view to organizing its many different parts or expanding them further.

Buying Brass is a large complex of material and runs to 174 pages in the standard German edition. In English, extracts were gathered by John Willett as *The Messingkauf Dialogues* in 1965, but this title does not adequately acknowledge the diversity of forms Brecht employed in the project as a whole. While there are certainly many dialogues contained in the collection, there are also monologues (which were presumably awaiting integration into dialogue form), poems, a translation of a scene from *King Lear*, instructions for actors, scenes for actors to perform and with which to rehearse, as well as notes on and plans for the project itself. What links all the parts is an interest in the potential purposes of the theatre and how these might be brought into being.

Literally, 'Messingkauf' translates as 'buying brass'. The curious title is derived from the analogy, given by one the figures, of going to a brass band not with the intention of buying a trumpet, but to buy the brass itself. Here the focus is on the raw material which, in the case of the band, has only been used for one specific purpose when it could be used for others. Brecht asks whether theatre-makers can take existing understandings of acting, direction, set design and all the other elements of a production and refunction them for a different set of ends. As John J. White observes, the brass-buying metaphor itself is a profoundly open one: the reader or spectator is continually asked whether the brass *can* be re-formed in such a way that it can satisfy in the same way that a trumpet can.[1] The 'Messingkauf' thus reflects Brecht's own hopes for his new kind of theatre: meaning does not reside solely on the page or the stage, but also with the audience, as they evaluate what is being proposed in the project.

Buying Brass primarily, but not exclusively, dramatizes Brecht's ideas in dialogue form and mostly puts the speeches into the mouths of four figures:

The Philosopher wants to use the theatre ruthlessly for his own ends. It must provide accurate depictions of incidents between people, and facilitate a response from the spectator.
The Actor wants to express himself. He wants to be admired. Plot and characters serve his purpose.
The Actress wants a theatre with an educational social function. She is politically engaged.

The Dramaturg[2] puts himself at the Philosopher's disposal, and promises to apply his knowledge and abilities to the conversion of the theatre into the *thaëter* envisaged by the Philosopher. He hopes for a new lease of life for the theatre.[3]

What is interesting about the description of the cast is its treatment of the Philosopher. He can be read as an ironic shorthand for Brecht himself, and at points he is referred to as 'the Augsburger' (Augsburg was Brecht's home town). Yet Brecht treats the Philosopher in such a way that he, too, is open to critique: the use of the adverb 'ruthlessly' indicates that the Philosopher has his own agenda that may blinker both the accuracy and applicability of his ideas. He is not, then, the soul of wisdom, but a figure with his own limitations, however convincing his arguments might sound. At times, he can get impatient and angry, and other characters try to calm him down. The cast list was, however, an early plan for the project, and, in some of the dialogues written later, the Philosopher can actually be quite flexible and accommodating, another indication that his views could be modified in the light of other arguments. The dialogues have a liveliness: they are not mere vehicles for Brecht to peddle his ideas to a sympathetic audience of on-stage theatre-workers, but a forum in which these ideas can be discussed and challenged.

Buying Brass's central theme of refunctioning the existing theatre is also to be found in the word 'thaëter', a word that appears in the description of the Dramaturg. Brecht coins the new word as an umbrella term for the new kind of theatre the Philosopher wants to bring about rather than using 'epic theatre' (a term explained in Chapter 3), which was already becoming something of a millstone for Brecht. In 1954, Brecht would reflect that the word 'epic' was 'too meagre and too vague for the kind of theatre intended'[4] and he finally exchanged 'epic' for 'dialectical' in his appendices to the 'Short Organon', which itself only included the word 'epic' once. In coining a new term that was no longer tied to terms that could be misunderstood, Brecht set out the principles of the 'thaëter' without directly referring back to earlier ideas about 'epic theatre'. He was starting with a clean theoretical slate, so to speak.

The possibilities of performing theory

The dialogue fragments of *Buying Brass* suggest the possibility of performance. The Berliner Ensemble was the first company to attempt a production in 1963 and set about editing the many drafts, scenes and fragments found in the Brecht Archive into a workable evening-long show. The company's management initially assumed that the piece was likely to be a low-key affair, only attracting those with a curiosity about Brecht's theories. Instead, the show proved so engaging that it ran for 100 performances over seven years, with changes made to the material performed during its lengthy run in a process of sustained, critical revision. *Buying Brass* had vindicated itself as a theatrical piece that discussed and enacted its own theories, and proved attractive to a fee-paying audience. Brecht's experiment with the proposition of staging theory was a success even though he set himself a remarkably difficult task.

White notes that *Buying Brass* 'attempts to expound, illustrate *and perform* theory by means of an ingenious presentational strategy largely dictated by the theatrical medium that is at the same time the work's subject-matter'.[5] It is worth investigating this 'ingenuity', because the dialogues are doing an amount of work that essays simply cannot.

The following extract considers ideas that underpin Brecht's new way of making theatre. To summarize, he criticizes 'old' theatre for offering superficial representations of reality. Brecht claims that an audience learns nothing about how such representations come about and what lies behind them. He sets out his stall in *Buying Brass* like this:

PHILOSOPHER: The mere fact of an incident occurring is not
   enough to teach the spectator something. The incident won't
   be understood simply by dint of being observed.
DRAMATURG: So you want some kind of commentary on it?
PHILOSOPHER: Or something in its portrayal that will be
   equivalent to commentary, yes.
DRAMATURG: And what about learning from experience?
   You don't just see things in the theatre, you experience them. Is
   there any better way of learning?
PHILOSOPHER: We'd need to look at how people learn from
   experience when no elements of commentary have been
   incorporated in it. The first thing to say is that there are many
   factors which prevent people from learning (i.e. becoming
   wiser) through experience. For instance, when certain changes
   in a situation come about too gradually – so gradually as to be
   imperceptible. Or when people's attention is distracted by other
   incidents happening at the same time. Or when people look for
   the causes of incidents and identify the wrong ones. Or when
   the person undergoing the experience has strong prejudices.

(*Brass* 37)

The extract unfolds in a fairly straightforward fashion: the Philosopher
makes an assertion, the Dramaturg asks for clarification and receives
a reply. The Dramaturg then develops his line of questioning and the
Philosopher gives a comprehensive set of responses. What gives the
exchange its liveliness is that the speeches are not merely arranged in
such a way that the Philosopher is either asked the 'right' questions
or that his responses are predictable. The Philosopher's 'clarification'
could have consisted of the simple 'yes' that is found at the end of
the speech, but instead he suggests that the direction and the acting
themselves might be able to comment on a performed incident – the
Philosopher complicates his answer. And rather than asking what
such practices might look like, the Dramaturg asks a question about
learning in the theatre. The Philosopher gives four possible reasons
why experience alone may not be enough to bring about learning.

There are a couple of features worth noting in this fairly typical passage from the dialogues in *Buying Brass*:

- The format of question and answer rarely ends in resolution, or, to use the language of dialectics introduced in Chapter 1, the thesis (the question) and the antithesis (the reply) rarely reach a synthesis (an agreed answer). The only person charged with reaching conclusions is the spectator.
- The dialogue itself is not formulaic. On the one hand, the Dramaturg does not 'feed' the Philosopher easy questions, but asks a genuinely searching question that is itself complex and well expressed. On the other hand, the Philosopher's replies are not simple, but acknowledge the complexity of the issues involved. If dialogue is not formulaic, it has the power to surprise the spectator and provoke thought either by challenging what a spectator might expect or by introducing new ideas.
- As a result, the *spectator* is invited to learn in the theatre. However, the learning itself is not the learning of a particular lesson – the Philosopher deals in ideas that are not translated into practice. Instead, the spectator is being asked to think about ideas, reflect on their validity and reach conclusions: the spectator learns how to learn in the theatre.

The dialogue form allows ideas to emerge and develop, so that the spectator can follow their evolution and the various figures' responses to them. In order to start from basic principles, Brecht separates himself from the Philosopher in an important way: the Philosopher is portrayed as someone who, unlike Brecht, has no experience of practical theatre. This aspect allows Brecht to use the Philosopher as a way of probing the theatre-people about their craft because he needs them to spell out the practices he will then go on to challenge. Brecht has made the Philosopher deliberately naïve; he asks questions with a view to teasing out the ways the theatre works at present. Take the following example, the response to the Philosopher's question about the nature of the 'fourth wall':

> THE DRAMATURG: Plays are usually performed as if the stage had four walls and not three, the fourth wall being on the side where the audience is sitting. The impression created and maintained is that what happens on the stage is a genuine incident from real life, in which of course there is no audience. Acting with a fourth wall, in other words, means acting as if there wasn't an audience.
>
> THE ACTOR: You get the idea? The audience sees very intimate episodes without itself being seen. It's just like somebody looking through a keyhole at a scene between people who have no idea they are not alone. In reality, of course, we arrange it all so that you get a good view of everything. We just hide the fact that it's been arranged.
>
> (*Brass* 63)

The Philosopher's ignorance allows the Dramaturg to offer a definition before the Actor qualifies it with his own 'inside' knowledge. That is, the standard definition of the fourth wall is revealed as something of a smokescreen because the actors *are* aware of the audience and indeed perform for them while pretending not to. The Actor's speech is an example of dramatic irony: the Actor says one thing (he proudly reveals the secrets of his profession) while the audience understands something else (the fourth wall is a sham). The audience can thus follow more clearly the Philosopher's arguments later that propose the removal of the fourth wall entirely. However, the dialogue form is doing more than just exposing the nature of the fourth wall. It also shows that conventional actors still feel that the fiction of a fourth wall is worthwhile and valid. If a new 'thaëter' is to be introduced, then it will need to convince artists in the old theatre of the merit of its innovations. Brecht's dialogues are thus not only about developing ideas, but also understanding the positions of representative figures from the theatre and how they respond to the Philosopher's proposals.

Of course, Brecht's ideas, as articulated by the Philosopher, are the focus of *Buying Brass* and the dialogues are designed to bring out his positions so that they unfold in all their complexity and subtlety. Thus the topics that are covered concentrate on Brecht's own interests, and it would be tempting to think that *Buying Brass* was simply a vehicle for Brecht to prove the correctness of his theories. Yet, as already seen, the Philosopher is not given an easy ride, and the other characters make convincing points that need to be dealt with if the Philosopher's ideas are to have any purchase. All the time the spectator observes the action from the auditorium and is charged with making judgements.

A Brechtian performance of *Buying Brass*

It would have been difficult for Brecht to propose a new way of making theatre while having actors play the parts of those involved in *Buying Brass* in the manner of the old theatre. Brecht proposes in one of his earliest notes on the project that the performance of the dialogues be contrasted with a failed attempt to stage a 'theatre of the scientific age'. In this scenario, the Actress has invited the Philosopher to the theatre after an unsuccessful performance of the new kind of theatre, and the theatre-makers are dissatisfied with their own inadequate results (see *Brass* 11). In another exchange, it may be the case that the theatre-people have been involved in a production of *King Lear*. In either setting, which may overlap with each other, the figures on stage want to explore the new theatre. If performance is to become a part of the argument in *Buying Brass*, then the dialogues themselves need to grapple with the methods of the new theatre, too. Thus, if the

Philosopher is to be portrayed critically, then his comments need not be accepted at face value, but questioned.

When the Berliner Ensemble performed *Buying Brass* in 1963, the Philosopher was presented in a deliberately ironic fashion in order to keep an amount of distance between him and the audience. He was dressed and made-up to look like Brecht, yet when he spoke, he sometimes had to consult a notebook to make his points; he was not a fluent and confident articulator of his own ideas, but needed help. The figure, then, was comic and not earnest, exploiting the audience's knowledge of Brecht and playfully undermining it. The same principles can also be applied to the others, too. They can be portrayed ironically, with the actors showing the distance between themselves and their figures. The Actor, for example, could be rendered in such a way that he does his best to resist the Philosopher's ideas because they attack all he has held dear in terms of acting practice. An actor could show *why* the Actor was so sceptical of the Philosopher.

All the figures can be analysed for the contradictions they display so that each one surprises the audience by revealing different facets of their behaviours. Rather than portraying the Philosopher in an overly positive light and the others as miserable relics of an outmoded theatrical past, a more Brechtian production could make the Philosopher's debate with the old theatre more credible by allowing each side to stand its ground so that all the ideas under discussion are treated seriously. A production of *Buying Brass* can use Brecht's own staging principles to treat the material being performed dialectically.

The dialogues in *Buying Brass* do work that discursive essays cannot. Brecht organizes the speeches in such a way that there is space for a spectator to stand back and process the arguments on stage and reach conclusions. Yet because the dialogues are not an acting manual, *Buying Brass* also asks actors and directors to develop the theoretical positions into forms of practice if they are to stage the work in such a way that it complements the thrust of the arguments.

Not only dialogues: *Buying Brass*'s scenes for actors

In Brecht's early plans for *Buying Brass* as a whole, one section includes material of a different type from that of the dialogues. Here Brecht indicates that he wants to see performances of scenes as a way of *demonstrating* his 'thaëter'. While it is unclear precisely what he meant by the headings 'experiments', 'exercises' and 'variations on Shakespeare' in his plans, there are scenes and exercises present in the *Buying Brass* documents that do not include the Philosopher and the others. Brecht divided his 'Practice Pieces for Actors' into four sections: two 'parallel scenes', two 'intermezzos', one poem and a scene aimed at bringing out qualities Brecht valued in his actors. I will take each example in turn.

The 'parallel scenes' are designed to reinvigorate classic plays by changing the actors' approaches to performing them. Brecht despaired of actors playing Shakespeare who got lost in the language without paying attention to the action that drove the speeches. The 'parallel scenes' emphasize action over character in a bid to reorientate the actors, and the two found in *Buying Brass* echo famous scenes from the dramatic canon. Brecht chose one from *Macbeth* and one from Schiller's *Mary Stuart*. I will concentrate on the former as it is better known to English-speaking readers.

This parallel scene covers the events concerning the murder of King Duncan and the discovery of his corpse. Brecht's new scene is set in a porter's lodge (although it has no connection with the comic 'porter scene' in *Macbeth*). Here a driver brings the porter's wife a valuable yet fragile Chinese good-luck talisman which she later accidentally decapitates when she stumbles over it. The porter and his wife, who are obviously working people serving rich masters, then blame a drowsy beggar who is staying in the lodge for the accident when the housekeeper arrives to collect the broken item. The parallels with the murder of Duncan are clear: the porter and his wife are Macbeth and Lady Macbeth, the talisman Duncan, the beggar the king's guards, the housekeeper the king's entourage. However, one immediately recognizes that there is no murder, that the 'decapitation' is accidental and of an object, and that there is no motivating factor, such as ambition. Brecht constructs a scene that is *reminiscent* of its original, but one that changes important details. What remains is the action itself: the blind panic in the face of the murder/the accident and blaming someone else. Brecht understood the scene as a rehearsal exercise, not as one to be performed for a paying audience. Actors work through the scene and then transfer its treatment of the action and the characters' responses back into the original scene's speeches. Brecht invites actors to *play the situation and not the character* in the parallel scene in a bid to inject the pressure of real events back into *Macbeth*.

The two 'intermezzos' have a similar status: they are to be rehearsed, but not performed, with a view to enlivening old plays that have lost their energy after years of performance in the old theatre. An 'intermezzo' is a scene that comes between two others. Brecht writes intermezzos for *Hamlet* and *Romeo and Juliet*. In the latter, he offers two short scenes that come between the first and second scenes of the second act, that is, before the so-called 'balcony scene' in which Romeo overhears Juliet's feelings for him prior to appearing below her in person. Brecht's scenes concern Romeo and one of his tenant farmers, and Juliet and one of her servants. In the first, Brecht reminds the actor playing Romeo of his social position in the upper echelons of Veronese society. Romeo is short of money and plans to sell the tenant's farm to raise funds for an elaborate present for Juliet. A stage direction indicates that the farmer should wander around in the background of the 'balcony scene', and one may interpret this instruction as a way of showing the audience and the actor playing Romeo that the social problem persists. In the other scene, Juliet questions her serving woman about her lover, Thurio. Juliet permits the servant to go to Thurio, something made urgent when she learns of his desire to see another woman as well. Juliet then hears a twig break and both women realize it is Romeo. Now Juliet needs the servant to distract the door-keeper below so that she can speak to Romeo undetected. Juliet's need is thus placed above that of her social inferior, and another stage direction tells the woman to be present during the ensuing scene, again as a means of retaining the presence of the social contradiction. In this pair of scenes, Brecht invites the actors of the famous roles not to neglect their social position when playing the famous characters, but to perform their parts mindful that they are not 'simply' star-crossed lovers, but members of a divided, class-based society. Their freedom of action is based on their wealth and the power it brings over those lower down the social ladder.

Brecht's third exercise is the performance of the following 'circular' poem:

> A dog went into the kitchen
> And stole an egg from the cook.
> The cook took his cleaver
> And cut the dog in two.
> The other dogs came
> And dug him a grave
> And put on it a headstone
> With the following epitaph:
> A dog went into the kitchen ...

That is, the speaker keeps repeating the poem for as long as is required. Here Brecht wants the actor to try out a new role with each repetition. Each character should establish its relationship to the events and show its opinion on them. A cook, for example, might consider the act justified; a judge might be more distanced; a dog-lover sympathetic to the hound's plight; a beggar jealous of the dog's achievement, etc.

This relatively simple exercise conceals an amount of complexity. The actor has very little time to establish each character and has to choose precisely which words or phrases might reveal the character's role and attitudes. The repetitious nature of the exercise also means that a spectator will have little difficulty understanding the nature of the task and so becomes an 'expert' quickly. The spectators are in a position to determine the success of the short performances and assess whether the actor has been inventive and accurate or whether the actor is relying on tricks and technique to sham each characterization. The exercise is thus not only about developing clear and well-observed approaches to acting, but having them validated or rejected by the audience.

The final exercise is another that can be performed to an audience. The 'Contest between Homer and Hesiod' is a dialogue between the two classical poets in which Hesiod puts questions to Homer. It is concerned with laying verbal traps and linguistic cunning, and is framed by on-stage commentary and narration. According to Brecht in his note preceding the text, the training value of the exercise is the study of speaking verse and the ability to portray two 'determined old men who present a struggle rich in gesture'.[6] Again, this scene is about developing actors' expressive skills, but whereas role and attitude is central to the poem about the dog, here the relationship between Homer and Hesiod is key as the rivals try to outsmart each other. When the Berliner Ensemble staged its version of *Buying Brass*, the two actors wore masks and flowing robes. Without the expressivity of their faces, they had to show their relationship through voice, physical gestures and positioning on stage.

Brecht also imagined that performance could play an illuminating role in *Buying Brass*'s dialogues themselves. In one fragment, he gives the stage direction '*the Actress plays a man*' (*Brass* 66). The Philosopher initiates the ensuing dialogue by remarking that a man playing a man would not draw attention to the character's masculinity in the way a woman would. This is because she has to observe what it is that makes a man's actions different from her own and can then emphasize this in performance. Her portrayal thus draws attention to qualities that would otherwise go unnoticed. In this dialogue, then, performance serves as a starting point for further discussion and is the measure by which the points of the discussion can be assessed.

Brecht's plans are not clear on how he sought to integrate these examples of real theatre practice into the performance of the project as a whole. It is difficult to see how the 'parallel scenes' or the 'intermezzos' would have proved engaging or useful for an audience because they were designed for rehearsal. Their value lies with the actors involved and in the performances that they would *later* give in productions of *Macbeth* or *Romeo and Juliet*. In the Berliner Ensemble production of 1963, the parallel scene to *Mary Stuart* was indeed performed, but it would not have had the function Brecht intended for it: the actors were not making discoveries because they had already rehearsed the scene several times.

The poem and the 'Contest', on the other hand, present exercises that can be evaluated by an audience as examples of approaches to acting in which the body as a whole, rather than the head on its own, makes meaning. They also reflect, in practical ways, some of the arguments made in the dialogue sections. When, say, an actor performs the poem, it is clear that he or she is not trying to 'be' a new character and deceive the audience with every repetition. Instead, the actor is consciously *displaying* each new character, with the audience very much in cahoots, judging, and hopefully enjoying, the actor's abilities. This is not the theatre of naturalism, but one in which actor and spectator acknowledge each other. The 'Contest' then builds on the skills developed in the poem and deploys them in a scene whose very essence is a public performance. So, even if Brecht only considered using the final two parts of the 'Practice Pieces for Actors', these still would have offered an audience an active role in reflecting on the new theatre in a different, more directly theatre-oriented performance than the other dialogues.

Montage, or: Structured disruption in the episodic form of *Buying Brass*

Buying Brass is a project that includes many different forms of performative writing. Its unfinished status makes it difficult to know just what Brecht intended for the work as a whole. He left behind dialogues, scenes and poems. In his own plans for organizing *Buying Brass*'s elements, Brecht divides the action into four 'nights' of thematically linked sections. It is unclear whether each 'night' was designed to take place over four real nights or functioned as an act in a four-part whole.

Each 'night' was to contain a number of different episodes. In the first, for example, one finds headings such as 'the theatre's business is good/the Philosopher's business is not so good/escape from reality into the theatre' (*Brass* 119–20). The form of each night is based on the assembly of related but different parts, or, as Brecht would have called it, a montage. Montage is the positioning of disparate elements to form a whole. To Brecht, montage was a powerful way of organizing material to activate spectators because *they* have to make the connections, not the actors. In the example of episodes from the first night, it is clear that the first two headings are related to each other thematically by considering the success of the old theatre and the Philosopher's failure to establish a new one. The third appears to be addressing a more direct critique of the old theatre – that its conventions and representations are out of touch with the real world. So, even though the episodes in *Buying Brass* all address tensions between the old and new theatres, they do not flow from the one into the other, but leave gaps to be filled by the spectators. With this in mind, the episodic organization of *Buying Brass* also contributes to the enactment of the Philosopher's theory. It jolts the audience out of a passive position into one where its members have to negotiate the relationships between the different parts. They can then construct ways of understanding the complexities of Brecht's ideas for a new theatre in their entirety. This does not mean, however, that the audience is obliged to agree with everything the Philosopher suggests: the montage makes it possible for spectators to approve certain facets while challenging or rejecting others. If *Buying Brass* represents Brecht's attempt to make his audience active and critical, then such responses are to be expected.

In Brecht's early planning documents, the relationships between the four nights also have a montage quality. The first two seek to criticize the old theatre and conclude with the tantalizing heading 'foundation of the thaëter'. The third night includes what appear to be demonstrations of thaëter, taken in part from material Brecht had already written, along with dialogues and perhaps sections of the 'Practice Pieces for Actors'. The fourth night opens with the heading 'reconversion of the thaëter into a theatre'. This movement from night to night dramatizes the mechanism of the dialectic. Here, the old theatre, or the theatre as Brecht found it, is the thesis. The Philosopher's 'thaëter', presented on the third night, is the antithesis. One might have thought that Brecht would stop there. Instead, he adds a fourth night in which he acknowledges just how difficult it will be to implement his innovations. As a good dialectician, he understands that he cannot simply do away with the old theatre, but meld its practices with his own proposals, and so the fourth night enacts another experiment, the synthesis of thaëter and theatre. Once again, this is an experiment aimed squarely at the audience: having followed the arguments in the first two nights and experienced the performance and discussion of the new theatre in the third, the spectators are offered various episodes that ask what *might* happen in future.

Brecht perhaps never finished the *Buying Brass* project because it was trying to do too much with too many disparate montage elements. His goal of setting out his theories and opening them up to the audience was a question of both constructing and organizing the parts. As has been shown, they can work remarkably well, and he had certainly found a practicable way of bringing theory off the page and into the theatre.

The importance of the *Buying Brass* project is not only to be found in the ways it performs theory, but in what it tells us about Brecht's understanding of theory. The theory that forms the project's subject matter is by definition unfixed. Characters take issue with and develop it, and, beyond the stage, it is offered to the audience for its consideration and judgement. This is the status of theory to Brecht: it is not final and it is open to further analysis. Theory can be criticized in discussion and in the light of its embodiment in performance, and this, indeed, is how Brecht treated his theories when he finally got his own theatre company in 1949. What *Buying Brass* also signifies is Brecht's desire to create a bridge between theory and practice, not to keep them as separate entities. Brecht took this idea further, and it can be seen in his rehearsal practice. However, before considering how Brecht rehearsed, I will turn to his thoughts on and ideas for a new theatre in the next two chapters.

Brecht and Difference

The centrality of change and its relationship to difference in Brecht's theatre

Ever since the mid-1920s, when he had become interested in Marxism and dialectics, Brecht had written short stories and parables that featured the fictional ̣   ̣ner One, called 'Meeting Again', runs as follows in its entirety:

> A man who had not seen Mr K. for a long time greeted him with the words: 'You haven't changed a bit'. 'Oh!', said Mr K. and turned pale.[1]

The simplicity of the two lines conceals a complexity of ideas surrounding Keuner's unexpected reaction. The anecdote surprises the reader because the man believes he is paying Keuner a compliment, yet Keuner is taken aback. The reader is thus invited to ask why Keuner blanches.

One answer is that Keuner feels that he *has* changed, but that the man who has not seen him for some time has not noticed. Personal change is often a gradual process; near-death experiences and large lottery wins – events that may alter someone drastically and quickly – are a rare occurrence. Yet anyone who keeps a diary can look back on episodes in their life and observe the changes in attitude, understanding and behaviour that have taken place over time. Observations, decisions and actions that seemed so clear and obvious at one point become questionable in the light of the knowledge and experiences accumulated in the meantime. So, because change can be slow and gradual, it is possible that the man who bumps into Keuner is simply unable to register just how much Keuner has changed: this is a problem of visibility.

Another answer is that the man does indeed register that change has taken place, but does not let Keuner know this, even though the man knows it has taken place. Perhaps the man felt he was being polite by not registering the changes, but such politeness is built on an assumption that change is in some way unwelcome or unwanted. Nowadays, such a response may be linked to one's outward appearance, that the aging process is not as apparent as it could have been. Being old and less attractive is frowned upon rather than acknowledged as a part of a natural process. Or perhaps the man felt obliged to trot out a popular cliché, that despite all appearances, Keuner was the same man he ever was. This sentiment is one that points to continuity in the face of change: however much one *appears* to change on the surface, there is still something constant underneath.

Such a position is essentially conservative and has implications for far greater political issues. At its heart is a model of human nature. The sociologist Charles Horton Cooley developed the idea that there is a relationship between how a society defines 'human nature' and the ways it organizes itself.[2] Cooley is not interested in *what* 'human nature' means. Rather, he concentrates on *how* any society's understanding of the self affects the way it creates laws, public institutions and customs. Cooley invites us to ask what kind of society develops when human nature is understood as unchanging. The answer, unsurprisingly, is a society that is unchanging.

Of course, no society remains the same, but here it is worth making a distinction between reform and revolution. Changes in the political or social situation, or in technology and ideas, have an impact on every society, yet politicians may seek to reform the system so that it can accommodate or adapt to the changes. The system remains the same at heart. Revolution, however, rejects the existing system and replaces it with another. A model of human nature as changeable is therefore a necessary prerequisite for a revolution.

If Cooley is right, then the West's social and economic structures, which have developed and endured for several centuries, reflect an understanding of human nature as stable. Such a narrative of human nature also acts as a way of *preventing* fundamental change from taking place because it suggests that such ambitions are futile: human beings are unable to go beyond their 'innate' limitations and transform society into something fundamentally different. Francis Fukuyama argues that history 'shows' that human beings cannot escape their nature: he reads the collapse of communism in the East after the fall of the Berlin Wall in 1989 as evidence that Western liberal democracy and free-market capitalism are the complementary systems best suited to human beings.[3] Brecht, on the other hand, objects to such a definition of human nature, as will become apparent later in the chapter, and wants to emphasize change over constancy.

The short Keuner parable highlights two significant aspects regarding Brecht's concerns for his theatre:

- Change occurs, but may not be visible. Brecht therefore sets about finding ways of showing change on stage.
- Change can be actively rejected or underplayed in the interest of a continuity that supports the status quo. Here Brecht looks at how to open a dialogue between human beings and their social and historical contexts on stage in order to show how they might influence each other.

This chapter focuses on how Brecht designed a theatre that sought to expose rather than to hide change and to understand its dynamics and its consequences. Again, the key word is 'dialectics'. Brecht was keen to find theatrical representations that allowed spectators to understand the world as one of instability, constantly defined by contradictions whose opposing parts bring about not superficial, but actual change.

If we read the parable in terms of theatre, with Keuner as a character on stage and the man as a member of the audience, the relationship is one in which change has been underplayed or ignored. The spectator looks at the character and finds someone who may have changed over the course of the drama, yet has kept his self intact. Keuner's response to the observation, however, suggests that much *has* changed, but that that has either been kept from the spectator or the spectator has willingly overlooked the change. Brecht thus needed to create a theatre in which change is foregrounded, and foregrounded in such a way that the spectator cannot ignore it. Change is intimately linked to difference: one is not the same after a change. Difference thus stands at the heart of Brecht's theatre, and it takes on many forms.

Forgetting 'character'

In the case of Mr Keuner, the man he had met again either did not notice or did not accept that change had taken place. For Brecht, the desire to keep things as they always are is dangerous: it suggests the proposition that if people do not change, then society either will not, or more worryingly, cannot change. Brecht's belief in the dialectic means he considers that neither human beings nor human society are stable, and it is thus drama's job to bring this out.

Brecht's model of character was radical and presumed that a unified character did not actually exist. On the contrary, what might be considered 'character' was only the accumulation of a character's behaviours over time, as his assistant Käthe Rülicke[4] notes:

> Brecht hardly ever gives directions that relate to the 'character' of the figures; on the contrary their characters emerge from their behaviour. Thus, no figure is a figure 'in itself', but rather 'in relation

to' someone else; something different 'in relation to' every other person. If Brecht ever does say anything about a figure's 'character', then he derives it from their social situation.[5]

Before proceeding to an interpretation of the lines, I will briefly note the linguistic distinction Rülicke makes between a 'figure' and a 'character'. This distinction is not unusual in German, but it is in English, and it is worth retaining it to show the difference between the two conceptions. To Brecht, a figure is something that is unfixed and flexible; a character has definite and persistent qualities.

Rülicke touches on a difficult set of ideas and it is worth approaching them one by one:

- First, characteristics are not something that come from inside, an in-born set of qualities. Instead, they are *exhibited* to others in the different forms of one's behaviour.
- Second, behaviour is not something that simply exists in itself, but rather is directed towards someone else and differs depending on who the someone else is. If we think of Lady Macbeth, for example, she drives Macbeth to murder Duncan and take the crown for himself. Yet once the deed is done she is sickened, eventually goes mad and apparently commits suicide off-stage. So, is she strong and ruthless or weak and remorseful? It is impossible to answer this question because we only have her speeches and deeds by which to judge her. She is a fluid figure: resolute when out of power and keen to grasp an opportunity through her husband, yet once the context changes, a different side is exposed and she behaves differently. What is her true character? We cannot say, but we can comment on the way she behaves under different circumstances. That is, Brecht is not concerned with psychology, a seemingly fundamental concept for an actor. Instead he invites actors to explore a figure's behaviour in context from the outside and understand relationships (between figures

or between figures and events) as defining elements in building
the dramatic figure.

- Third, Rülicke acknowledges that when Brecht does talk about a
  figure's character, it is based squarely in terms of social context.
  By this Brecht means that one's place in society may give a clue
  to why someone behaves like they do. Would Lady Macbeth
  incite her husband to murder the king with a view to becoming
  king himself if they were not nobles? This is unlikely. Thus, she
  may not 'naturally' be so scheming and cold-blooded, rather, she
  might be trying to take advantage of her position as a privileged
  member of a hierarchical society in which those at the top might
  pursue personal gain.

A figure to Brecht is something that an audience can never know;
spectators only see an individual's different behaviours in a series
of different contexts. What would an audience make of a manager
who lords it over the employees while kowtowing to the company's
owner? Is this person a bully or a coward? Brecht would argue that the
manager is a contradictory mixture of both and would trace this back
to the way the business was run. The manager is looked down upon by
the owner and made to know his place. He, in turn, displays the same
behaviour to his staff. But what would happen if the manager worked
in a co-operative where everyone owned a part of the business? Would
the same behaviour emerge? Brecht might suggest that it would not. A
figure is thus susceptible to changes in circumstance and environment
in opposition to a character that exists as a stable entity, independent
of social context.

The task of the actor is thus to build a raft of contradictory
characteristics not from speculating on the figure's 'inside', but by
observing the figure's 'outside', its behaviours towards different
people in different situations, without neglecting the overarching

social contexts of the play. The aim is to *show* different behaviours in different situations in a bid to emphasize difference.

How to build a contradictory 'figure'

Brecht recommends that actors do their best to point to, rather than to pass over, contradictions in an instruction written in the early 1940s: '*memorizing the first impressions*' of a role.[6] Here Brecht acknowledges that familiarity with a role can have a negative effect on its contradictory realization. That is, an actor may be surprised by a figure's behaviour when first reading the part. Yet, over the rehearsal period the actor becomes more familiar with the figure and risks turning it into a character. The actor may either forget the initial astonishment and treat the behaviour with increasing understanding, or find ways of explaining the behaviour, reducing the extent of the contradictions that initially led to astonishment. In either case, the actor has taken something unexpected and turned it into something accepted. By memorizing first impressions, the actor can preserve the sense of wonder, shock or surprise, and retain these qualities in a discontinuous performance. Actors with the Berliner Ensemble noted that the study of their figures was based on locating 'turning points' and 'breaks' in a figure's behaviour. They were then asked to perform their roles with an emphasis on showing these discontinuities.[7] What Brecht wanted to counter on stage can be seen in the following quotation from Naomie Harris, a British actor who plays Winnie Mandela in a screen biopic of Nelson:

> She's a very difficult woman to capture because she is like seven different people in one and I think because of her experiences as a person she is fractured. Trying to pull all that together was my greatest challenge.[8]

It is the last sentence, in which Harris seeks to reconcile contradictory features that Brecht wanted to challenge. He was keen to draw attention to disparity and ask the audience why the same person might act in such opposing ways. While film, as a more 'realistic' medium, may seek to harmonize contradictions, Brecht made use of the theatre's artifice to expose them.

Brecht offers a tool for constructing figures in this vein in the form of the 'not – but'.[9] He asks actors to think not only about what their figures are doing, but also what they are not doing. In the scenario sketched above, the manager is *not* treating the staff decently, *but* treating them poorly. Or, Lady Macbeth does *not* celebrate the murder of Duncan, *but* regrets it. In each case, the actor shows that their figure is not fixed: under different circumstances the figure may have behaved differently. In the 'Short Organon', Brecht recommends establishing the 'not – but' as an exercise in constructing a figure. The idea is that figures are kept open; they are sites of possibilities and do not act in ways predetermined by their 'character', but under the influence of their situation. Performing the 'not – but' is about showing alternatives:

- Imagine that a figure exits stage right rather than stage left. This is a normal enough action. Yet an actor could show that there was an *alternative* by looking stage left while exiting stage right. Such a gesture might prove significant: stage right may lead to the kitchen in which the figure toils, while stage left leads to the living room that offers leisure and relaxation.
- Or consider when Richmond kills Richard III at the end of *Richard III*: Richmond can show that he is *not* sparing the defeated king, *but* killing him. This has a different meaning from Richmond just killing Richard: it shows that Richmond views the murder as a necessity, although the precise reasons for his conclusion have to be answered by the audience. Showing that

mercy *was* a possibility points to the fact that Richmond has dismissed it.

The 'not – but' is a device in the actor's arsenal that helps to open up behaviour on stage as changeable. The actor performs difference: the difference between not doing one thing but another. The 'not – but' generates two important effects in the auditorium:

- First, it invites the audience to speculate on why one decision was taken over the other.
- Second, it depicts a stage world in which action is not inevitable, but the product of pressures that, in Brecht's theatre, are social in nature.

Brecht's understanding of 'character' is that there is no such thing as an 'essential' character. Figures respond differently to different situations. Any figure's 'characteristics' are only as durable as the most extreme test of them. Lady Macbeth reveals that her strength and determination collapse when she is confronted by the consequences of her murderous plan. Her husband's deed has changed her and will transform her into a gibbering wreck, obsessed with purging herself of guilt. Yet all 'characters' exhibit these contradictions, and they serve to unfix the character from their characteristics. Characteristics *emerge* from events that provoke responses. They are also connected to someone's place in society. As a result, the *same* action can have *different* meanings to different figures. It is unlikely that a Scottish peasant would assassinate King Duncan to gain the crown, but that peasant might consider undertaking such a drastic action to rail against an unfair feudal society. So, both Lady Macbeth and our imaginary peasant might carry out the same act, but they would be doing it for very different reasons because of their different social positions.

The emphasis on difference in the performance of a figure is not the result of actors' understanding of their figures as 'characters', but an acknowledgement that figures are in a dynamic relationship with their environment and with other figures. The actor is thus invited to start with the *situation* and to derive behaviour from the situation rather than to impose behaviour on a situation. Actors in Brecht's theatre play the situation and not the character, a crucial idea I will return to in Chapters 5 and 8. This fundamental change of perspective means that events and actions come first, not a predetermined conception of character. Brecht believed that such an approach was simply more realistic, a better model of reality than one that assumes that human beings retain unchanging qualities in the form of 'character' that exist independent of their experiences. To put this into context, it is like asking the question, 'how would you react if you picked up a wallet full of money that also contained a return address?' You might *speculate* on what you would do, but the only test would be to experience the situation. Would you really send it back with all the money? Might you send it back, but retain a banknote as a 'finder's fee'? Would you send it back at all? Brecht invites us not to speculate on situations and not to base our potential behaviour on aspects of our 'character', but to perform such situations and perhaps be surprised at our responses in the light of our social context. In this way of rehearsing, where situation trumps 'character', Brecht believes that contradictory actions in response to different situations not only mirror reality, but point to reality's potential for change.

The dangers of empathy in theatrical communication

Brecht often refers to his new ways of making theatre in relation to the Greek philosopher Aristotle, the author of the first recorded work of theatre theory in the West, the *Poetics*. For the most part, Brecht objects to the centrality of empathy in Aristotle's understanding of theatre. Empathy has a range of meanings in different disciplines, but in theatre it has come to mean a relationship based on identification. Bruce McConachie offers a useful definition taken from the field of cognitive neuroscience, the field that investigates how our brains learn. He notes that empathy is a process 'by which one person can come to know something about what another person is intending and feeling. In this sense, empathy is a kind of mind-reading that allows one person to step into the shoes of another and experience that person's world from her or his point of view'.[10] Thus, we do not simply register other people's expressions, we *understand* them as representing happiness, anger or sadness, for example. The definition also helps to unpick a potential confusion between empathy and sympathy: the former is a process of sharing experiences, regardless of whether they are pleasant or unpleasant; the latter is an emotional relationship of concern for another.

The process of empathy alarmed Brecht for the following reasons:

- First, empathy is a universal human process: we have no choice in whether we empathize or not, unless we have certain neural deficits (as is the case with psychopaths).[11]
- Second, empathy is immune to differences in context: a person empathizes with a worker and an aristocrat in the same way (that the person might choose to respond differently to the experience of empathy afterwards is another matter entirely). The fact that empathy simply 'happens' means that there is a risk that we experience another person's point of view without understanding *why* he or she holds it. As a result, we might find ourselves identifying with something that is more complex than it appears.
- Third, and in a similar vein, empathy is value-neutral, so we can as easily empathize with a saint as with a sinner. It is not the case

that empathy 'turns itself off' to protect us from experiencing something particularly nasty. Consequently, we may find 'bad' behaviour alluring or simply acceptable, and this might remind readers of the example Brecht gives of his experience of the film *Gunga Din* in Chapter 1.

The dangers of empathy were all too evident to Brecht as an exile from the Nazis. In a theoretical dialogue akin to those of the *Buying Brass* project, Brecht criticizes the Nazis for using theatrical techniques to get the German people to agree with them.[12] Here, empathy creates a link between an irrational and hateful set of ideas, and a mass of people who should know better. The emotional appeal of a passionate Adolf Hitler or the spectacle of hundreds of thousands of Nazis at the Nuremberg Rallies could have the effect of bypassing human reason and generating unquestioning feelings in the audience. Yet Brecht also acknowledged that empathy was an undoubted element of any experience of theatre in section of *Buying Brass* (*Brass* 33–4). He thus had to find a way to short-circuit empathy because it was impossible to eliminate it. In addition, he tried to find productive uses for it, too.

Interrupting empathy in Brecht's theatre

Empathy, as Brecht understood it, manifests itself in two major contexts in theatre: in the relationship between actor and character (where the term 'identification' is more fitting), and in the relationship between audience and characters. Here I am deliberately using the word 'character' because empathy will arise in a more consistent manner when an actor is playing a character as a unified whole rather than playing the situation, which may fundamentally change the way a figure behaves.

I will take the actor–character relationship first. The actor, who
may have little in common with the figure he or she is playing, can
assume the figure's qualities and perform the character in a mode of
acceptance, embracing all that is found in the character due to the
bond empathy can create or identification can promote. Brecht does
not exclude identification as a way for an actor to approach a character.
After many experiences directing with the Berliner Ensemble, Brecht
formalized his understanding of identificatory relationships between
actor and role in 1953. Here he sketched three stages in the process
of constructing a character. The first is the hunt for contradictions,
of searching 'for the ugly in the beautiful, for the beautiful in the
ugly. In the first phase, your most important gesture is shaking your
head'.[13] Identifying with the character is the second phase: 'the search
for the truth of the character in the subjective sense, you let the
character do what *it* wants, how it wants, [the actor's] criticisms [of
the character] be damned'.[14] The third phase takes the actor outside
the character once again and returns him or her to the first phase,
in which the contradictory nature of the character returns. Only
this time, the actor, having identified with the character, can bring
the understanding gained from this process to the contradictions, as
opposed to the 'head shaking' of the first phase.

Brecht thus introduces the dialectic into actor training. The actor
moves from incomprehension (why does the character behave
so contradictorily?), to apparent understanding (so this is what
the character feels when doing these divergent things), to fuller
understanding (I have combined the contradictory nature of the
character with an appreciation of how it behaves). Brecht notes,
however, in the light of his experiences with the Berliner Ensemble,
that the three phases are not separate and may not follow the scheme
as neatly as he maintains: his reflections abstract a process that is
in fact more complex. Evidence for the inclusion of identificatory
rehearsal phases with the Berliner Ensemble is registered from the

first production Brecht directed to the last.[15] So, identification to
Brecht is indeed something that can give an actor depth and insight.
It is just that such a process is not an end in itself, but a part of a larger
scheme for creating a figure rather than a character.

The need to construct characters that are not unified, but
contradictory, with whom the actor does not always identify, is part
of a greater plan because, in Brecht's theatre, the focus is always on
the spectator. Everything on stage, however elaborately theorized
and practised, is for the benefit of the spectator as the person who
ultimately learns from the action on stage. Brecht feared that the
audience would empathize with the characters on stage and experience
what they experience without standing back and understanding why
the characters acted as they did. That is, spectators would be more
likely to be passive, get caught up in the fiction of the story being
told and thus ask no questions. An opportunity to provoke a response
that might lead to the analysis of the action would be lost. Ultimately,
the audience might simply accept the world as it was presented on
stage as in some way inevitable or unchangeable. This, after all, was
the response to the 'theatricality' of the Nazis: significant parts of the
German populace were taken in, did not question the Nazis' premises
or consider the alternatives to them, and followed the Führer headlong
into disaster. Brecht's argument runs that any good theatre will not
unify an audience because the audience itself is divided along social
lines. He believes that unencumbered empathy produces 'an audience
that reacts in a unified fashion'.[16]

To understand how a production might divide its audience, I return
to the example of *Macbeth*. What might an audience think about the
murder of Duncan? The obvious answer is that it is repulsed by the act.
Duncan has done nothing to provoke Macbeth to murder; indeed, the
king has just rewarded his general for victory in battle. An audience
may well feel a sense of outrage, that one human being has slain another
in the pursuit of his own self-interest. This might be considered a

'universal' response. But Brecht asks his audience for a differentiated reaction. Those in positions of power may well feel enraged by the act and/or compassionate for Duncan, whereas those lower down the social scale might respond with more indifference: the privileged are hacking each other to pieces but my lot hardly improves. In a production that emphasizes social position instead of human tragedy, the horror of one class might contrast with the shrugs of indifference from another. By disrupting the audience's empathetic relationship with the stage, a production can open up a differentiated set of responses.

Brecht, then, was critical of complete identification and empathy, but nonetheless recognized that they were fundamental parts of the actors' and the audience's experience of theatre. What he wanted to achieve in his new theatre was a way of frustrating the simple, undisturbed processes of empathy. We have seen how he approached this with respect to the actor (and I will return to how Brecht actually rehearsed his actors in Chapter 6). The next section examines how the stage itself can disrupt unproblematic communication between itself and the audience.

Separating the elements of the performance and the meaning of 'epic theatre'

Brecht deliberately sought out theatrical means to make empathy problematic for the audience; frustrating its processes was key to Brecht's political ideas. In the notes of 1930 on his opera *The Rise and Fall of the City of Mahagonny*, Brecht suggests a 'radical *separation of elements*' that make up live opera: the text, the music and their performance.[17] Here Brecht is responding in particular to Richard Wagner, the great opera composer and theoretician, who proposed an aesthetic known as the *Gesamtkunstwerk*. This term denotes a work of art in which each of its constituent elements helps form a unified whole. Theatrical performance is, in part, the simultaneous transmission of different signs. The actor's body, the actor's voice, the actor's gestures, the actor's position, the other actors, the lighting, the sounds, the set and other elements encode meaning for a spectator to decode. A *Gesamtkunstwerk* harmonizes the different sign systems. So, put crudely, a sad scene features sad words sung by singers sadly to sad music against sombre lighting. Brecht criticizes such an arrangement not so much for what the stage is doing, but for the effect it has on the audience. He notes that agreement between the signs on stage allows the spectator to sit back and become passive: the stage is not asking questions, but simply transmitting a single impulse – something sad is taking place – and it is simple for a spectator to decode this.

A 'separation of elements' means that the signs being transmitted from the stage to the auditorium do not agree with each other and thus provoke *the audience* to make sense of them. Again, Brecht deploys difference as a means to make the spectator productive. Here are a couple of examples of how this might work, taken from Brecht's productions with the Berliner Ensemble:

- Brecht directed his own play, *The Caucasian Chalk Circle*, in 1954. He had planned to end the show with a grand musical parade in which each figure would dance on stage. One of his assistants noted, however: 'the music must not be illustrated. Dance against the music!'.[18] Here it would have been easy to choreograph a pleasing finale, but instead Brecht wanted to show each figure's relationship to the celebration through their relationships to the music. In this way, the stage could pose questions to the audience born of the differences between the figures' bodies and the music.
- The Berliner Ensemble's production of Brecht's play *Mr Puntila and his Man Matti* separated text and its delivery to create a different kind of work for the audience. The scene 'Tales from Finland', for example, was an important one to Brecht.[19] It features

stories narrated by four female figures that reflect on issues of injustice in the social sphere. After the production, assistant Peter Palitzsch wrote that the women were not treated critically, like the other figures were.[20] One might then expect a jarring piece of propaganda, but he continues: 'the scene should emerge tenderly and strangely: the women are right'. The team achieved this in the following way: 'the accusation is not in the tone, which remains easy-going, but in the construction of the respective tale'.[21] In other words, while the women may well have been telling the truth in their stories, the audience was not required to empathize with them to reach this conclusion, but to discover the correctness from the lines themselves, uncoloured by appealing phrasings or deliveries: the tension between the texts and a dry articulation means that the *spectator* has to work to create meaning.

Brecht was also keen to vary the ways in which a *play* communicates with an audience in order to create discontinuity and to disrupt the simple consumption of signs in the auditorium. Here he wanted to interrupt the dramatic flow by inserting different forms of narrative into dialogues, thus creating a different kind of 'separation of elements'. Indeed, he named the combination of dramatic and narrative 'epic theatre'. Here 'epic' does not mean 'on a grand scale' as in a Hollywood epic. Instead, it refers to Aristotle's division of the literary arts into the epic (that is, narrative poetry, like Homer's *Iliad*), the dramatic and the lyric. Brecht's aim was to switch between different modes of theatrical presentation in a bid to disrupt the relationship between a figure and the audience. This procedure is found in a variety of forms in Brecht's plays:

- He uses narrators in plays like *The Caucasian Chalk Circle*. Here a figure stands outside the action, introduces it, comments on it, adds context and draws it to close.

- Elsewhere, figures from the drama itself can fulfil similar tasks, as when, in scene eight of *The Good Person of Szechwan*, Mrs Yang narrates a series of episodes concerning her son, Sun, and his dealings with Shui-Ta.
- Brecht also opens scenes with 'epic banners', texts to be displayed or spoken that sketch the action or themes of a scene, such as in *Mother Courage* or *Life of Galileo*.
- In addition, the inclusion of songs does not exclusively serve the purpose of telling an audience more about the figures or an episode, but the songs comment and reflect on figures, events or themes, as in *The Threepenny Opera*.

In each of the examples, Brecht gets outside the action and in doing so acknowledges that the drama is a construction, it is not real but a fiction. Brecht acknowledges that the performance is taking place in the theatre and that it is not to be confused with real life. It should not be forgotten that Brecht was writing at a time when cinema was only beginning to become a mass phenomenon and television was in its infancy. Nowadays both media can create highly convincing forms of illusion that make even the most naturalistic theatre seem stagey and artificial. Spectators in the auditorium can always turn their heads and take in the theatre's apparatus, its stage, its lighting, the edges of the set, etc. There is little to persuade anyone that they are not partaking in art rather than reality. Today, then, Brecht's 'epic' devices are more about making the reception of the theatrical event complex rather than banishing illusion. They invite an audience to compare different kinds of theatrical communication or to challenge them to process a scene in a different kind of way. Viewers of a crime drama, for example, clearly have a different experience if they are watching a whodunit or a show in which the killer is identified from the outset. So, if an epic banner tells us that Mother Courage is going to lose a child, we will not focus on the outcome of that scene (will she? won't she?) but on the *way* she loses the child to the war. The device emphasizes the process rather than the outcome. Similarly, a commentary or a song will add extra material to a scene or an action rather than drive it further.

The separation of elements of a performance fulfils Brecht's call to activate the audience. The stage offers material that cannot be easily assimilated without reflection on the part of the spectator, and so the *difference* between the sign-systems helps complicate the reception process and disrupts the processes of empathy. The audience is invited to question what is seen and heard because the material on stage is not being presented in a way that allows for passive reception. However, there is an additional aspect to this practice: it poses the question as to *why*, for Brecht, the material on stage should not be easily consumable. The answer is to be found in the dialectical basis of Brecht's theatre theories and practice: what is seen and heard on stage is never simple, but the result of processes itself.

To Brecht, the decisions we make may seem to be our own, but can turn out to be connected to values born of or developed in response to our social position. Brecht again suggests that if we change society we might change the way we make decisions and the way we act in general. He is keen to show that human beings are not 'natural' as such, merely doing what they want to do, but social creatures who do this or that for reasons that may not be initially obvious. Take the following text, the second article of the UN's Universal Declaration of Human Rights, written in 1948, as an example of values that appear to be self-evident:

> Everyone is entitled to all the rights and freedoms set forth in this Declaration, without distinction of any kind, such as race, colour, sex, language, religion, political or other opinion, national or social origin, property, birth or other status.[22]

The sentiments of the article may appear to be utterly straightforward and obvious, yet why is it that such rights have taken so long to be recognized and why are they not observed and nurtured the world over? If sex is not a reason for discrimination, then why was New Zealand the first nation to give women the vote in 1893 and why did Switzerland only bring in such legislation nationwide in 1991? Values that may seem obvious to one group of people may not be so to others. Brecht wants the theatre to investigate such differences with a view to promoting insights, but not so much into the values themselves, rather, into the complex relationships that generate such values. However, while the separation of theatrical elements might activate an audience to process rather than merely to accept what is happening on stage, Brecht also proposes that the material itself be treated in such a way that it raises its own questions, and again the concept of difference plays a central role.

Historicization and/as *Verfremdung*

One of Brecht's main aims in pointing out difference on stage is to counter the process of naturalization. The values we have and the ways we behave today may appear self-evident or simply be taken for granted. However, a simple comparison with another place or another time can reveal how views or behaviours are not the same at all. One need only consider the relationship between the sexes to expose that they have changed a great deal over time and are different in different parts of the world. Values like these are not 'natural', but the result of social processes that could have led to very different opinions, had the processes themselves been different. In other words, very little in terms of our values, beliefs or behaviours is 'natural': Brecht's theatre sets out to expose what we *perceive* to be natural and show how it has been constructed. Brecht proposes that the theatre submits everything we hold to be natural to scrutiny. He notes in the 'Short Organon', as already noted in Chapter 1: 'we must be able to characterize the field in historically relative terms' (Organon §36), and we can now consider what this means for theatrical performance.

Brecht asks that we do not treat the past as if it were the same as the present, but understand how things were different. He calls the process 'historicization' and it serves to show the audience how actions and behaviours are relative rather than absolute. Historicization thus means looking at figures, actions and relationships in terms of what they meant in their own time rather than today. So, if one were to stage Chekhov's *The Cherry Orchard*, it would be impossible to historicize it without researching and understanding the state of Russian society at the turn of the nineteenth century. Why is it that Madame Ranevskaya has to sell the cherry orchard? How did she come to possess it in the first place? Why is the former peasant Lopakhin able to buy it off her? Such specific questions ultimately give way to more general ones: what are the figures' social positions, and how do these positions affect the ways that they relate to one another? These questions force the actors and the director not to take the figures and their relationships at face value, as if they were in some way 'natural' from today's perspective, but to make connections between the scenes' actions and their time. In short, little exists 'in itself', but is in dialogue with social forces that may well surprise us as actors or spectators, and it is the establishment of difference that brings about the surprise.

'Making theatre politically' is all about emphasizing difference in order to provoke audiences into asking where the discrepancies between today and yesterday originated. But Brecht's aim is not to present museum pieces that remain locked in the past and are divorced from the present. Clearly, that would be of interest to very few spectators. Instead, historicized productions have to connect with an audience's interests today as well. Contemporary productions of *The Cherry Orchard*, then, are not supposed to be faithful recreations of how Stanislavsky directed the play in 1904. Brecht is asking for the figures and actions to be presented to the audience so that we might *compare* them with our own society today. So while Stanislavsky may have portrayed social relationships as they were in his time, in the way that a contemporary director might stage characters 'as they are' in a contemporary play, Brecht is asking for something discernibly different. Historicized productions are not only called on to imagine how different two different periods are, but to point out the differences as well, to stimulate the audience's curiosity and invite them to consider why such differences exist.

One of Brecht's key means of 'pointing out the differences' is the deployment of *Verfremdung*. The term has been rendered in English over the years as 'alienation', 'estrangement' and 'defamiliarisation', among other things. A better translation, however, is 'making the familiar strange', and I will be retaining the German word *Verfremdung* as it encapsulates this activity in a single distinctive word. An early reference to Brecht's ambition to change the way theatre-makers portray people and situations on stage reads:

> What we are looking for is a kind of representation in which the familiar is striking, the normal amazing. Everyday things should appear strange, and much that seemed natural should be recognised as artificial. If you give an unfamiliar quality to the actions, then all that they lose is a familiarity that is derived from fresh, naïve observation.[23]

An important part of the process is thus located in observation, that one can look at a figure or a situation in a naïve way. 'Naïve' has two primary meanings in English: it has the more negative connotation of being inexperienced and a more neutral one when it means 'innocent'. Brecht favours the latter meaning here and asks theatre-makers to look on dramatic material with fresh eyes, to wonder at what is happening rather than to take it for granted. In this sense, 'naïvety' means the ability to perform or respond to material without reducing it with prejudices or preconceptions. This is the ability to perceive reality without collapsing it to fit particular agendas. It does not mean, however, that there is something simplistic at work here. Brecht writes disapprovingly that 'our narrow bourgeois [spectators] can't imagine naïvety and complexity living together'.[24] That is, naïvety about approaching the world does not equate with the world itself being in some way uncomplicated. The idea is that the naïve work of the actors is passed on to the audience so that they see the action on stage in a fresh, new way, too.

'Making the familiar strange' is about questioning things we may take for granted. In Brecht's *The Caucasian Chalk Circle*, a servant, Grusha, becomes the surrogate mother to a royal child when he is inadvertently abandoned by his mother, the Governor's Wife, during an uprising. The real mother is too busy looking after her possessions and forgets the child. This, in itself, is shocking: it reveals that the Governor's Wife is more concerned with her goods than her son. In the light of such action, it is tempting to see Grusha as someone who helps the helpless baby through her own 'natural' motherliness. Yet Brecht has his narrator emphasize how long it takes Grusha to reach her decision. Yes, Grusha is maternal and she does not turn her back on the child. All the same, the time she takes shows that this is not a simple decision. By doing good, she is putting herself in grave danger, and this is one of the central contradictions of the play. Thus, Brecht makes what could have been construed a 'natural' decision, born of pity and sympathy, something far more complex and shows how perilous it is for a servant girl to harbour a well-born child. Brecht imports the social dimension into the decision: while Grusha hesitates, the audience is invited to ask why. If soldiers were to be seen running about behind her, the production could construct a possible answer.

Verfremdung is not about making the familiar strange for no reason; it also has a political thrust. As noted at the beginning of this chapter, modern society has a self-preserving interest in understanding people in terms of an unchanging 'human nature'. Brecht puts an emphasis on difference as a way of taking issue with such claims. The aim, as always, is to suggest that human beings are in a dynamic, dialectical relationship with society and that if they seek to change society they will also change themselves. *Verfremdung* helps to point out difference rather than to ignore it, and this is why Brecht instructed his actors actively to seek out contradictions in their figures and their actions: these were to be stressed and not repressed. That Grusha spends so long deciding to do 'the right thing' not only shows just how hostile social conditions are to such behaviour, but also how she triumphs over what is deemed to be 'human nature' (looking out for oneself instead of others), albeit after much internal debate.

In addition, *Verfremdung* is not only about calling old assumptions or ideas into question, but creating a new understanding. Brecht makes this clear in his notes on *Buying Brass* that *Verfremdung* transforms the '*self-evident*' into the '*evident*' (*Brass* 122). Thus, if we see *The Cherry Orchard* in a 'traditional', character-based staging, the production would do nothing to disrupt a comfortable reception of the story; everything seems 'self-evident'. Brecht, on the other hand, wants directors to expose social and historical connections in a production so that the audience can see the figures and their surroundings anew. Productions can explain, or at least give clues, as to why the scenes take place as they do by providing the relevant contexts. I will consider the ways in which such a production might work with reference to Patrick Marber's play *Closer* in Chapter 8.

Making the familiar strange is intimately linked with historicization. To bring out historical causes and effects is to make the figures and their actions strange: they are not self-evident but striking. However, historicization does not only apply to the past. As noted above, views, values and beliefs we hold today are also products of our society and our history, yet while we might indeed view the past as odd or peculiar, the present can at least *seem* to be more comprehensible and self-evident. But this may simply be because we encounter all its strangeness on a daily basis that it ceases to be strange. The present is just as 'historical' as the past, if 'historical' means constructed by different social forces at a given time. One could thus argue that the present is actually in more need of historicization than the past because we take so much for granted: the theatre can expose the historical forces acting on the figures in the present. In order to achieve this, Brecht suggests that *Verfremdung* be applied to any point in history,[25] including the present, in order to make audiences wonder about figures, their actions and their times, rather than merely to accept them.

Theatre as a site of contradiction, not merely conflict

As I observed at the beginning of this chapter, Mr Keuner was disappointed that his old acquaintance did not notice that he had changed since last they met. Brecht's proposals for the theatre invite theatre-makers to show how people change and how they have changed for a number of reasons. Brecht sees change as a fundamental human quality and experience: we go through life and encounter a great many people and events, and these affect us in ways that are conscious and unconscious. People may, for example, be appalled when they discover that certain large corporations exploit loopholes in tax law in order to pay less than their own workers, and consciously decide to boycott such firms. But there are also behaviours that one adopts without conscious decision. There is a propensity in the UK to adopt certain Americanisms, presumably due to their frequent use in UK media. The word 'research', for example, is often heard pronounced with the stress on the first syllable (US) and not the second (UK). This, on the one hand, is hardly earth-shattering, but on the other, it says something about how change occurs without people necessarily registering it. If we were only ever to see male experts interviewed on the TV news, for example, would both men and women unconsciously change their attitude to women? There are perhaps many assumptions we live by that we have not consciously chosen, but absorbed, and these changes in our thinking may need to be challenged in order to make sure that they actually serve our best interests.

The following example shows how conscious and unconscious attitudes might provide productive material for Brecht's understanding of theatre. After centuries of marginalization, women began to campaign for the vote, but the suffragette movement was not universally embraced. In some quarters women themselves actively opposed the movement.[26] One might have thought that all women would have welcomed the right to participate in representative democracy, but this clearly was not the case. It is worth noting, however, that Brecht would not be that interested in considering whether the women's views were right or wrong in the campaign against universal suffrage; instead he would have focused on the conditions under which such opinions could flourish. He would be pointing to the social contradictions of the times, and these may have included the tension between a lack of female representation in public life and female centrality in the home. One could ask why women were trusted with running the home but nothing more, for example.

Change is brought about by resolving contradiction, and so one could see Brecht's as a theatre that is continually seeking to articulate contradiction in order to dramatize difference for the audience. Yet it is important not to mistake contradiction for conflict. Drama, since its emergence in ancient Greece, was founded on conflicts that drive the action forward. In Brecht's theatre, *contradiction* frames the conflicts. The theatre, with all its different sign-systems (the body, the voice, the text, the gestures, the placement on stage, etc.) and its inherent artificiality (we know that actors are representing figures and actions), is in a perfect position to dramatize contradiction. It can do one thing and show another (separation of elements) without raising eyebrows about strict adherences to surface realism (because of the agreed pretence between auditorium and stage at the theatrical event). Actors can exaggerate gestures, foreground words, lines or movements, and acknowledge and develop a relationship with the audience. All the things that 'real life' tends to hide or leave unspoken can be addressed in a theatre of contradiction in which difference is not something to be passed over, but willingly set out and presented to the audience.

Difference is a central idea for Brecht's theatre. It allows the audience to compare one thing with another and speculate of how the two relate to each other. Brecht creates differences between the different signs in the theatre, between figures, between contexts, between drama and narrative. Difference is concerned with discontinuity and interruption. The theatre is no longer about stability, but change, and by highlighting difference in its many forms, Brecht is trying to prevent the easy consumption of the material on stage and asking spectators to confront contradiction.

4

Method Trumps Styles

The Brechtian method: Greater than
the sum of its parts

When people talk about a 'Brechtian' production in the theatre, it is not uncommon to find it broken down into its constituent parts: direct address to the audience to dispel theatrical illusion, epic banners (see Chapter 3) to pre-empt a scene's action, or on-stage narration to contrast with dramatic dialogue. However, to treat Brecht's theatre as a series of 'aesthetic features' that have to be included in a production misunderstands their role in the overall ends of his theatre. Each 'feature' helps to support Brecht's political aims, and when they appear by themselves they can have very different functions. After all, how many of the 'features' listed above appear regularly in television commercials? It would be difficult to argue that vehicles designed to sell products have anything in common with Brecht's critique of capitalism. Brecht makes the same point in a journal entry written during his stay in the USA:

> Eisler [one of Brecht's main musical collaborators] quite rightly recalls how dangerous it was when we were putting purely technical innovations into circulation, unconnected to any social function. The postulate then was rousing music. You can hear rousing music on the radio here 100 times a day, jingles encouraging the purchase of Coca Cola.[1]

Brecht notes how it is not just politically committed art that can stimulate action in an audience, and so it is always important to bear

the ultimate aim of Brecht's theatre in mind, something he here calls
its 'social function'. In a more specific attack on playwrights of his own
time, Brecht writes:

> That epic theatre was developed with the aim of providing realistic
> representations of society must always be kept in mind since some
> of its features, due to the appeal of their novelty, have been adopted
> and perverted by certain writers (Wilder, Eliot, Claudel) in order to
> make a 'new' theatre of illusion.[2]

Here Brecht accuses fellow playwrights of aesthetic 'asset stripping' in
order to give their own work the flair of the new while ignoring the
central purpose of his theatre: 'providing realistic representations of
society'. (Brecht's use and understanding of 'realism' are discussed at
the end of this chapter.) In short, an understanding of 'the Brechtian'
in performance must not confuse the means with the ends: Brecht's
is a theatre with an undeniable desire to critique and, through this,
to change society. It seeks to do this by revealing instability and
changeability in what we might have considered fixed and enduring. A
dialectical theatre is thus concerned with using Brecht's new ideas for
staging, but with a definite aim: to jolt the audience out of a position of
acceptance of the world as it is and to suggest that it could be different.

This chapter, like this book as a whole, emphasizes the Brechtian
method of analysing and staging drama as a prerequisite for the means
Brecht designed to bring it about. The following discussion outlines
how a series of processes can be understood as a practical realization
of Brecht's method because, *when taken together*, they present a viable
system to achieve a social and political end: representing the world
dialectically.

The Brechtian method, then, is the dialectical investigation of
dramatic material. Brecht proposes an overhaul of the way dramas
are performed in order to present the world in ways that stress its
alterability and its potential for further change. For example, as seen

in the previous chapter, he wants to get behind what is usually called 'character' in order to show its debt to its place in both its society and its time. If such connections can be made, then character becomes something less independent and self-governing, and more subject to social structures and their contradictions. In turn, social structures themselves can be revealed as dynamic mechanisms rather than immovable institutions. This is thus a theatre based on making the familiar strange, *Verfremdung*, but again it is important to note that *Verfremdung* is a device deployed to achieve Brecht's social ends, too. After all, it could be argued that all art makes the familiar strange, makes readers, viewers or spectators approach its themes and motifs from a fresh point of view. For Brecht, *Verfremdung* is a set of means that shakes spectators out of a position of passivity or acceptance of the world on stage. It can make them more detached and critical in order for them to question how society works. Through *Verfremdung*, a Brechtian production initially surprises the audience by presenting a character, an action or an event they thought they understood in a different light. They are then invited to draw the consequences of the change of perspective. As will be shown below, *Verfremdung* runs through Brecht's method, it does not exist independently of it.

In the following sections, I will offer an explanation of the practical method Brecht develops to approach the business of staging dialectical theatre. It has four principal terms: *Fabel, Arrangement, Gestus* and *Haltung*. The first two primarily concern the work of the director; the second two that of the actor. This chapter, therefore, introduces concepts that will recur in the rest of the book.

The centrality of the *Fabel*

Work on staging dramas dialectically at the Berliner Ensemble did not start in the rehearsal room, but in meetings beforehand. The aim of these meetings was to establish the play's *Fabel*, something that would become the thematic blueprint for the rehearsals that were to follow. The word *Fabel* may remind the reader of the word 'fable', and while the term is intimately connected to the events of a play, it is not simply a summary of them and has its own special meaning.[3] I have retained the German *Fabel* in order to distinguish it from its English counterpart. Brecht offers a useful explanation of the term in his appendices to the 'Short Organon', written after extensive experience with the Berliner Ensemble:

> The *Fabel* does not just correspond to an episode from people's lives together as it might have taken place in reality, instead we have rearranged incidents in which the *Fabel*'s inventor articulates ideas about people's lives together. In the same way the characters are not simply depictions of living people, but are rearranged and shaped in accordance with ideas.[4]

A play's *Fabel* is therefore *an interpreted version of events*, not simply the events themselves (examples are given in Chapters 5 and 8). Carl Weber, one of Brecht's former assistants, elaborates on the nature of the interpretation: '"Fabel" was, of course, Brecht's preferred term, designating a play's plot as it is retold on stage from a specific point of view [...]; a *Fabel* was always to reveal the contradictions of a plot'.[5] The *Fabel* is thus an account of a play's action from a dialectical point of view because it teases out contradictions in order to emphasize them in performance.

The *Fabel* works on different levels. It can offer a short 'master interpretation' of a play as a whole. According to another assistant, Käthe Rülicke, Brecht summed up the *Fabel* of his own *Life of Galileo* in the English rhyme 'Humpty Dumpty':[6]

- In this play, the great scientist recants his theory that the Earth rotates around the Sun (and not the other way round) when he is threatened with torture by the Catholic Church, an institution that has preached that the Earth was the centre of the universe. That is, once Galileo has recanted, there is no way for him to repair the damage; he cannot be 'put back together again'. He has placed personal well-being above the social good his theory could have done by challenging the authority of the Church. Consequently, the production as a whole was concerned with building Galileo up in order to knock him down, although, as always, Galileo was not simply one thing or another, but dialectically both at the same time. As Brecht reportedly put it, 'by the end, he is a champion of science and a social villain'.[7]

Brecht applied the *Fabel* as an overarching interpretation of the events to plays by other dramatists, too:

- Johannes R. Becher's *Battle in Winter*, staged in 1955, is about a young, middle-class German soldier, Hörder, involved in the Battle of Moscow (1941–1942). He starts off as a Nazi war hero, but gradually discovers how brutal the war machine can be. When he is told to bury partisan prisoners alive, he is unable to carry out the order and shoots himself dead instead. A play like this could be told as a human tragedy, and Becher himself described Hörder as a 'German Hamlet'. Brecht, on the other hand, wanted to trace Hörder's gradual process of awakening, of how he *learns* to make the right decision despite his upbringing. Brecht's *Fabel* runs: 'at the beginning of the play, Hörder is blind; as he starts to see, his eyes are violently closed'.[8] This short description traces a line of development in which Hörder experiences episodes that change him. Once he reaches a level of consciousness that leads him to reject his Nazi beliefs, he can take only one course of action. The tragedy is therefore one of its time; Hörder is unable to act on his insights because of historical circumstances that need to be changed.

The *Fabel* can also address smaller units of a drama, the scenes themselves. Here the *Fabel* helps to identify the contradictions at work in a scene and to understand the figures' roles within them. This is a method for getting actors to play the situation and not the character, an important shift in their way of approaching their task (see Chapters 3, 5 and 8 for examples). Yet even here, the idea of a 'micro-*Fabel*', as I will call it, has two different manifestations. It can be used

1. To trace the development of a play, from scene to scene
2. To identify the way a scene itself develops dialectically

In the first sense, the *Fabel* is equivalent to the 'epic banners' with which Brecht opened all the scenes to *Mother Courage*, for example. The second sense is a more analytical way of understanding how a scene moves from action to action. Such a rendition of the *Fabel* acts as a commentary for the actors involved.

Take, for example, the following events in a scene from *Mister Puntila and his Man Matti*:

- This is a play all about class relations between Puntila, a rich landowner, and his chauffeur Matti. At one point in scene five, Puntila's daughter Eva decides to distract herself by flirting with Matti. Egon Monk, one of Brecht's assistants on the production, observes in the show's rehearsal notes how Matti recognizes the manoeuvre and puts her off. This is something she was not prepared for and Monk writes 'such lessons were not on the timetable in Brussels', a reference to the expensive finishing school Eva attended.[9]
- This 'micro-*Fabel*' digs out an amount of social material from what could have appeared to have been nothing more than a failed attempt at flirting.
- In the dialectical version, Eva is clearly a representative of the moneyed middle class: she toys with Matti because she believes

he will be an easy conquest. Yet he is brighter than she thinks, and herein lies the social contradiction. All her expensive education has given her a distorted understanding of the world, whereas reality has shown her that the socially inferior chauffeur is not necessarily dim or passive, but the very opposite.

- This is a sequence interpreted through the lens of social contradiction, of a clash of expectations born of the tension between the middle and the working class. This, of course, is a mere detail, yet is shows how such details are not to be overlooked, but integrated into the contradictions of the *Fabel* as a whole.

Brecht unequivocally states in §65 of the 'Short Organon' that the *Fabel* is at the heart of the theatrical event. It provides the direction for the actors because it sets out the social contradictions that exist beyond their individual figures. In an appendix to the 'Short Organon', Brecht confirms that the study of a role is actually the study of the *Fabel*, or that this is at least the starting point for such work.[10] He elaborates further when he writes, reflecting on the work of the Berliner Ensemble: 'we work out situations, and the *Fabel* has the final say. We construct the *Fabel*, not characters that are then thrown into the *Fabel*.'[11] The idea that the *Fabel* can be developed underlines its status as an *interpretation* of the events, and interpretations can be wrong and can thus be altered in the light of new discoveries made during the rehearsal process.

The *Fabel* is concerned with interpreting *fictional* events through the lens of *real* social contradictions. Brecht maintains that any play has to defend itself 'against the most inartistic questions' in order to qualify as a proper work of art.[12] That is, questions of a sociological or historical nature are asked of the work when establishing the *Fabel*, as to whether people really do behave in such ways in such situations, and only then can production work proceed. Here, Brecht attempts to compare dramas with reality in order to make sure that the action obeys society's laws and rules. In the same note, Brecht also recognizes that the scope of a play 'emerges in its variability, or rather in its service to varied interests that are antithetical to one another'. The *Fabel* is therefore open to a number of readings; there is no single interpretation because a good play is not a piece of propaganda, but a lively exploration of different positions. A production team may thus spend quite some time settling on a particular *Fabel* and then find, in the course of rehearsals, that they have not got their interpretation right across the board.

Arrangement as the *Fabel* made flesh

An *Arrangement* is the visual representation of the *Fabel* on stage. I have italicized the term to retain its specifically Brechtian meaning and thus to distinguish it from other meanings of the word in English. An *Arrangement* organizes a scene's contradictions to make them clear for an audience. An *Arrangement* is a tableau that makes the social relations on stage readable for an audience. This is a way for contradictions to be clearly articulated so that the audience can understand the nature of the tensions.

Brecht's rendition of the climax to *The Caucasian Chalk Circle* gives a clear example of how the positioning of bodies on stage points to their social relationship as well as to the figures involved in the scene:

- Here, the judge, Azdak, asks the two women who claim to be Michael's mother to pull him out of a chalk circle he has drawn in the middle of his courtroom. Through this, Azdak hopes to establish the identity of Michael's mother.
- The Governor's Wife is the biological mother who inadvertently abandoned Michael when fleeing her palace during a revolt.

She needs Michael to regain control of her estates and possessions.

- Grusha, the servant, took Michael and raised him as a surrogate mother. She wants Michael because she believes she will be a better mother to him.

- The *Arrangement* of the episode tells the audience about the nature of the contradiction between the two women. In Brecht's production with the Berliner Ensemble in 1954, the Governor's Wife has positioned herself in such a way that, had we not seen what she was pulling, we may have assumed it were an object rather than a human being. Grusha, on the other hand, is not even set to pull Michael out of the circle at all, but offers him her hand in friendship.

- The *Arrangement* thus not only deals with the action, but tells the audience more about the figures involved: the Governor's Wife has no real human concern for her own child – he is simply a means to an end based on her position at the top of the social scale. Grusha, on the other hand, indicates her unwillingness to engage with the contest at all and shows the difference between herself and her adversary.

Yet an *Arrangement* need not necessarily limit itself to a single tension:

- In Becher's *Battle in Winter*, one finds the following situation: 'the unsettledness that Trenk has provoked in the General must be felt throughout the dressing down given to Oberkofler'.[13] It is not that important to know much about the figures themselves: Trenk is a major in the Nazi's army, and he and the General are both members of the officer class. The General is superior in rank to Trenk. Oberkofler is a working-class cook critical of the officers' war against the Soviets.

- The three-way tension of the scene disturbs the hierarchical power structures of the army: an officer has prevented his superior from rebuking a regular soldier properly.
- There are thus *two* power relations in play in this section: Trenk has brought news that has undermined the General's status; the General is then unable to assert his authority over the working-class cook.
- The General is at the centre of the *Arrangement*: he stands over the cook, but there is an irony for the spectator because his words are not having the effect they should have because he cannot concentrate properly. The cook can register the unusualness of the encounter not by looking down as one would expect, but by raising his head in disbelief, registering that he is not being punished. Behind the General stands Trenk, as his rank dictates, yet he can show his influence on the dressing down by looking uncomfortable.

Visually, the image is perfectly clear: events on the battlefield have brought about a breakdown in order. The army is not an impersonal machine, but an organization made up of people. When the relationships between those people change, so does the nature of the organization. In the above example, the audience views two social relationships simultaneously. Real events have undermined the General, something registered by Trenk. At the same time, the working-class cook realizes that the existing order is starting to crumble and that he might be able to effect resistance more successfully.

The movement from *Arrangement* to *Arrangement* in a scene tells the spectators how contradictions develop, get resolved or how new ones emerge; they let the *Fabel* unfold. As changes take place in the *Fabel*, changes take place in the *Arrangement*. Consequently, the figures on stage are always in dialogue with the events of a play: they respond to their twists and turns, and have to come to terms with them. This is a major shift in the understanding of how actors move on stage. As one assistant notes from the rehearsals of *Puntila*, 'on principle: we try to keep the groupings in place until the need for change arises'.[14] The actors do not simply move because they feel that they have stayed in one place for too long, but rather they move to show the audience that the *situation* has changed. Actors thus do not think about their characters first, but rather the conditions under which the character is acting.

Brecht organized a play's *Arrangements* early in the rehearsal process; they were usually the first thing to be established on stage. Brecht arranged the actors before they had spoken a single line, and they effectively became pawns as the director and his assistants tried out ways to make the *Fabel* clear to the auditorium. Today, this might sound like a profoundly disempowering process for the actors: they had virtually no input at this stage. As will be shown presently, the actors actually had a very important role to play, once the basic *Arrangements* had been established. However, the centrality of the *Fabel* and its representation in the *Arrangements* also served to reorientate the actors: they had to become conscious of the fact that they were making a type of theatre in which character was no longer the focus, but instead served the political aims of staging social contradiction.

Locating the actor in society: The discovery of a figure's *Gestus*

So far, readers might be excused for thinking that Brecht's theatre sounds mechanical: the director agrees on an interpretation of the play's action ahead of rehearsals in the form of the *Fabel*, and this is then reproduced visually in a series of *Arrangements*. The actor appears to be little more than a puppet at this stage. However, it is also

well known that Brecht was a keen talent-spotter and recruited some
of the best young actors to the Berliner Ensemble in the early 1950s.
The actors certainly played an active role in embodying their roles, yet
Brecht redefined that process in a bid to develop his dialectical theatre
as one that reflects reality more accurately. Brecht made the following
observation after a couple of years' work with the Berliner Ensemble:
'most characters on the German stage are not taken from life, but from
the theatre'.[15] We should be clear about what Brecht wants to achieve,
however: he is not arguing that the stage should merely reproduce
what is found in the 'real world' – that, after all, was naturalism's aim.
Instead, he is asking for his figures to understand their place in society
and the ways in which that place influences how they behave.

One of the primary elements involved in dramatizing figures
on Brecht's stage is to understand how their social context *prevents*
them from doing what they want to do. Figures do not have infinite
possibilities for action; instead Brecht makes an analogy with a game
of which he was fond: 'the "moves" are thus to a certain extent a
figure's [available] moves as in a game of chess, not merely a person's
expressions (reactions to stimulus) in response to wholly external
influences'.[16] Brecht thus seeks ways to anchor his figures to the kinds
of restrictions they encounter in the outside world. He does this by
introducing different yet complementary ways of connecting his
figures to their place in the social world.

Gestus is a word Brecht coined and it thus has no translation in
English. Brecht was somewhat vague in his use of the word, and it
has assumed different meanings in theory and practice since its
first, undefined mention around 1927.[17] Meg Mumford offers the
following definition with respect to the actor: '*Gestus* entails the
aesthetic gestural presentation of the socio-economic and ideological
construction of human identity and interaction', adding that is it 'the
externalization of the socially significant'.[18] Mumford explains that
a figure's gestures, or indeed its body-shape, can say things that go

beyond the individual and reveal important things about their place in the social and economic situation. That is, the actor's body is involved in a dynamic relationship with its social contexts as a way of establishing a visible connection between the two. It may be useful to consider how gesture may well betray more about the figure than merely its own internal feelings:

- Imagine a scene in a fine restaurant: dining there is a marker of high social status. An audience may then view the different ways in which different social types reveal something about themselves in the way they deal with wine, for example.
- Wine is a drink that is suffused with class associations (as is beer, if one wanted to imagine a similar scene in a pub). Wine was once the preserve of the upper classes. It then became a sign of middle-class refinement, and is now available to all by virtue of its lower price in supermarkets. However, it is still imbued with a set of social codes. As a result, actors can show their place in the social order in the way that they deal with the drink in public.
- Choosing a bottle is itself a challenge: who makes the choice? Is the chooser at ease with the menu or does the chooser struggle with the distinction between a Bordeaux and Beaujolais or the use of foreign words or place names? Does the price elicit a response?
- When the waiter approaches the diners and offers the man, and not the woman, the bottle, does he accept the traditional yet implicitly sexist role imposed on him by the waiter? Does he show that this is just 'one of those things' and go along with it, or does he clearly direct the waiter to offer the bottle to his partner? Or is he surprised by the ritual, thus betraying his unfamiliarity with the up-market setting?
- When it comes to drinking the wine itself, the actors can show their relationship to the drink in the context of an expensive restaurant: do they handle the glasses like wine glasses or beer

glasses? Do they sip elegantly or sup heartily? Do they look at home with the act of drinking fine wine because it is an affordable luxury, or instead display their unease because it costs so much?

- The acts of ordering, receiving and drinking a bottle of wine in a restaurant can show an audience a great many aspects about the figures' social status without them speaking a single word.

This gestic approach to articulating the actor's body can be applied to many further situations, of course. Yet *Gestus* need not only restrict itself to a series of socially significant gestures.

Actors can also consider the effects of society on their bodies as a whole. A figure who has led a life of hard toil will not have the same body-shape as a figure who has not had to lift a finger to get something done. However, a figure's social background does not dictate how that figure's body will appear. In the case of the labourer, for example, the actor has a number of choices to make. At the extremes of this figure's gestic representation, the actor could present a body that announces its own decrepitude as one that is bent-over and unable to perform normal physical tasks. Alternatively, the actor could inhabit a body that is muscular and agile, one that has made the most of the manual labour and has not been defeated by the burdens placed upon it over time. There is, of course, a whole spectrum of variants that could also inform the actor's decisions. But whatever is chosen, the actor is acknowledging that body-shape reveals information about its social situation and its history.

With several gestic actors on stage, an audience can compare the ways the social environment has affected the different figures so that a complex sense of each figure can emerge. To return to the example of the labourer: the image of the strong, powerful worker says something about both the nature of the work and the figure's relationship to it. *Gestus* thus combines the general and the particular. The aim of a gestic theatre is to show the interrelationship between individual and society in order to dispel a sense that people behave 'naturally' in or independently of any given situation. Instead, spectators are invited to speculate on the relationships and consider how society affects the figures on stage.

The body is no longer in some way neutral, but actively displays its connections to its social environment. The actor emphasizes certain physical gestures as a way of pointing to connections that lie beyond the scope of naturalistic representation. *Gestus* will also acknowledge the contradictions of any given social position. In the above example of the manual labourer, the actor might show how his or her work is necessary to bring in an income, but that such work has also cost the worker his or her health. Alternatively, the fit worker at the other end of the scale can show how hard labour that could have kept him or her 'in their place' has actually been a benefit and allows the worker to engage in activities, such as fighting for his or her rights, with a clear mind and a strong body. *Gestus*, as well as the *Fabel*, can thus point to society's contradictions.

A figure is the sum of all its *Haltungen*

Brecht notes in §58 of the 'Short Organon' that 'the smallest social unit is not "the" human being, but two people. In life too we develop one another reciprocally'. That is, actors must acknowledge that other people and situations have an effect on them, too – individuals do not exist in isolation, but through social interaction. Brecht proposes that actors should become conscious of how they relate to other people and that different situations will call for different responses. A figure's behaviour towards a manager is likely to be different from, say, a figure's behaviour towards a spouse or a friend. Brecht uses the German word *Haltung* (plural: *Haltungen*) to draw attention to this aspect of a figure on stage. *Haltung* combines what is usually a mental state in English (attitude) with physical expression (bearing), and I shall retain the German *Haltung* so as not to emphasize either aspect unduly. Brecht wants the actor to embody *Haltungen* and to show how they change as the situation changes. The most important aspect of *Haltung* is that it is never passive; it denotes a relationship *towards* someone or something; as the 'someone' or 'something' changes, so will the *Haltung*.

To return to the episode from *Puntila*, referred to above in the discussion of the 'micro-*Fabel*', well-to-do Eva seeks a flirtatious dalliance with her father's chauffeur Matti. Her *Haltung* towards Matti at first will be assured and perhaps a little arrogant. Yet she has to revise this when Matti does not play along and demonstrates that he is not simply her plaything. The shift in Eva's *Haltung* registers her poor understanding of class relations in the scene.

In the previous chapter, I noted how Brecht was unwilling to ascribe characteristics to a figure. It should now be clear that, to Brecht, a figure is in fact the sum total of its *Haltungen*. *Haltung* changes with the situation and so a figure can display its contradictory behaviour without 'falling out of character'. Thus, Eva may start out snobbishly looking down on Matti, but her experience of an intelligent working man can change her *Haltung* towards him and extend her range of behaviours. Her shift from arrogance to surprise to understanding is contradictory, but not unrealistic. If Eva were defined by the characteristic of arrogance, she would not be able to learn and would remain a prisoner of that trait. Brecht thus invites actors *not* to approach characters from the inside, but to observe figures and their behaviours from the outside in order to create lively, dialectical representations that are in dialogue with situations and other characters.

In a gestic theatre, actors are charged with locating themselves socially in their *Gestus* and showing how this social position interacts with the world around them through changes in their *Haltung*. The result is a *dynamic* actor on stage, always conscious of a new situation (while the figure the actor is portraying may indeed be unaware of the connections between him or her and society). This can be illustrated in the following scenario:

- A play set in a school might feature a pupil, a teacher and a headteacher. Each figure adopts a *Gestus* based on their position in society and in the school. The actors thus need to know what kind of school it is and how they fit into it. There is, of course, a great deal of scope for work here.
- The headteacher may be someone who has successfully led a smaller school, but now finds the new task more difficult. He or she may show how they need to adapt to rise to the challenge or how they fail because they cling on to methods that are no longer suitable to the new environment. The teacher and the pupil offer similar scope from a range of gestic interpretations.
- The actors then consider the question of *Haltung*. The teacher will have a very different *Haltung* towards the pupil (to show who is in charge in the classroom) than towards the headteacher (to acknowledge who is in charge of the school), and an audience would be able to contrast the two and understand the different dynamics involved in the two relationships. The teacher's two *Haltungen* are contradictory: one is about maintaining authority, the other is about submitting to it. However, they both make sense in the context of the school.

The actor blends *Gestus* (position in society) with a repertoire of contradictory *Haltungen* (responses to specific situations). Both facets limit the figure's room to manoeuvre, just like a character's psychology limits possibilities. Yet in the case of the gestic actor, limitation comes from society and the behaviours it either permits or forbids. With society 'present' on stage in the form of the actors' gestures and actions, Brechtian theatre cements the link between individual behaviour and larger social questions.

Such an approach to acting may raise questions about a figure's individuality. Brecht certainly believes that human beings are more connected to each other than one might initially think, when he states, 'the realisation "how very different people are!" is a partial realisation'.[19] Brecht is not denying that every individual has a different life and a unique set of experiences. Instead, he invites actors to see beyond the perspective of the isolated individual and acknowledge the commonalities shared by individuals that might manifest themselves in terms of class, sex or ethnicity. A figure's individuality is guaranteed by the choices they make, yet those choices are always limited and always dependent on the social conditions of the time.

Brecht's theatre of showing

Brecht wrote a poem about the theatre in the mid-1940s, with the title 'Showing has to be Shown'. It opens like this:

> Show that you are showing!
> Among all the varied *Haltungen* which you show when showing
> how men play their parts
> The *Haltung* of showing must never be forgotten.[20]

The lines are addressed to the actor. The actor is charged with performing 'out' to the audience rather than keeping things small or private on stage. Every decision the actor has made in rehearsal and every *Haltung* adopted on stage is to be shown to the audience. This directive fundamentally affects the way the actor approaches the business of acting. The actor not only carries out an action, but also points to it, shows it off to the audience. Yet the emphasis on showing is to be found at every level of the Brechtian dialectical method.

Benno Besson, one of Brecht's assistants at the Berliner Ensemble who went on to become a major and influential director himself, notes, 'a detail is either itself large or it's nothing. It belongs to a great *Fabel* or it doesn't exist and has no meaning'.[21] Details are what prevent a production from becoming indistinct or bland. Besson shows how a *Fabel* is in fact composed of dialectical details that unfold to tell the play's story. For Brecht, details, grounded in specific situations, always point to larger issues.[22] Consider the following details from a scene from *The Caucasian Chalk Circle*:

- Grusha decides to leave Michael on the doorstep of a peasant couple in the hope that they will give him a better life.
- The peasant woman who discovers the abandoned child was directed to respond as follows: first, she is sceptical because she does not know why it is there. Then she notices the fine linen and changes her view. She finally realizes that children cost money.[23]
- In this short assembly of moments, the actor can use closely observed details to say more about her social situation. On discovering the child, she does not pick it up immediately: the audience is asked why sympathy for a helpless baby is not instinctively aroused. We then see how the woman recognizes the expensive fabric and how she thinks she may gain by the discovery. Finally the realization hits her that even the child of wealthy parents will drain her resources.
- The details give a picture of the wider social context through clear observations: poor people cannot afford simple acts of charity and seek financial advantage where possible in order to lift themselves out of their poverty.

Showing is all about highlighting one aspect at the expense of another, as is clear when Brecht discusses the construction of *Arrangements*:

Epic theatre makes use of the simplest imaginable groupings for
expressing the meaning of the actions in a comprehensible manner.
There is no longer the 'accidental', 'everyday' grouping that 'pretends
to be real life': the stage doesn't mirror the 'natural' disorder of
things. The desired opposite of natural disorder is natural order.
The standpoints that shape this order are socio-historical.[24]

Brecht is concerned with making *Arrangements* as clear as possible
for the spectator, and this means eliminating the accidental and the
superfluous from them. An *Arrangement* can only function properly
if it clearly communicates its social relations and contradictions;
there is no room for material that will distract the audience from the
image's focal point. Thus, showing is about de-cluttering the image
and making sure that its composition draws attention to important
material. In theory, the director in a theatre of showing should direct
the spectators' gaze from point to point, from detail to detail.

Clarity also stands at the heart of the actors' performances
themselves. Brecht insists on dividing up a figure's different *Haltungen*
so that they can be compared with one another separately, rather than
bleeding into one another. In the rehearsals for *Battle in Winter* he
notes, 'don't put everything under one hat; on the contrary, always pull
out a new rabbit from the hat. This is an art that's hardly understood
in the theatre'.[25] The director wants everything set out clearly so that
contradictions in *Haltung* can provoke questions of the audience
about why a figure might behave in such diverse ways.

Showing and clarity go hand in hand, from the *Fabel* to the
Arrangement to *Gestus* and *Haltung*. This is a theatre of making the
familiar strange, of drawing attention to that which goes unspoken or
unmentioned. It is a theatre that points out difference and contradiction
in order to break society's harmonious surface to reveal what might be
going on underneath. Only by shining the light of clarity and drawing
attention to significant details can a Brechtian production emphasize
the dialectical nature of society, the contradictions upon which it is
built, and the kinds of behaviours it brings forth. Brecht offers clear

visual contrasts to the audience: there is no room for material that does not contribute to or diverts attention from the issues at hand. Brecht's method of examining the world of a play dialectically by focusing on its contradictions requires precision, otherwise crucial distinctions and differences can be forgotten, ignored or never even revealed in the first place.

Realism and Brecht's dialectical method

Realism in the theatre is usually understood as reproducing people and events in a fashion that equates with the way we encounter them in everyday life. It is primarily an *aesthetic* term, associated with a style of performance in which the accuracy of the imitation provides the yardstick by which it is measured. In the discussion below, I will refer to this as 'stylistic realism'. However, the words 'realism' and 'realistic' occur with remarkable frequency in Brecht's theoretical writings, and they thus appear to sit uneasily with the approaches to staging described above. After all, Brecht's starting point, the *Fabel*, from which all else follows, is an *interpretation* of a play's events, a re-telling of reality rather than its mere re-presentation. And the emphasis on showing is itself selective: it highlights the elements Brecht considers most important (social context and the articulation of contradiction) rather than offering a comprehensive picture of 'reality' itself. It is clear that Brecht's understanding of 'realism' is at odds with the way the term has been understood in the theatre for over a century. Nonetheless, it is Brecht's contention that his theatre be judged on its realism. So, how did Brecht understand realism as something that did not merely reproduce everyday reality?

Brecht's focus on dialectics already suggests that he would not be satisfied with merely imitating reality. To a dialectician, reality is the *result* of processes in which contradictory demands struggle with each other, and so Brecht's realism is not so much about what appears to be happening but, to him, what is really happening. Brecht noted in his journal during the rehearsals of *Mother Courage* in 1948, the East German production that relaunched his career as a director, that realism is not a style, but a stance, a positioning of oneself towards reality.[26]

A true 'stylistic realism' would be deadly dull. It is obvious that plays, TV drama and film abbreviate 'reality' and offer up its most interesting and significant parts. For example, any soap opera, despite its 'stylistic' approach to realism, will omit unengaging details of people's lives and focus on what is perceived to be more attractive aspects for viewers, and these are generally negative rather than positive. The soaps' time-scheme also generally imitates 'reality' (episodes on a Monday in the spring take place on a Monday in the spring), yet weekends tend to get conveniently forgotten. And each instalment almost unerringly ends on a cliffhanger, something that contradicts most people's experience of reality. Thus, even 'stylistic realism' has a stance towards reality and is not reality itself. This stance tends to be based on sensationalism despite the fact that reality is remarkably unsensational for the most part.

Brecht compares 'stylistic realism' (which he calls 'naturalism') with his own understanding of realism in the following chart:

Naturalism	*Realism*
society regarded as a piece of nature	society regarded historically
segments of society (family, school, military unit, etc.) are 'little worlds of their own'	the 'little worlds' are sectors of the front in the great struggles
the milieu	the system
reaction of individuals	social causality [...]
copies	stylisations [...][27]

A quick comparison of the first four pairings reveals that Brecht understands 'reality' in far more complex terms than naturalism does. As is to be expected, he emphasizes the ways in which the incidents that make up one's experience of the everyday cannot be approached in isolation, but are connected to larger issues concerning society and society's place in history. People's behaviour is not independent of these factors and is certainly not 'natural', but indebted to context. Brecht's critique of naturalism is that it offers the spectator no means of criticizing reality because reality is presented 'as is', as unchangeable. Brecht's response to his dissatisfaction with naturalism is found in the final pairing: naturalism is content merely to copy while Brecht's realism acknowledges that it must stylize reality in order to understand it properly. Brecht's stance to realism is thus concerned with distrusting reality's surfaces rather than taking them for granted. This is a critical stance, one that is not satisfied with what reality *seems* to offer, but one that wants to probe and discover what makes it tick and *why* people behave as they do.

It is important, however, to understand the nature of 'stylisation' in Brecht's theatre. Lee Strasberg, who transformed Stanislavsky's Russian 'system' into the American 'method', wrote about Brecht's own production of *The Caucasian Chalk Circle*, which he saw on tour in London in 1956:

> Whatever was not done simply and naturally in the production was stylized, but it was not unreal. It was not unconvincing. It was professional. Each moment and each gesture was chosen and composed. Every detail was just so. Everything [...] was part of the composition. This is what stylization means in its true sense.[28]

While the meaning of 'true' stylization might be debatable, Strasberg at least gives a concrete sense of how he read the moments that did not conform to his sense of 'stylistic realism'. Stylization here means that Brecht created representations of reality that signalled their own artificiality, rather than representations of reality that were so distant from their point of reference that they were unrecognizable. 'Stylisation' for Brecht thus means a way of retaining the surface of reality while probing the ways in which it is constructed. He offers heightened realistic signs on stage.

Brecht adds that realists, in his sense, must also be able to employ 'the art of abstraction'.[29] This means that whatever takes place on stage always and consciously stands for something greater than itself. The figures, their actions and the situations in which they occur thus have an exemplary quality. This aspect connects with the point I made earlier about a figure's individuality: unique experience is always influenced and bounded by social conditions. Figures on stage thus exhibit a form of *typicality*; they behave in ways that can be connected to their place in society with respect to the situation in question. Typicality is another word for 'realistic' in Brecht's vocabulary: spectators recognize action and behaviour on stage as credible: 'would a person *really* behave like that?' is a central question here. In the example given above about the peasant woman discovering an abandoned child on her doorstep, Brecht may well have objected to the actor simply picking up the child without thinking. Instead, he wanted to show her thought processes by including the important social fact that she was poor. This aspect of her figure prevents her from helping the child initially, and this, to Brecht, embodies typicality. However, there is a difference between the typical and the stereotypical, and this will be discussed with respect to Brecht's thoughts on acting in the next chapter.

If Brechtian realism is understood as a way of including and highlighting material either not seen or hidden from the surface of our everyday experiences, then it is clear that his realism thinks first and represents later. Realism as Brecht defines it is thus primarily a *philosophical* term that he then translates into an appropriate aesthetic. Naturalism, conversely, starts with an aesthetic position which then has, to Brecht, wholly negative philosophical implications: it disempowers the spectator and leads to an acceptance of reality rather than to its critique. Steve Giles proposes the term 'cognitive realism' as a way of understanding Brecht's brand of realism:

> Instead of motivating action in terms of the individual's character or inner life, cognitive realism will concentrate on the typical external behaviour of figures performing specific functions and this means in turn that it is necessarily anti-empathetic. Cognitive realism [...] seeks [...] to enable its audience to derive causal relationships inductively from the behavioural attitudes presented in the work.[30]

Cognition is, in part, concerned with how one acquires knowledge. Giles's term helps us understand the relationship between Brecht's theatrical project and reality by pointing out an important feature of the nature of reality to Brecht: human beings have to bring their own input to the process of making sense of reality – it does not simply 'exist' by itself. Brecht can articulate contradictions in his productions, but spectators are required to learn about reality's nature if they are to make sense of it and to change it. Again, it is the *structures* of reality spectators learn about. Giles points out several key features of Brecht's 'realistic' theatre. In order to understand human action, it can no longer be taken 'as is', and so bonds of empathy between spectator and character must necessarily be interrupted to pull the spectator away from an uncritical relationship with the events on stage. There is thus a link to *Verfremdung*, making the familiar strange, in a bid to challenge popular conceptions of 'how people are' and to introduce instead 'how people have come to be'. *Fabel, Arrangement, Gestus* and *Haltung* can all produce *Verfremdung* in Brecht's realistic theatre of showing because they process reality in ways that offer new perspectives on human beings and their actions. The striking nature of these approaches confronts spectators with surprising or unexpected representations, thus distancing them from the action on stage and disrupting empathy.

'Cognitive realism' underpins Brecht's dialectical method. The dialectic is Brecht's means of interpreting reality, of getting behind its appearances in order to understand what *produces* what we take for reality. For the dialectic to have any meaning, it has to engage with the ways real people behave in real situations. 'Real' here implies the inclusion of social context as a prerequisite for any consideration of behaviour or action on stage.

Brecht's tools for approaching the business of staging (*Fabel, Arrangement, Gestus* and *Haltung*) might be considered as contributing to something of a mechanical or a formulaic process, moving from the one phase to the other. While rehearsal tended to establish the *Fabel* and embody that in *Arrangements* first, there are recorded instances where actors' difficulties in finding dialectical and contradictory solutions on stage resulted in a rethink of a scene's *Fabel* and *Arrangements*. However, we will see in the following two chapters how the work of the actor and the director made realizing Brecht's dialectical method on stage more organic, creative and inventive than the scheme in this chapter might suggest.

Brecht and the Actor

There is no 'Brechtian Style' of acting

As late as the late 1940s, when, after his lengthy absence from the theatre, Brecht was working again with actors on productions, he used the term 'the epic style of acting [die epische Spielweise]' on at least two occasions.[1] It would thus be reasonable to assume that there *is* such a thing as a 'Brechtian style' of acting. In using this expression, it is possible that Brecht was trying to differentiate his approach to acting from that of others at the time, yet a closer inspection of his work with actors reveals that there was no single 'style' as such. Instead, it is more helpful to view Brecht's relationship to the actor and to acting through a different lens.

John Rouse wrote in 1984 that 'Brecht was far less concerned with acting method than he was with the interpretive basis of the actor's work.'[2] This significant observation, based on Brecht's work with the Berliner Ensemble from 1949 to 1956, appears to have been overlooked by those who derive an 'acting style' from Brecht's writings, yet it offers a perspective on Brecht and the actor that is a helpful corrective to such a view. 'Acting method' is a way for a teacher to train an actor to perform dramatic material in a particular way; the development of 'the interpretive basis of the actor's work', on the other hand, puts more emphasis on the actor's ability to negotiate dramatic material *before* making decisions about how to perform it.

Of course, as noted in earlier chapters, Brecht insists on certain ways of understanding a figure: the exposure of contradiction and difference are central ideas, as are a grounding in realism, the primacy of figure over character and the sense that each figure is built on its relationships with other figures and its place in society. The work of the actor, then, is to accommodate these fundamental understandings in a production *without* Brecht imposing particular ways of representing them. Brecht did not engage with anything as formalized as 'actor training'; a better term would be 'actor sensitization'. Once actors were sensitized to Brecht's dialectical worldview, they could find the most appropriate ways to perform their roles.

In short, acting, like the different elements involved in staging plays discussed in Chapter 4 (*Fabel, Arrangement, Gestus* and *Haltung*), is always to be seen in the context of Brecht's method: the dialectical interpretation of dramatic material. Thus, the actor does not exist independently of the method by exhibiting a 'Brechtian style'. Instead, it is the method, the way of approaching the representation of reality, that asks certain questions of the actor, and the actor's performance will respond to the different challenges of different texts, rather than conform to a 'Brechtian style'. The chapter is thus concerned with the ways in which Brecht seeks to sensitize the actor to certain ways of interpreting reality rather than establishing and fixing a characteristic style of performance.

Brecht and casting, or: Cleaving the actor from the role

As should be evident from the previous chapters, a theme that runs through Brecht's ideas about theatre is that of difference. Difference presents a productive means of activating an audience: it is provocative to spectators because (at least) two disparate elements are presented to them, and they have to make sense of the discrepancy. Brecht finds that the actor can serve as a site of difference, too. In order to understand his reasoning, it is necessary to appreciate an important distinction between Brecht's and Stanislavsky's understanding of what an actor was supposed to do on stage. Brecht notes:

> An actor's efforts to transform himself [sic] into the dramatic character to the extent of extinguishing his own personality – a notion given theoretical and practical grounding most recently by Stanislavsky – serves to bring about as close an identification as possible on behalf of the spectator with either this character or its counterpart.[3]

Unsurprisingly, Brecht criticizes Stanislavsky for the ways in which his actor training leads spectators to empathize with characters. Brecht's implicit suggestion for a strategy to resist such a relationship between the stage and the auditorium is, however, the point of interest in the quotation. Brecht proposes that actors should both play their roles *and* display their personalities. That is, the audience should never believe that the actor on stage *is* the character, but rather that there is an actor *playing* a character by showing the difference between actor and role. The maintenance of this division helps to emphasize artificiality by 'separating the elements' (see Chapter 3): the actor simultaneously transmits two sets of signs. One set encodes the qualities of the figure; the other encodes the reality that this is an actor performing the figure. The result is that the spectator is not drawn into the action too deeply, but can remain at a distance and contemplate larger issues than a particular character's words or actions. Brecht asks actors not to submerge themselves in their characters, but to 'show the join', to signal the difference.

The quality that appealed to Brecht in actors was their ability to contrast their personalities with their roles:

- For example, while Brecht was in Switzerland, before his move to Berlin, he auditioned a young actor, Regine Lutz. She was a doctor's daughter from a comfortable suburb in Zurich.

Brecht asked her to deliver a poem. Having completed the task satisfactorily, he asked her to read the poem as if she had never read a poem before.[4] Brecht was interested in the friction created when the young middle-class woman tried to act against her background. He was clearly impressed by the result because he recruited her to the Berliner Ensemble, where she played several important figures.

However, the ability to 'show the join' between actor and figure is not only a way to show that an actor is playing a role, thus disrupting empathy by generating contradictory signs. It can have other effects as well:

- Brecht praised Ernst Busch, an actor whom he cast in several central roles with the Berliner Ensemble, because he brought his working-class biography on stage, along with his role.[5] Busch was on the verge of being arrested by the Nazis in 1933 for his left-wing activities, but escaped by lucky hap; he fought for the Republicans against the Fascists in the Spanish Civil War between 1936 and 1937; and he was arrested as an exile by the advancing Nazi army in Belgium in 1940. Busch thus embodied the revolutionary tradition, and Brecht found this fascinating. He believed that Busch could not only 'show the join' between himself and his role, but that his experiences could also inform the way he played a role. Brecht thus badgered Busch to play the upper-class general Coriolanus in his adaptation of Shakespeare's play, but Busch turned him down.[6] Brecht wanted to show how a staunchly working-class actor could comment on the noble figure in performance. One can only imagine how Busch might have delivered speeches contemptuous of the working people in Rome while playing Coriolanus: perhaps there would have been clear acknowledgements to the audience that contradicted the sense of the lines, perhaps there would have been particular deliveries that showed how Busch disagreed with the figure's sentiments. Busch declined the role, believing that there was simply too great a divide between himself and the figure, yet this was precisely what Brecht was keen to exploit.

In Chapter 2, I noted that one of the dialogues in *Buying Brass* was preceded by the direction '*the Actress plays a man*' (*Brass* 66). By observing the differences between the male and female body, and between masculine and feminine behaviour, the Actress can draw attention to those aspects that a man may simply take for granted and ignore in performance. The distance between actors and their roles allows them to identify difference (in class, in age, in opinion, etc.) and to expose it, not to submerge it by 'completely transforming' into the role.

Casting against type was a strategy Brecht employed to highlight difference in a bid to offer the audience two perspectives on the material being performed: that of the figure and that of the actor. This was not, however, always the practice at the Berliner Ensemble and, indeed, there are no recorded instances of women playing men at all, except when the script called for a woman to disguise herself as a man. Young actors sometimes played older figures, and Brecht instituted the practice of 'alternating' two different actors in the same role. Over the years, actors were paired successfully and the flyers for the 1954 production of *Don Juan* show that the two lead roles alternated on different nights.[7] This was a feature of many Berliner Ensemble productions and one aimed at the actor rather than the spectator (who may have been blissfully ignorant of the dual casting). Actors could observe their peers' approach to playing a particular figure and consequently note the differences between their own and the other actor's gestic performances.

Observation, realism and *Gestus*

Brecht wrote in 1951:

> In my opinion the true actor both wishes and is able to display *other* people, to perform for the audience people who are completely different than himself, and it is the wish and ability to observe people that make the true actor.[8]

It is clear that the theme of difference recurs here, too: to Brecht, actors should not want to play figures similar to themselves, but show their skills by performing the unfamiliar and the strange. The key to achieving such an end is the ability accurately to observe other people – but observation itself has a special function for Brecht. The activity is not about identifying similarities but differences; it helps the actor appreciate the distance between the observer and the observed. In addition, Brecht calls for precision in observation. The following example, taken from a speech by the Dramaturg in *Buying Brass*, asks the actor to differentiate between similar-seeming qualities in a bid to represent them with clarity: '*relaxed* and *loose, quick* and *hurried, imaginative* and *digressive, thought out* and *elaborate*' (*Brass* 68).

Observation is about registering the variations found in reality. The emphasis on precision marks Brecht's desire to connect gestures and actions on stage with those found in the world outside the theatre. He thus found his wife's performance in *The Caucasian Chalk Circle* laudable for the way she understood the role of the Governor's Wife:

- The first actress to play the role exercised power over her servants by moving around the stage excessively and getting people to do her bidding like that.
- Helene Weigel, on the other hand, remained mostly static, while all those around her carried out the same reactive movements

as before. Brecht enjoyed this depiction of the Governor's Wife because it showed how little she needed to do to in order to have her commands obeyed.[9]

- This 'realistic' observation of a socially superior figure showed that the existing power relations had become so ingrained that great effort did not have to be expended to further the Wife's ends. The audience was thus invited to ask why she could do so little, but achieve so much.

For Brecht, there is another, more political benefit to the act of accurate observation. During the rehearsals of *Life of Galileo* in 1955, one assistant made a note under the heading 'How do Great Actors Rehearse?': 'Nothing is obvious to them – everything's open to question. *Verfremdung* is thus also a part of their approach to building a role, not just the result of that work for the spectator'.[10] *Verfremdung* here has the meaning, discussed in Chapter 3, of turning the apparently obvious or self-explanatory into the understandable or the explanatory. Observation is not only concerned with noting difference, but accounting for it too. And in Brecht's rehearsal room, that process did not ignore the social dimension.

Thus observation is not merely about considering exteriors, how things look or seem. Brecht promotes what might be called 'dialectical observation', the marrying up of a 'strange' phenomenon and its explanation. He draws attention to this in a comment from 1940 in which he suggests that a stupid actor can play a clever character 'simply by copying the *Gestus*'.[11] This comment begs the question as to what a clever person's *Gestus* might consist of. A clever man might exhibit arrogance because he looks down on those around him. A clever woman might be more understated because she does not want to draw attention to her intellect. In both cases, the quality that accompanies the 'cleverness' is interpreted in relationship to its situation, and the actor can work further on *why* the man wants to exhibit his cleverness and *why* the woman does not. Arrogance and modesty are not 'natural' qualities in this reading, but the product of a person's relationship with their surroundings. One may not need to be arrogant if there were no sense of competitiveness in a group; similarly, modesty may not be necessary if one is not made to feel guilty for making a contribution to a discussion. Observing a person's *Gestus* connects actions to (social) context; it asks the actor to look beyond the surface and ask why such actions might be taking place. Observation is no longer an activity of merely registering difference, but one in which difference is the starting point for further observation and inquiry.

Sensitizing the actor to dialectics

In an entry in his journal, Brecht notes an evening he spent with the celebrated stage and screen actor Peter Lorre in 1943. Lorre had worked with Brecht in Berlin before they both took different routes into exile in 1933. Lorre reproaches Brecht for not spending enough time on the 'actor's technique' in rehearsal. Brecht accepts the criticism up to a point, but concludes, 'what I want to do is base the actor's interestingness on the interest he brings to the social phenomenon with which he is concerned in his acting'.[12] This acknowledgement informs much of what Brecht wants to achieve with the actor: he is not so much concerned with perfecting technical ability, but with developing the actor's consciousness, such that the actor no longer ignores social factors, but actively builds them into the rehearsal and performance of dramatic material.

The process of sensitizing the actor to the principles of a dialectical theatre was a slow one. One of Brecht's leading ladies, Angelika Hurwicz, writes that her experience of Brecht was

entirely one of a normal director, different from conventional direction only perhaps in his greater patience. It was only after some time that Brecht's characteristics as a director converged from many single qualities to form a complete whole.[13]

Rather than develop a systematic methodology, Brecht asked targeted questions of his actors in rehearsal in order to bring about dialectical performances (I will discuss Brecht's work as a director in the next chapter). The aim was to make them think more carefully about the approach to their craft. Käthe Reichel, another leading actor at the Berliner Ensemble, said that actors had to 'learn to think "dramaturgically"' under Brecht.[14] They are to function as their own dramaturg, analysing their roles and their relationships with others through the dialectical prism. Actors are encouraged to think and locate themselves in the context of the *Fabel*. This stance may remind us of Brecht's contention from the 'Short Organon', quoted in Chapter 1: 'without opinions and intentions one cannot represent anything' (§55). Actors have to be aware of themselves, their relationships with the other figures on stage and their context if they are to represent anything with meaning. Showing cannot be achieved if the actor does not understand what is being shown.

Over time, Brecht developed a way of rehearsing in which actors brought their discoveries to their fellow cast members. He expected his cast to make 'offers' to each other and the director, in order to solve performance problems rather than to wait for the director to make suggestions. By sharing the burden of creative input with the actors, Brecht sought to make the rehearsal process a *collective* activity rather than one based solely on the ideas of the director.

Manfred Wekwerth, who joined the Berliner Ensemble as an assistant director and went on to run the company from 1977 to 1991, notes concisely how the process worked: 'the actors are to make "offers". The director develops [the offers] through correction. To repeat: the *Fabel* decides everything. The final understanding of a figure only comes about through this interplay.'[15] The 'offer' process thus represents a dialectic of its own. Actors bring their embodied ideas to a particular situation (thesis) and these are processed through the lens of the *Fabel* (antithesis). Only when the offer responds appropriately to the *Fabel* can it be integrated into the performance (synthesis).

It was very important to Brecht that the actors made discoveries, derived from their observations of reality. One of the greatest crimes an actor could commit at the Berliner Ensemble was to arrive with something divorced from reality and designed to achieve an end that was not supported by the play or the *Fabel*. Brecht said in a discussion:

> There is a strict ban on achieving a desired effect. Actors can't resist it for too long. They start to get embarrassed when offers they make that have nothing to do with reality are taken as impudence.[16]

While Brecht's insistence on realism is clear, it is his process of enforcing it that is of more interest here. He develops a practice that simultaneously asks for input that is tentative while discouraging ideas that are forced or run contrary to the material itself. Brecht thus sensitizes his actors by suggestion rather than explanation (an offer is either accepted or rejected), in a mode founded on experimentation within the social bounds of the *Fabel*.

The actor-as-demonstrator in theory and practice

In Brecht's ideas on acting, there is one area that poses particular problems for an actor because it is not clear how to translate the ideas into practice. Brecht wrote the 'Street Scene' in 1938 and subtitled the essay 'a basic model for an epic theatre'.[17] The essay proposes that actors stand apart from their roles rather than immerse themselves in them:

- Here Brecht asks the single actor to *demonstrate* the behaviours and attitudes of different people involved in a car accident. The actor is thus a narrator who is always at a remove from the figures being portrayed.
- At the same time, each reported figure retains his or her own liveliness and individuality, just as is the case when one is retelling a story involving other people.
- The new model has features that Brecht prizes highly: 'the street demonstrator's performance is essentially repetitive. The event has taken place; what you are seeing now is a repeat'.[18] Here, Brecht stresses that the actor is signalling to the audience that the event, the car accident, is past and invites them to consider its meaning in the present. As a result, every 'character' the narrator performs is a quotation.

For Brecht, speaking lines as if one is quoting has a number of virtues:

- Actors can put distance between themselves and their figures, disrupting empathy in the process, because they are *not* their figures, but actors referring to figures.
- The quotability of a line or a speech puts the emphasis on the text rather than the person who first spoke it. This peculiar paradox takes us back to the question of typicality, raised in the previous chapter. An individual is at once unique *and* typical, displaying qualities that are the result of singular experience *and* of his or her place in society. Brecht wants to underplay the peculiarity of the individual in favour of its more general social role, and thus the idea of treating lines as quotations is a way of shifting the focus from the particular to the general. What counts is what the text tells an audience about a more general social attitude to a particular incident.

- By treating speech as quotation, the actor can compare different *Haltungen* towards the incident. The actor becomes a summarizer of positions, and the audience can then develop its own views on the material presented in a performance mode that has already disturbed the free flow of empathy.

While the advantages of the actor-as-demonstrator require some explanation, the way in which the practice works is hardly complicated. We have all told friends stories that involve other people: we are able to vary our voices and give the reported speech a different quality to differentiate the various 'characters' from one's own voice that is narrating the episode. However, plays simply do not work like this: they contain characters acting in the present and not the past, and it is rare (although not unheard of) for a character to recall previous events and retell them. So, how does Brecht propose actors of drama use the qualities of the actor-as-demonstrator?

Actor Angelika Hurwicz provides a reply to how actors at the Berliner Ensemble dealt with the issue. She stresses that acting at a remove from or standing next to a figure is actually about locating it in the context of the play as a whole, to establish its role in the events, noting the moments of social importance.[19] This may sound like a complicated set of instructions, yet they actually tie together the skills of observation discussed above and their place in the development of *Gestus* and *Haltung*.

Brecht devised an exercise for actors, initially described in 1940[20] and later used at the Berliner Ensemble, and it consists of rehearsing one's figure in the third person in the past tense, while contextualizing the lines with stage directions created by the actor.

The following example of dialogue is taken from Strindberg's naturalist drama *Miss Julie*. The extract features Jean, a servant to a Swedish Count, who has planned to run away from the country estate at which he and his fiancé Kristin work, together with the Count's

daughter, Miss Julie, with whom he is now in love. He and Julie intend
to set up a hotel in Italy. Jean is thus seeking to liberate himself from
servitude and climb the social ladder – until Kristin brings him down
to earth:

KRISTIN: So – you intended to run away?

JEAN: [Rather shamefaced]. Run away? That's putting it rather
strong. You heard Miss Julie's project, I think it might be
carried out.

KRISTIN: Now listen to that! Was it meant that I should be her
cook –

JEAN: [Sharply]. Be so good as to use proper language when
you speak of your mistress.

KRISTIN: Mistress?

JEAN: Yes.[21]

Brecht asks the two actors to preface each line with 'And then
Kristin/Jean said' in order to put a distance between actor and role:
'she' or 'he' is no longer 'I', and the events have already taken place in
the marker of reported speech, 'said'. Although this might appear to
be a simple technical detail, two practitioners noted that when they
tried using the exercise, but had their students use the first person
and the present tense ('and I say') instead of the third person in
the past, as per Brecht: 'we discovered that the difficulty here was
for the actor to avoid revealing subjective internal life and to keep
the narrative purely descriptive'.[22] Their procedure simply did not
deliver the distance inherent in Brecht's original instructions and
obscured the central focus of the exercise: to contextualize the lines
themselves.

How might actors describe their lines in the example taken from
Miss Julie? In the following revised version, the extra stage directions
are what an actor might say before delivering his or her lines as way of
putting distance between actor and text, and of providing themselves
with additional information that might help deliver the lines:

And KRISTIN said with surprise:

So – you intended to run away?

And JEAN said defensively:

[Rather shamefaced]. Run away? That's putting it rather strong.
You heard Miss Julie's project, I think it might be carried out.

And KRISTIN said, outraged that she would be cooking for
someone who fled with a servant:

Now listen to that! Was it meant that I should be *her* cook –

And JEAN said, in an attempt to restore order by referring to Miss
Julie's social position: [Sharply]. Be so good as to use proper
language when you speak of your mistress.

And KRISTIN said, with irony, given the circumstances:

Mistress?

And JEAN said, trying to reinforce his position with a single short
word:

Yes.

The scene, that could be played in such a way that Kristin is only
jealous at being replaced in Jean's affections by Miss Julie, can be
viewed here in its social context, too: Kristin registers the shift
in the social hierarchy if Miss Julie and Jean view themselves as
equals. Jean tries to re-establish the hierarchy, but Kristin is having
none of it.

The exercise sensitizes the actors to issues other than their own
feelings to each other. By processing the lines in this fashion, the
actors can locate their figures in their social context, and this will
affect the way they deliver their lines. After working through scenes
like this in rehearsal, the actors deliver the lines *without* the 'and x
said' and should notice a difference in the way they perform their
dialogues as a whole. Their awareness of the social issues at stake will
be greater and they should be able to view their figures at a distance
rather than completely 'inhabiting' them.

This, then, is one of Brecht's main rehearsal exercises, designed
to drive a wedge between actor and figure, and to bring out social

context. This comes after the actor's 'memorizing the first impressions' (see Chapter 3) that was used to register the aspects of a figure that surprised the actor on first reading the part, and the actor's hunt for a figure's contradictions. So, the actor first becomes aware of certain social issues affecting the role, and then the exercise helps to make these visible in performance. Brecht's exercise does not fully realize the ambition of the 'Street Scene' essay for the actor-as-demonstrator, but helps develop the essay's principles (gaining distance from the character, understanding its social position) for performing roles in a drama.

Playing the situation and not the character, or: The problem of saying 'I'

Brecht understands the individual not as a lone, autonomous entity, but as a person in constant dialogue with his or her social surroundings. This dialectical understanding of the individual undermines one of the central ideas of Stanislavsky's actor training. Stanislavsky divides dramatic scenes into smaller, manageable units, much as Brecht divides them up into the step-by-step unfolding of a scene's *Fabel* (see Chapter 4). Yet at the heart of Stanislavsky's units are the characters' objectives, goals that are to be achieved through action. Bella Merlin, an expert on using the practitioner's theories in practice today, states: 'the best way to express an objective [...] is to start by saying "I want to ... [*do* something]" '.[23] 'I want' suggests a degree of control over events. The problem with this position for a Brechtian actor is that the 'I' is not in some way detached, but enmeshed in a variety of social forces: the figures in Brecht's and other dramatists' plays often act under the pressure of events they are often unable to control.

Here are a couple of examples:

- In the third scene of *Mother Courage*, Courage's son, Swiss
  Cheese, has been captured by the enemy army. Courage tries to
  sell her wagon, her only means of generating income, to raise
  money that will be used to bribe the soldiers and save her son's
  life. However, she spends too much time haggling over the price,
  and Swiss Cheese is shot by firing squad.

  What does Courage want here? She wants *both* to save her son
  and to get the highest price for her wagon. The two desires
  are, in this case, mutually exclusive, because the time taken to
  agree the price for the wagon is that time it takes for the firing
  squad to execute the prisoner. If Courage's desire is 'I want to
  save my son', then she would have accepted the lower price
  offered, *but* her behaviour has already been conditioned by the
  laws of the market: a sale is only worth making when it brings
  the maximum yield. It is thus *not* Courage who is acting in the
  bargaining process, but the logic of doing business that she has
  absorbed over time. A Brechtian theatre can deploy the 'not – but'
  (see Chapter 3) to show that Courage is not acting in her own
  interests, but in those of the market here.

- Arthur Miller's *The Crucible*, a play about the Salem witch-hunt
  trials of the late seventeenth century, shows how hysteria can be
  manufactured and exploited to achieve certain ends: members
  of the community denounce each other as witches in order to
  settle old scores or gain material advantage over each other. The
  action reaches a climax at the end of the third act. The play's hero,
  John Proctor, tries to put an end to the persecution of his wife
  as a witch by exposing Abigail, the ringleader of the group of
  girls accusing other citizens of witchcraft. Proctor's first attempt
  fails. His maid, Mary, is also in attendance: she once lied that she
  had seen spirits, but now wants to tell the truth. Mary is thus a
  potential threat to Abigail, and so Abigail, supported by the other
  girls, pretends that Mary has sent a 'bird' to attack them, that

only they can see, of course, and they scream and writhe in its presence. In order to clear herself, Mary denounces Proctor for trafficking with the devil, and he is duly arrested.

In this example, 'I want' is mostly supplanted by the pressure of events. Proctor wants to exonerate his wife, yet in doing so sets off a chain of actions that lead to his own incarceration. Mary wants to tell the truth, but finds that she has to lie in order to avoid punishment herself. Even Abigail is locked into the events: her initial fiction has brought her a 'starring' role at the hearings, but it is also one that could expose her as a fraud and have her hanged, too. She thus has to attack Mary whether she wants to or not.

To Brecht, the problem with Stanislavsky's 'I want' is that *situations* make the phrase meaningless because 'I want' suggests a degree of choice that situations either limit or deny.

The question now arises as to how Brecht rehearsed such an approach. In the 'Short Organon', Brecht writes, 'each actor's learning process must be co-ordinated with the learning process of the other actors, the development of their figure[24] co-ordinated with the development of the other figures' (Organon §58). That is, actors rehearse as a unit: they do not start with ideas of an isolated 'character', but respond to each other as the situation demands. Rehearsal is about combining a figure's *Gestus* with a range of *Haltungen* brought about by the changing situation. 'Playing the situation' means combining the pressures that a situation exerts together with material taken from each figure's social context in a bid to perform behaviour that is appropriate to the situation. The emphasis on behaviour returns the actor to the issues raised about 'character' in Chapter 3: Brecht believes that what the theatre calls 'character' is in fact merely the accumulation of a person's many and varied behaviours over time. The task of rehearsal is thus not to establish a figure's 'character', but to expose the figure to new situations and to see how he or she responds.

This shift of emphasis can be seen in an analysis that engages with the example taken from *The Crucible*. Situations are complex and so it is necessary isolate their component parts and then to establish their *Fabel*. The action described above includes a couple of figures not mentioned in my summary: Reverend Hale, a clergyman who does not believe in the girls' accusations, and Deputy Governor Danforth, who presides over the trial. The following table lists the events of this sequence and their interpretation as a *Fabel*:

Events	*Fabel*
Hale defends Proctor and accuses Abigail	Hale tries to re-assert the rule of law to counter the obvious injustice
Abigail invents the 'bird'; the other girls join her; the credulous adults look for the 'bird'	Abigail seeks to cover the truth with more fantasy and uses the most fitting means available to her in the hope that powerful adults will believe her
Abigail accuses Mary of sending the 'bird'	Abigail attacks the person most likely to expose her and the girls
Mary defends herself and is supported by Proctor	Mary still has faith in the justice system
The girls continue; Danforth believes them	Abigail gains an important ally
After sustained pressure, Mary is about to change her story	Mary doubts the court's ability to deliver justice
Proctor tells Mary that God damns liars	Proctor invokes an alternative source of justice that exists outside the court: divine justice
The girls intensify their 'performance'	The potential for Proctor's stratagem to succeed evinces greater vigour from the girls
Mary denounces Proctor	Mary opts for deliverance on Earth rather than in heaven

This form of analysis, that takes events and interprets them as *Fabel*, helps actors to develop *Haltungen* to each other and the events, rather than just to rely on psychological aspects of their 'character'. In this example, the actor playing Mary can move through this section by negotiating her relationship to two systems of justice, the earthly and the divine. What changes over the course of the extract is her *Haltung* because justice in this courtroom is not determined by law and argument, but by superstition and theatricality. Each time the events progress, the figures can show a change in their *Haltung*. Proctor enters the court with faith in its ability to deliver justice, and even after his first attempt to convince the court fails, he persists in his bid to discredit the girls. He shows his resourcefulness by deploying the Bible to keep Mary honest, but what triumphs is her will to stay alive on Earth and not to be hanged as a witch.

With reference to his work on a scene in the 1949 production of *Mother Courage*, Brecht writes, 'what's going on inside [the figures] is not to be shown; the audience can work it out for themselves'.[25] Brecht values a figure's behaviour over its psychology. Is Proctor a God-fearing Christian or does he invoke the Bible to suit his own ends? Such a question about 'motivation' does not arise in this interpretation of the play. Instead the audience watches a series of actions and reactions, and is invited to ask what kinds of *conditions* bring them about: Proctor uses all his wits to expose the truth.

It is also difficult to attach rigid moral judgements to the figures, too, because their 'characteristics' are always in dialogue with their social contexts. Abigail may well appear to be the villain of the piece. In the first act, we learn that she and the other girls have indeed been involved in occult activity. Her skill as a liar helps her deflect attention away from the group and onto other people. Yet her initial actions cause far greater repercussions, and she is no longer able to control events: this is because the locals have seen how the charge of witchcraft can act as an effective weapon against their neighbours. Abigail's personal culpability cannot be denied, yet a more socially sensitized interpretation and performance of the play implicates the society in which she is operating, too. She propels herself into the role of 'star witness' at the hearings, yet this role both brings her celebrity and power, and risks exposing her. It is this contradiction that a Brechtian production can reveal, rather than speculating on whether or not she is a vindictive attention-seeker. The precariousness of her position is shown in the fourth act: we learn that Abigail has skipped town as a way of escaping the monstrous situation she has helped to create.

Brecht's emphasis on situation over character helps to account for characters' actions in their social context. In the excerpt discussed above, the actors can adapt their behaviour with every new event: this is a battle, based on a series of *material* interests. Abigail, the other girls, Mary and Proctor are all under threat of death, and so their performance can be shaped by that pressure. Each new event allows each actor to show how their figure responds. It may be tempting to play Abigail, for example, as a confident manipulator when she 'sees' the bird, but the theatre can reveal to the audience that this is actually a gamble that only pays off once Mary denounces Proctor.

'Relational rehearsing' is a way of starting a scene with actions rather than characters. Actors are invited to work through a series of *events* and to understand how each event affects the way they relate to each other. In highlighting events, Brecht proposes that the figures on stage have less control than Stanislavsky's 'I want' suggests. Instead, they are subject to pressures that they constantly have to negotiate. To Brecht, the interactive form of rehearsing results in a far more accurate reflection of reality.

The pursuit of naturalness and lightness in a stylized theatre

It may come as something of a surprise to find that, in his writings on acting and in the records of his rehearsals with the

Berliner Ensemble, Brecht regularly refers to the quality of naturalness – despite the frequent mention of stylization, showing and *Verfremdung*. Naturalness appears as an essential quality in the retelling of other people's stories in the 'Street Scene' essay and is praised in a list of Stanislavsky's virtues,[26] yet it is also clear that Brecht's theatre is also one that seeks to criticize behaviour that may be taken to be 'natural'.

Brecht offers a solution to this apparent contradiction in his notes to his production of *Antigone* in 1948:

> The stylization which turns the actor's performance into art must not in the process destroy the naturalness, but should on the contrary heighten it. [...] Stylisation means a general elaboration of what is natural, and its object is to show the audience, as part of society, what is important for society about this *Fabel*.[27]

Brecht suggests that stylization is not about making things less recognizable, but more. Naturalness is important in that it connects with Brecht's understanding of realism. It offers an unforced way of representing people and actions: an audience can recognize such behaviour. It is then subjected to the stylization – primarily in the act of showing – and can then be located within the bigger picture, that of social relations. Stylization is thus another form of *Verfremdung*, making the familiar strange.

How does Brecht help nurture naturalness in his actors? The first imperative has already been discussed above, and is also found in of the 'Short Organon': 'observation is a major constituent of acting' (Organon §54). Observation is certainly essential when working on the physical aspects of *Gestus* and *Haltung*. However, delivering lines presents a different set of difficulties for achieving naturalness, primarily because dramatic figures may use words, phrases and linguistic structures with which the actor is unfamiliar or ill at ease. Brecht also notes the influence of the stage and its linguistic traditions on dramatic writing: 'it must never be forgotten that our stage German is artificial. The actor's lines gain reality when they are practised in the vernacular, that is in local dialect'.[28] When Brecht's actors encountered problems with speeches, especially ones taken from the classical canon where the language itself was old-fashioned, he asked them to speak the lines in their own regional dialect.

One of the great appeals of this approach is that it can bring out *gestic* material in the language. Vernacular speech, by its very definition, reveals class positions because it is the language of particular social groups. There is a difference between the 'pub', the 'watering hole' and the 'boozer'; the 'police', the 'cops' and the 'filth'; to 'have sex', to 'make love' and to 'get laid'. Each variant reveals something important about the speaker's relationship to the concept or action in question, and that relationship is social. A note made by an assistant on a rehearsal of the Berliner Ensemble's adaptation of J. M. R. Lenz's *The Tutor*, a play written in 1774, shows the process through which more informal renditions of text developed Brecht's theatrical aims:

> At first, the action was performed entirely naturalistically, the actors spoke their lines in [their own] dialect. They then attempted a realistic delivery without the dialect, then an accentuated realistic version. The scene was then performed in epic fashion, incorporating and emphasising realistic aspects: individual gestures and movements are emphasised and isolated, the words flow well (not evenly but with meaning).[29]

The 'naturalness' of the dialect version serves as the raw material for further development, for identifying the social features Brecht wants to show to the audience. The actors' initial rehearsal makes them aware of the lines' meaning to them, they have a more concrete relationship to the words, and this is then imported back into the original lines. In the UK, such practices can be found in the work of Northern Broadsides, for example, a company that has largely performed classic plays, especially those by Shakespeare, in regional accents.

Naturalness is a way of understanding social material in everyday speech and behaviour, and it offers a Brechtian theatre details taken from reality that can then be refined and processed in rehearsal, and exhibited in performance.

A problem, however, with Brecht's attention to detail and its precise exhibition in performance was the risk that the show itself could become little more than the movement from detail to detail, a mechanical progression devoid of naturalness. To counter this very real consequence of Brecht's rehearsal strategy,[30] Brecht endeavoured to give his productions the quality of lightness.

Brecht writes about lightness at various junctures. In what appears to be an address to actors in *Buying Brass*, the anonymous speaker sees lightness as a way of dealing with difficult material (see *Brass* 111–13). Lightness means finding clear solutions to potentially complex problems. Brecht is more specific after a couple of years' work with the Berliner Ensemble when he notes:

> [The actor] must divide up, modulate, and get the flavour of his lines in such a way that he's comfortable with them. He must 'arrange' the movements [of the lines], whatever they express, in such a way that their rhythm and form are pleasing to him. These are all sensory tasks, and the training for it is physical.[31]

Actors are invited to approach complexity by dividing it up, understanding its constituent parts and finding a simple and enjoyable route through it. As Brecht adds, if actors do not make it easy for themselves, then they will not make it easy for their audience.[32] If they do not understand what and why they are doing things on stage, then their audience will have little chance of making sense of the performance, either.

Acting and emotion

The role of emotion in Brecht's theatre has been something of a bone of contention ever since Brecht drew up a now almost infamous table in 1930 that listed the contrasting qualities of dramatic and epic theatre.[33] The very last pairing is 'feeling' and 'reason'. What appeared to be a separation of the two was nothing of the sort, as Brecht endeavoured to argue in the years that followed. His understanding of the role of emotions on stage is subtle and requires further examination.

Brecht makes the following points in an essay on acting, written in the early 1940s:

> The rejection of empathy is not the result of a rejection of the emotions, nor does it lead to such. The crude aesthetic thesis that emotions can only be stimulated by means of empathy is wrong.[34]

The two sentences address common misapprehensions concerning emotion in the theatre, its origins and its effects. The first seeks to decouple the role of empathy or identification (see Chapter 3) from the presentation of emotion on stage, while the second proposes that empathy is not the sole source of emotional reaction in an audience. The related points, which take issue with apparently 'commonsense' opinions on theatre and emotion, rest on a common premise: the audience need not see emotionally charged action to experience an emotional response. Newsreaders, for example, usually do not gush when reporting on disasters or massacres, but the effect on their audiences may be profound and moving. In the theatre, documentary productions can report the most harrowing tales of hardship and suffering in the most cold and neutral terms, but a sense of sympathy, pity, anger or outrage will not necessarily be generated by the mode of transmission. Brecht proposes that the stage can have an emotional effect on its audience without employing empathetic communication.

Actors can depict all manner of highly charged incidents by engaging alternative approaches.

However, emotions themselves can also provide the subject matter for performance. Brecht continues:

> The emotions always have a quite definite class basis; the form they take at any time is historical, restricted and limited in specific ways. The emotions are in no sense universally human and timeless.[35]

Here he proposes that human emotions, like human values, are not in some way disconnected from society, but produced and shaped by it. An anthropological study of, say, when men and women are 'licensed' to cry at different points in history and in different cultures would reveal a huge divergence in both sorrowful and joyous instances. Emotions are products of complex physiological functions, as Bruce McConachie observes: 'human beings don't simply "get emotional"; our bodies are constantly experiencing emotions and affects. In addition, these emotions and affects always take time to run their course in our bodies and brains'.[36] Brecht's theatre is not only interested in frustrating the simple communication of emotion to the audience because it wants to resist an automatic empathetic response, but also because emotions themselves are worthy of investigation.

As already mentioned in Chapter 3, Brecht understood the actor's preparation process as one involving a dialectical movement that synthesized distance and proximity. Consequently, actors could both know their figure and stand back from it. In this way, a figure's emotions can appear just as 'strange' to an actor as its opinions or actions. Examples of this curiosity towards emotions can be found in Brecht's final production with the Berliner Ensemble, *Life of Galileo*, which he rehearsed in early 1956:

- In scene four, Galileo takes a Philosopher and a Mathematician to task, and he insults the Philosopher's beloved Aristotle in

the process. Brecht directed the Philosopher to roar his rebuke
to Galileo, and the actor playing the Mathematician wanted to
follow suit. Brecht, however, asked the Mathematician to calm the
Philosopher instead. The use of contrast marks the Philosopher's
outburst as one *possible* response rather than a universal one.
Indeed, the Mathematician's move to pacify the Philosopher
shows that he considers this approach to counter Galileo's
position ineffective.

- In scene fourteen, Galileo is visited by his former student, Andrea,
  while under house arrest. This is an emotional confrontation
  between the compromised master and his disappointed
  apprentice. Galileo is more distant and wistful; Andrea feels
  the loss of what he considers Galileo's moral authority after his
  teacher has recanted his scientific discoveries in the previous
  scene. Brecht, as director, was keen for the actor playing Andrea
  to *display* his feelings when he noted, 'these are Schillerian lines,
  lots of emotion'.[37] Here, the actor is asked to foreground emotion,
  but the reference to Friedrich Schiller signals that Brecht wanted
  a delivery provoked by a different kind of dramatic writing. The
  actor openly points to emotion as an emblem of distress, not as an
  invitation for the audience to identify with Andrea.

In both examples, emotion is 'displayed' to the audience, not to
forge a bond, but to *signify* aspects of a figure's responses between
the stage and the auditorium. The aim is to perform emotion as if in
speech marks, so that the audience does not get caught up with the
figure's feelings, but rather considers what they signify. Emotion is
thus viewed, as are most things that actors perform on the Brechtian
stage, as a part of a complex set of contradictory behaviours that help
construct a figure in its entirety.

However, actors nonetheless have to perform lines that carry all
manner of emotional charge, and the question arises as to whether

Brecht made more general proposals on this issue. In 1955, he was reported to have asked for 'an "epic performance"' of *Don Juan* at the Berliner Ensemble as a present to himself for his birthday. He was said to have characterized the acting in such a presentation as being 'completely without pressure or tension, really just delivering'.[38] This was Brecht's ideal: a radical separation of the elements (see Chapter 3) in which the lines would be divorced from their usual mode of delivery in order to open them up for the audience. This empathy-defying mode reflects the ambition to cool down the action on stage so that actors might not cloud an audience's responses with too much proximity to their figures. As is evident from Brecht's reported sentiments, this was not the norm at the Berliner Ensemble, even though the production had been directed by one of Brecht's closest and most experienced assistants, Benno Besson. It was perhaps not possible for Brecht to realize all his aims for his actors with the company in his seven years as artistic director. Brecht showed the way with such practices, where actors stand at a palpable remove from their figures, and later practitioners took them up and radicalized them (see the Epilogue).

To return to the opening argument in this chapter, Brechtian actors do not develop a style of acting, but an approach to acting. The ideas and the exercises discussed above all provide *means* for actors to process dramatic material dialectically and to show their findings to the audience. Difference and distance, naturalness and lightness are all Brechtian principles, but their deployment is not a style as such; rather, it is a performance philosophy than runs through the action of a play and is the product of a dialectical worldview. The same can be said of the way Brecht understood the role of the director, and that is the subject of the next chapter.

Brecht and the Director

Inductive direction, or: The 'invisibility' of the Brechtian director

Towards the end of the 'Short Organon', Brecht sketches the different creative professionals required to bring about a successful dialectical production:

> The *Fabel*[1] is expounded, developed and presented by the theatre as a whole, by the actors, stage designers, mask-makers, costumiers, musicians and choreographers. They all unite their various arts for the common undertaking, without of course sacrificing their independence in the process. (Organon §70)

The *Fabel* is, of course, at the centre of the work, and Brecht proposes a 'separation of the elements' (see Chapter 3) to generate productive tensions from the stage for the audience to negotiate. Yet one role, central to the staging of any play, is conspicuous by its absence: Brecht makes no reference to the theatre director. This may strike the reader as a curious omission; after all, Brecht's theatre company, the Berliner Ensemble, rose to international prominence after a mere five years' work, and this was due, in no small measure, to Brecht's artistic leadership in general and to his work as director in particular. In order to resolve this apparent contradiction, it is necessary to understand the special role Brecht assigns to the director.

Brecht was critical of the ways theatre directors imposed their 'vision' of a play upon a production. He felt that the 'vision' was fixed and turned rehearsal into an exercise that forced through an interpretation without due engagement with the text itself.[2] Brecht believed that it was only in rehearsal that discoveries could be made, together with the actors. For Brecht, the director's work is not to provide grand ideas, but to enable productive practical investigation.

Brecht is also wary of an obsession with novelty as an end in itself among directors, and he makes the following comment with respect to other directors' approaches to staging his own plays: 'the talented directors I would fear most would be the ones who were the most original.'[3] Here, too, 'originality' is a false god: it may sell more tickets, but it can obscure what is actually happening in the drama itself.

As an antidote, Brecht proposes what he calls the director's 'inductive' approach to developing dramatic material for performance.[4] 'Inductive' and 'deductive' reasoning are terms taken from philosophy, and while I will not dwell on their specialist definitions, it is worth noting the difference between the two. The deductive method usually takes one general and one particular premise, and deduces a consequence, as in the following example:

> Premise one: Any user who borrows a library book for more than two weeks will be liable for a fine of £1 per day.
> Premise two: Stuart has had a book on loan for three weeks.
> Deduction: Stuart owes the library £7.

However, the deductive process is not as useful as it may at first seem, as has been noted here: 'the ability of valid deductive arguments to guarantee their conclusions derives from the fact that deductive reasoning merely draws out or makes explicit information that is already contained in the premises.'[5] So, deductive reasoning only really tells us what we already know.

The inductive method of producing knowledge, on the other hand, is based on the movement from observation towards the tentative establishment of patterns and principles. It is thus particularly well suited to works of art, because it can strive to make connections between the often unexpected behaviour of people in situations and the bigger social picture. The method is concerned with interrogating dramatic material rather than coming to it with preconceived ideas. The director and the actors thus begin the rehearsal process with no fixed ideas about their figures, but probe and experiment in order to establish relationships and behaviours.

Consequently, the director's role, as Brecht understands it, is more that of facilitator than visionary. The director does not impose a concept on a production: today, it would not be appropriate for Mother Courage to do e-business on an iPad, for example, because such 'novel' ideas fail to capture the nature of commerce in the seventeenth century. Instead, it is the director's job to support the actors in their journey through the contradictory text, ensuring that they identify and embody their *Gestus* and their repertoire of *Haltungen* with respect to the social relationships encoded in the text. Only then can the director connect the figures' behaviours to issues that may affect a contemporary audience. An inductive director might understand Mother Courage as a figure stuck in a similar set of problems to those of an audience today: she strives to survive and to protect her family, but finds that capitalism does not support the two simultaneously.

The director is no longer required to have great ideas that may or may not be supported by the play. On the contrary, the director becomes 'invisible', a servant of the dialectical method. It is not a question of imposing a novel style or feel on a production, but working through a method that exposes contradictions and presents them to the audience.

The tasks of the Brechtian director

At the end of the 1930s, Brecht speculated on the work of a director involved in an inductive process with a cast. The essay's title, 'The

Attitude of the Rehearsal Director (in the Inductive Process),[6] already says much about the newly conceptualized role. There is no talk of a 'production's director', but a person who is in charge of the rehearsal process. And this person adopts an 'attitude' towards the process; that is, the rehearsal director seeks to influence the way rehearsals are carried out by making certain interventions rather than imposing a vision or dictating a concept to the passive actors. The evidence from the Berliner Ensemble's own copious rehearsal notes bears out all the positions sketched in the essay, and I will go through them one by one to understand their function in the inductive rehearsal process:

1. The rehearsal director understands the rehearsal process as one of 'trying out' approaches to performing lines or scenes. This is, by definition, a slow process that involves 'several possibilities' for addressing the issues generated by a text. The inductive method is thus speculative: it does not deliver hard-and-fast solutions, but acknowledges that there are many ways to deal with the contradictions of the dramatic material.

2. This is, in part, because a cast is composed of different people who have 'their own diverse interests, which need to be fully developed in order to enhance the overall solution'. Here Brecht sees each cast member as representing a certain position or point of view, born of his or her unique experience: all input needs to be acknowledged in order for the work to retain its liveliness and its realism. The rehearsal director is involved in a process the draws out these different perspectives from the actors and sees what tensions they generate in performance.

3. This aim is effected by abandoning 'all the schematic, customary and conventional solutions to these challenges'. So, the rehearsal director is not against novelty in itself and actually wants to promote new ways of confronting issues, yet these go beyond the standard solutions found in the theatre of the time. Brecht

wants the actors to approach the questions that surround the construction of their figures by adopting his innovations, primarily the twin concepts of *Gestus* and *Haltung*, that reveal contradictions otherwise overlooked in more traditional theatre practice.

4. The rehearsal director is the catalyst for new ways of thinking about roles and relationships on stage: 'he must unleash *crises*'. It is the rehearsal director's task to ask difficult questions and *not* to settle for apparently adequate solutions. Brecht adds that the director should not be ashamed to admit that he or she does not have all the answers to the 'crises' themselves. This stance reinforces the understanding of the rehearsal director as facilitator, the person who is charged with continually exposing contradictions that have been overlooked or ignored.

5. The rehearsal director also ensures that the pace of rehearsals is kept slow. This is a strategy designed to achieve two ends: Brecht notes that more experienced or famous actors can intimidate younger cast members with their swift solutions to theatrical problems. He thus wants to allow *all* the actors the requisite time to make discoveries. He is also wary that hastiness may simply equate with taking the well-trodden, conventional route, and thus wants to promote the questions 'why do I say this? And why does he say that?' from *every* actor.

6. Finally, the rehearsal director is there to ensure that the solutions the cast arrives at are realistic: 'the healthy kind of surprise emerges when the logical solution is surprising'. So, Brecht has nothing against novelty in the form of surprises for the audience, either, but these surprises cannot be forced or manufactured; they have to be plausible in terms of everyday experience. Indeed, the excavation of contradictions should be an activity that is rich in surprises; surprise, after all, is the bedrock of *Verfremdung*, making the familiar strange.

The rehearsal director thus plays roles that are concerned with working through a method, not a vision. The director accompanies the rehearsal process and makes sure that it does not result in tired, stagey ideas, but engages with the material afresh, leading to lively and surprising performances, grounded in the realism contained in the fictional situations. The director short-circuits tried and tested approaches and invites the cast to think through the specific problems that arise in specific texts with fresh, or naïve, eyes. Yet the director has to have a critical mind that is continually asking actors to park a particular solution and try out a new one, to take what has already been achieved and to question it. 'Crises' can only be provoked if the director can criticize the existing state of rehearsal. The dialectical director is restless, testing all the material the actors offer for conventionality and 'un-realism', and driving them on to find solutions that go behind the surface and dig out social contradiction.

The prerequisite for a Brechtian director: A vibrant ensemble

It is no surprise that Brecht's theatre company was called the 'Berliner *Ensemble*' (my emphasis). The redefined work of the director, set out above, is dependent on an active and 'sensitized' group of actors who can identify contradictions in their figures, embody and present them to the rest of the cast (in the form of 'offers' – see Chapter 5), and respond to the offers of the other actors. Brecht's understanding of an ensemble has a number of distinctive features:

- An ensemble is not a faceless mishmash of actors setting out on a joint venture. Rather, it is a productive unit for the very reason that each actor brings a new point of view to rehearsal. Brecht noted while still working in the theatre before his exile, 'some theatres have tried to foster an "ensemble spirit". What this usually boils down to is that all the actors are expected to sacrifice their own egoism "for the good of the play". It is actually much better to mobilise this egoism in each and every actor.[7] The ensemble does not defer to the process, but enlivens it. Consequently, the ensemble becomes a lively group of competing voices, all of whom can make a valid contribution to rehearsals by fighting their own corner. The ensemble thus creates a dialectical tension of its own, between the collective desire to stage a play and each individual actor's interests in the project.

- An ensemble is an active *collective*. Brecht values collectivity because it can democratize the rehearsal process: 'the act of creation has become a collective creative process, a continuum of a dialectical sort in which the original invention, taken on its own, has lost much of its importance'.[8] In a hierarchical rehearsal room, where the director gives instructions and the cast carry them out, the 'original idea' is preserved. In a collective, the 'original idea' can come from the director or a member of the cast and is then subjected to scrutiny and modification with each successive 'offer' or comment that is made. It is continually re-shaped along the 'dialectical continuum' of a rehearsal until the 'original' idea has effectively been made unrecognizable.

- Brecht also notes (echoing Stanislavsky's dictum that there are no small parts, only small actors) that there is no difference between the ways a leading actor and an extra make meaning on stage; they are both significant, regardless of their prominence on stage.[9] A director can thus treat every member of an ensemble in the same way. The Berliner Ensemble often drew praise for its 'ensemble spirit' in newspaper reviews, which meant that even the smallest roles displayed the same sensitivity to the unfolding action and degree of concentration as the larger ones. The Berliner Ensemble's rehearsal notes similarly detail just how

closely Brecht worked with small roles and how he was not afraid
of casting lead actors in secondary parts. While Brecht would
rarely cast a novice in a major role, he certainly believed that
newcomers could learn a great deal from far more experienced
actors when the latter played smaller roles.

- An ensemble is a group of actors that can potentially stay together
  for some time because they are contracted to a certain theatre or
  company. Nowadays in the UK, ensembles are virtually unheard
  of: actors join productions for particular projects and then
  leave at the end of the run for another job. Germany, however,
  had and still has a tradition of theatre ensembles, and Brecht
  valued an ensemble's ability to learn together and develop over
  time. He could sow the seeds of his approach to directing and
  watch over the years as more-experienced actors passed on
  their ways of working to new members. Viewed as such, an
  ensemble could become self-sustaining as it worked away on the
  dialectical method by testing it over time, adding this, discarding
  that and ensuring that the method did not become stale and
  conventionalized.

Brecht's interest in collective creation necessarily dethrones the
director and helps to undermine the hierarchies that can exist in
theatre systems. Brecht, together with his assistants, was, of course,
responsible for agreeing the *Fabel* and for pushing through his
dialectical method. He thus retained a centrality in the rehearsal
process. Nonetheless, his faith in collective creative practice meant
that he was prepared to give the actors a greater say in their own
performances, and the development of the practice of making 'offers'
provided actors with a real platform for bringing their own embodied
ideas to the stage. Brecht was not happy to take the lead as director,
and the Berliner Ensemble's rehearsal notes sometimes record Brecht's
disgruntlement at too much passivity in the ensemble.[10] The practice

of rehearsing inductively with an ensemble of active participants can lead to a shift in power relations *and* the type of work produced. Meaning-making is no longer solely the responsibility of the director, but is negotiated over time as the ensemble engages with the concrete problems of the play.

Rehearsing with an inductive director

If a director is not barking orders or staging a 'vision' of a play, then what is he or she actually doing in the rehearsal room? Brecht's interventions at the Berliner Ensemble reveal what his practice, described in the previous chapter as 'sensitizing the actor', actually entailed.

Brecht's close collaborator and sometime mistress Ruth Berlau lists the words she most frequently heard Brecht use in rehearsal: 'show, try out, contradiction, dry, speak, *Fabel*, why?, why?, and again: why?'.[11] This short list may contain imperatives to cool down delivery ('dry', 'speak'), but it is more concerned with activity, activation and interrogation. The inclusion of 'contradiction' and *Fabel* show that Brecht emphasized central ideas from his dialectical worldview, but also sought input in terms of practice to answer the recurring question 'why?'. The answers, however, were not to be provided by discussion or debate: Brecht considered both unproductive because they did not lead directly to *practical* solutions. Instead, he wanted actors to answer his questions with performance.

It is worth lingering a little on how Brecht embedded the innovations he was introducing into the business of performing the dialectical method. Brecht hardly ever used the word *Verfremdung* in rehearsal. This has led some critics to conclude that Brecht left his theories at home when he entered the rehearsal room.[12] It is true that Brecht did not ask an actor to perform a 'Verfremdung', but this was because making the familiar strange would actually be produced as a result of inductive rehearsal itself. Indeed, the very business of performing a figure dialectically is about identifying and then negotiating the contradictions, as the following examples show:

- In one rehearsal Brecht spelt out his plan clearly when referring to the presentation of one of the figures: 'I'm in favour of dialectics: irreverent *and* reverent. In his daily life, Ruprecht is certainly an upstanding peasant – in court he bends' (my emphasis).[13] Thus, the figure can show how a change of social situation, from his normal environment to the formal one of the court, affects his behaviour. The actor engages in *Verfremdung* in his depiction: the audience believes that they know the irreverent Ruprecht, but observes how the court turns him into someone who must submit himself to the power of the law if he stands any chance of being taken seriously. He surprises the audience, but the audience is then able to make the connection between behaviour and context. Brecht was thus able to embed complicated theoretical views into clear and understandable directions that more often emphasized contradiction instead of terminology like dialectics and *Verfremdung*.

- The figure of the Little Monk in scene eight of *Life of Galileo* presented a range of problems because he is such a contradictory figure. He is both a practising Catholic, of course, and a student of science. His divided loyalties make his conversation with Galileo painful and protracted. Brecht noted that the Monk was the son of poor parents whose studies the Church had paid for. All of a sudden, his benefactor had been called into question. Brecht advised the actors he was auditioning to ignore the technical problems of the Monk's long speeches with Galileo: 'speak slowly and relatively softly; you're thinking as you're speaking'.[14] He thus wanted to dramatize the contradictions not by playing off one side against another (as was the case with Ruprecht), but by showing the difficulty such contrasting demands made on the Monk.

Brecht himself gave direction in two forms. As one would expect, he gave verbal assistance. Yet, as far as the records show, he often gave *metaphorical clues* that the actors then had to translate into the concrete context of a particular scene:

1. In *Mister Puntila and His Man Matti*, Matti sees Puntila drunk for the first time in scene one. Puntila, a monster when sober, is friendly and kind when inebriated. There is obviously the temptation for the actor playing Matti to embrace the new Puntila, yet the suggestion offered was: 'meeting of two patrols, reconnaissance in no-man's land'.[15] The direction is evocative and captures a specific mood, one of mutual suspicion in the face of danger in a place that is unknown to both parties. Such a direction also acknowledges Matti's social situation: as a working man, Matti is better off regarding the transformed Puntila with wariness because he knows how wily Puntila can be.

2. In the Berliner Ensemble adaptation of *The Tutor*, Brecht told two figures not to play a love scene as if they were both smitten with each other, but like a game of chess, with each lover responding in turn to the latest 'move'.[16] Here the direction is more concerned with realism, of getting the tentative nature of a budding relationship right. But once again, it is clear that Brecht was directing in metaphors, allowing the actors to find their own way through the lines under the gestic guidance of the instruction.

Brecht was also fond of performing a speech or an action to his actors, but here, too, there is no evidence to show that he actually wanted the actors to copy him directly. Many of Brecht's assistants and actors have commented on his exceptional performance abilities. Actor Käthe Reichel recalls: 'he always ran up onto the stage. [...]

He wanted to provide a spark'.[17] This 'spark' was suggestive rather than concrete and was performed in such a way that direct imitation was impossible. Actor Angelika Hurwicz talks of an 'understatedness' in Brecht's performances while assistant Egon Monk says his actions were 'almost always exaggerated'.[18] Assistant Carl Weber adds that Brecht often spoke the lines in gibberish.[19] At the heart of Brecht's performance was, as actor Regine Lutz adds, an implied *Haltung* towards an action or another figure, 'but you could distil the *Gestus* and develop it further'.[20] Thus, actors who had learned to play with *Gestus* and *Haltung* could read Brecht's either over- or understated demonstrations and re-direct the example into the specific context of their scene. Brecht was not, then, involved in inhibiting the actor with his virtuosity. Instead, he enlivened actors with his own gestic renditions that offered a *starting point* for their further development.

It is clear from Brecht's approach to inductive direction that his own skills – with language and performance – were deployed to produce suggestive direction, when required, that did not diminish the actor's art, but set it further tasks. It respected the ensemble's abilities by avoiding the patronizing stance of giving literal directions and instead encouraging creativity.

Abolishing the read-through, or: The status of the text in rehearsal

Brecht, as the Berliner Ensemble's artistic director, introduced a special format for the rehearsal process whose very structure was designed to support his aims of implementing inductive direction.

The starting point, as with most rehearsal processes, was the read-through, yet Brecht was not overly in favour of the practice. In the company's early years, Brecht made concessions to the convention, but insisted that the actors read their lines as drily and as neutrally as possible. There were no discussions of what the lines meant or how they were to be delivered.[21] In his later years, Brecht virtually abandoned the practice entirely. The reason for this curious relationship to the traditional rehearsal schedule was that Brecht did not want his actors to form opinions about their figures, other figures or the action before entering the rehearsal room itself and encountering the text in performance.

Once in rehearsal, actors were often allowed to carry their scripts, or the in-house prompter would be used extensively. Brecht feared that if the cast learned their lines too early, they would also learn specific ways of delivering them, something that would make rehearsals themselves less open and productive. The idea was that actors should rehearse under the influence of the *Fabel* rather than under their own steam: the *Fabel* interpreted the play in terms of its action rather than the figure's individual roles. Actors were to make their discoveries not in the privacy of their homes, but in direct confrontation with the other actors.

Brecht, too, wanted to approach the dramatic material with fresh eyes, even when directing plays he had written himself. There are several reports of how he appeared to be completely unfamiliar with his own figures, lines and scenes.[22] While some co-workers wondered whether this was genuine or feigned, the result was the same: Brecht asked questions of the text in a spirit of inquiry and could also criticize his own writing on occasion.[23]

This stance towards the dramatic text was one that he advocated in general, and he was thus leading by example when directing his own plays. He advised actors not to be inhibited by their speeches, however famous they were, and to avoid the 'mistaken reverence for the playwright that makes them forget reverence for the audience' and that 'prevents them from comprehending the play's mistakes'.[24] The sentiments are interesting because they reflect Brecht's priorities when dealing with a play as a director:

1. The audience is placed firmly at the centre of the theatrical production: everything is for their benefit. This is because they are the ones who are to learn from the work, although we should not forget the kind of learning Brecht wants to bring about, as set out in Chapter 1: not the learning of lessons as such, but learning how society works and how it might be changed.

2. The actor, supported by the director, is crucial to the development of a *relationship* to the text. Any play does not exist 'as is', but is there to provoke a response. What is the actor's *Haltung* to his or her figure, or to the action? Such questions drive a wedge between the text and the performer, and confer a special status on the actor: the actor is no longer subservient to the text, but stands apart from it, judging its norms and its biases, and adopting an opinion on them.

3. The play itself is no longer the hallowed text of the dramatist, but a complex, poetic negotiation with the writer's time, place in society and views on the events and situations depicted. It is open to criticism (the 'play's mistakes') and these need to be addressed in rehearsal. For Brecht, a play's Achilles heel is often to be found in its treatment of social issues. His adaptation of Shakespeare's *Coriolanus*, for example, shows reverence towards the playwright's language and the situations he describes, yet it shifts the focus away from Coriolanus himself, contextualizes him in Roman society and gives a more balanced portrayal of the lower ends of society.

Brecht's approach to staging plays is all about focusing on their social function, on how people behave under certain conditions and how society influences people's behaviour. The only way to establish such relationships was to have actors work with each other on the text: they should not defer to existing interpretations or be intimidated by a play's or a playwright's reputation. Both the director and the cast have to approach the material naïvely (see Chapter 3) in order to explore its possible meanings in the light of the *Fabel*.

The rehearsal process and its social goals

In many ways, the very form of rehearsal, described in Chapter 5, is designed to sensitize the actor to dialectics and the social dimension in performance: 'Relational rehearsing' is concerned with each figure in each scene acknowledging how the dialogue and the action affect and possibly change their opinions or behaviour. Brecht compares the process to a game of tennis:

> An actor must respond to their partner's reply like a tennis player to their opponent's shot. This is brought about by catching the tone and returning it so that it produces modulations and variations in the delivery that resonate through whole scenes.[25]

In effect, Brecht is asking the actors to demonstrate their debt to the other actors by tracing the contradictions in the dialogue rather than concealing them under a veneer of unchanging 'character'. As actors become more familiar with this way of rehearsing, they are less dependent on the input of the director. Rehearsing like this is about transferring the responsibility for creating dialectical performance from the director to the actor, while, of course, the director is always on hand to make suggestions, corrections and to ask questions.

Once the actors were placed in a series of *Arrangements*, they entered into what Brecht called 'rehearsals of details'.[26] Here the director worked inductively on identifying and bringing out the 'details' of the figures' relationships to each other under the conditions set out by the *Fabel*. The idea of a 'detail' is central to Brecht's understanding of the way theatre communicates its most important elements: 'the *distinguishing features* [*Merkmale*] stand as

realistic parts to the realistic whole'.[27] The German word 'Merkmal'
contains a particle from the verb 'merken', 'to notice' – and so the
details were not in some way minor or accidental, but significant and
designed to catch the spectator's eye. The inductive director is thus
also involved in pointing out what needs to be emphasized or 'shown'
to the spectator, and, again, over time, the actors can develop a feel
for a type of performance that moves from detail to detail, exhibiting
them for the audience.

However, as noted in Chapter 5, such a way of working can lead to
something mechanical emerging on stage: actors can simply perform
their details one after the other and offer the audience something
that lacks the naturalness Brecht demands of a dialectical theatre.
Brecht proposed 'lightness' as an antidote, but how was it to be
brought about?

Brecht introduced a final phase to rehearsals, called the 'speak-
through run' (Durchsprechprobe). In contrast to the more
conventional 'run-through' that represents that culmination of a
rehearsal process, the 'speak-through run' was used to help the actors
process their detailed and precise movements by moving through
them at speed. Brecht had them retain all their gestures, positions
and movements while delivering their lines quickly and neutrally.
The reported results were positive: the actors approached the 'speak-
through runs' in a relaxed fashion because they were not being asked
to execute their performances with the usual care and precision, but
merely to mark out where they were supposed to be and what they
were supposed to be doing. This helped replace mechanical execution
with something that flowed, due to the speed with which the actors
were required to perform. After such runs, they would return to
normal speed and import the lightness they had acquired back into
their performances.

Brecht could see the great value of dwelling on details because
of their social significance (see below), but acknowledged that they

could undermine the naturalness and realism that were so central to his overall conception of a production. His approach to *structuring* rehearsal was thus dialectical: the search for social detail and relationships is the thesis; their potentially ungainly performance the antithesis; and the reintroduction of lightness the synthesis.

Connecting the individual to society: Details, customs and monologues

Brecht as director wants to bring out the social dimension in performance, and, as has just been shown, he does this by foregrounding significant details in a figure or a situation. Details become a way of connecting figure to a context that reveals something important about the relationship between the two. But what does this mean in practice? The following examples shed light on the different ways the deployment of well-focused emphasis can suggest connections:

- In *Battle in Winter*, which follows a Nazi battalion during the Battle of Moscow, Brecht insisted that drunkenness be socially contextualized. Thus, he wanted to differentiate between an officer's inebriation and that of a regular soldier. German officers of the time were often of higher social class, and so Brecht had them remain stiff and upright when drunk, struggling to control themselves, rather than the men, who were happy to stumble and reel. Drunkenness, something that may appear to be a 'natural' state, was given a politics: the socially superior officers showed that even when drinking hard, they preserved class division, displayed discipline, and thus managed to differentiate themselves from the ranks.
- In *Life of Galileo*, Galileo travels from Venice to Florence. It would be easy for a director to stage the scenes set in different

cities in a similar way – after all, they are both in Renaissance Italy. Yet Brecht wanted to show that the two cities were run along very different lines at the time: Venice was a democracy of sorts while Florence was ruled by the powerful Medici family. By scene eleven, Galileo, who is residing in Florence, is about to be summoned to Rome to account for his scientific discoveries to the Inquisition. The whole city knows what is going to happen, yet Vanni, an iron smelter, greets him heartily. Brecht directed Galileo to take him to one side because such public approval, in the earshot of the royal court, could be damaging. Here, Brecht used a relatively simple instruction, not found in the script, to give the situation a realistic detail: a different form of government brings forth different types of behaviour.

- In Synge's *The Playboy of the Western World*, the creative team worked hard to establish the social context of the play, the poverty of a village in Ireland. In a love scene, the directors made the playboy, Christie, warm his hands by a fire while declaiming his passionate speech like an aria. The scene could have been played in a more 'traditional' manner by having the lovers embrace, but the production emphasized that love is not enough to keep them warm, and so the issue of priorities arises.

Well observed details, which may seem minor when viewed in isolation, help establish the complexities of the larger social picture when performed in combination with each other. Brecht also had a fondness for staging customs and ceremonies. These, however, should not necessarily be considered grand occasions, but gestures and *Haltungen* that point to social rituals. Such practices are important because they show people acting not on their own initiative, but deferring to customary behaviour, and customary behaviour will have its roots in the way society works. Again, a couple of examples:

- In *Mister Puntila and his Man Matti*, Puntila the landowner has a number of dealings with unemployed locals looking for work on his estate. At one point, Brecht refused to cut the gestures of the men doffing their caps to Puntila, even though the scene was running over time and cuts had to be made. He was not prepared to sacrifice the ritualized sign of class division for the sake of a quicker running time.

- Customs can also come together to form whole systems of behaviour, as in the following case. Brecht was dissatisfied with the work of a fellow director, Emil Burian, who had started directing *Battle in Winter* before Brecht intervened and took over. He found that Burian had neglected to represent the workings of the German war machine: 'this colossal chain of command with its particular customs, military ranks and traditions has to be right not only because the majority of our audience are familiar with it, but all the more so because our hero is stuck in its mechanisms'.[28] Thus, Brecht did not merely want to depict the army as a group of soldiers and officers, but as a complex interplay of rituals and practices that serve to produce certain behaviours – different ones at different levels. Again, the emphasis is on the way that behaviour that may *appear* to be natural or self-explanatory, but is actually the result of hierarchy and power relations.

Customs and rituals can say much about a society and people's places within it. If a group of workers, for example, doff their caps to a boss, but one refuses, spectators can observe whether he will be fired, disciplined or tolerated – each response will say something different about the relationship between the boss and the workers. In addition, the gesture of resistance shows that workers *can* refuse to respect the custom, and suggests that if enough followed the example, they might be able to change the conditions that appear to be encoded as unalterable in the custom itself.

Brecht continually sought to connect the individual with the social. However, monologues, a not uncommon form of speech in drama, threatened to frustrate this aim. He was concerned that monologues were too private, cut off from society and thus contributed little to the social dimension of a production as a whole.[29] As a consequence, Brecht *manufactured* a dialogue wherever possible. In one case, in *Battle in Winter*, one figure has a monologue that Brecht redirected in such a way that he brought out nationalistic lines of thought, so that the addressee was a concept – 'Germany's grandeur' – rather than a person.[30] This solution may appear somewhat contrived, but its effect was nonetheless concrete: rather than directing the speech inwards, the actor developed a relationship with a political idea. This gave the audience a context for understanding the monologue in terms that were no longer only private.

The difference between the treatment of realistic details and of monologues is not as great as it may initially seem. Both procedures are about connecting text to society by uncovering material that may have been hidden or simply not signalled in the script. Brecht's approach was to use a play as *material* for further exploration, and he focused, as a director, on making connections between figures and their social circumstances in a bid to draw the spectators' gaze away from the individual and towards his or her interplay with society.

Bringing out the social in performance: Focus on *The Broken Jug*

On three occasions during his seven years with the Berliner Ensemble, Brecht took over the direction of a production because he found the original director wanting with respect to the social mission he had ascribed to the work of the company. In this section I will consider one of these instances, the production of Heinrich von Kleist's *The Broken*

Jug (1811). The example shows how Brecht's direction responded to perceived shortcomings in another director's work and repositioned a well-loved classic in order to bring out its politics.

Kleist's comedy deals with legal corruption in rural Holland. A lowly local judge, Adam, has injured himself while pursuing an erotic adventure with Eve, breaking a precious jug in the process. The play follows his attempts to cover up the incident when the jug's owner, who is also Eve's mother, seeks redress in Adam's courtroom. To make matters worse, the court is being inspected by Walter, an official from Utrecht. Both Walter and Licht, Adam's scribe, have an interest in unmasking Adam: Walter wants to reform legal practices; Licht wants Adam's job. Finally, the truth is exposed and in the confusion Adam escapes. Suffice it to say, there are many more twists and turns in the plot involving Adam's desperate gambits to hide the truth and trade on his status as a judge.

Brecht took over from the original director, the renowned actor Therese Giehse, in late 1951. The list of criticisms of her work reads thus:

1. The play's *Fabel* was not recognizable in performance.
2. Giehse's treatment of the characters' language was praised, but it achieved little because it was not organically connected to the flow of the action – it was more a series of set-pieces.
3. The characters were approached psychologically and not socially.
4. Giehse had taken the traditional reception of each character as her starting point rather than exploring the text for qualities and behaviours of the characters as figures.[31]

In short, Giehse had directed the play in a conventional fashion, without inductive exploration or the guiding principles of a socially constructed *Fabel*. Brecht's interventions in the rehearsal process reveal how he brought out class conflict and derived behaviours from it.

The play's cast has a clear social hierarchy, with Walter at its top, Adam beneath him, then Licht as a member of the court, and at the bottom the local peasants and people of the Dutch village. Brecht's directions for the first scene set up some of the play's contradictions from the outset. The production opened with Adam alone as a miserable creature after the injury of the previous night. Yet when Licht entered, Adam had to transform himself into the role of rustic dictator. The audience saw how power could be created to emphasize social superiority. The rehearsal notes indicate a difference in the way the two directors treated Adam's opening lines:

GIEHSE: Bark at Licht out of insecurity.
BRECHT: Report for his subordinate.[32]

Giehse's direction imputes a characteristic to Adam, while Brecht's places the figures in a social hierarchy. The notes suggest two different types of delivery: the first reactive; the second more controlled and authoritative. And because Brecht had Adam look like a picture of wretchedness just beforehand, the social contrast was all the greater in his version, as Adam struggled to re-assert his place in the pecking order.

Brecht's treatment of Walter was also sensitive to the class issues involved. Walter was clothed as an educated bourgeois and acted in a quiet, gentlemanly way. His understated behaviour made him all the more powerful because of the responses it brought forth in Adam. Early in their relationship, for example, Walter notes the suicide of another shabby country judge. In Brecht's new version, Walter found the judge's act completely understandable – this is what happens when corrupt officials are exposed – while Adam was horrified by the news. This represented the start of Adam's downward spiral because the news threatened him in two ways: he was not as safe as he thought he was, and the authorities would be ruthless.

The villagers were also, of course, subject to the contradictions brought out by class-based analysis. In the text, Eve criticizes the powers that be, but Brecht was keen to show that this was the criticism of the peasantry and not of all the characters in general. The insistence on delivering lines from each figure's place in society helped to bring out the comic tensions of the play as interests could be played off against each other. The play's *Fabel* centred on how one bad form of justice could not be replaced by a better one because, to Brecht as a Marxist, justice in any unequal society always serves the interests of those in power. The peasants, once at the mercy of Adam and his whims, will find themselves subject to the laws of the moneyed middle-class, represented by Walter, once Adam has been deposed.

The production showed the kinds of behaviours a corrupt legal system could produce in people who had to negotiate its structures in order to get anything approaching justice for themselves. This was expressed in the antagonistic note: 'every figure speaks out against the other, all the figures are in opposition with each other'.[33] This basic position helped the actors understand their changing *Haltungen* to each other: as the comic action progressed, the figures had to reposition themselves to defend their respective interests.

By moving away from time-honoured interpretations of the characters, Brecht breathed new life into the figures. Productions of comedies, after all, tend to emphasize funny situations and characters without necessarily investigating *why* either is funny. In the case of *The Broken Jug*, Adam's attempts to extricate himself from the consequences of his amorous disaster were usually considered reason enough to stage the play. Yet Brecht sought to locate the comedy in the class relations of the piece, and to allow them to expose the licence social positions confer on the way the figures behave. The almost farce-like structure of the play helped him to refine his actors' decisions in that each new stratagem changed the terms of the argument, and the figures would either find themselves at an advantage or under more pressure. Brecht saw the humour of the play as secondary to the class-based behaviours on display;[34] it was these discrepancies that generated laughter rather than comic lines or twists.

The reviews of the production were overwhelmingly positive, especially in the East, and praised Brecht's new class-based interpretation of the figures and the action. What is interesting is that the critics often noted how the whole approach radically altered the reception of the play without changing a single word of the text. Brecht had applied the dialectical method to the comedy and had his actors rehearse from the social point of view by developing a *Gestus* for each figure and a series of active and reactive *Haltungen*. The result was enlivening and *accounted for* the laughter rather than simply taking the witty lines and changes of fortune for granted. In addition, such a production was, almost by definition, a model of how a class-based focus could bring out *Verfremdung* almost automatically: the familiar lines of the classic play were performed anew due to Brecht socially grounding the action. There was no need for clever effects, simply a considered and well rehearsed change of focus.

This example helps to show how the input of an inductive director working through the dialectical method can achieve a great shift in the way a classic play is performed and received. Brecht was not working with a 'vision' that he imposed on the dramatic material, but with an approach that contextualized the figures and their action in the social conditions of the time. The director's task was to make the connections that often went unmentioned in productions of the play in order to shed new light on the piece. This he achieved by engaging actors whom he and his assistants had introduced to dialectical contradiction and who could respond actively to its movements through the text.

Brecht, Documentation and the Art of Copying

Imitation and innovation

The first six chapters of this book provide readers with the raw material for their own acts of copying: they set out Brecht's ideas and practices, and readers with an interest in 'making theatre politically' might seek to imitate Brecht's approaches. Brecht as theorist thought about the meaning of copying and imitation (terms he used interchangeably) on many occasions and as practitioner developed a form of documenting his theatre work, the 'modelbook', that was expressly designed to be imitated by other theatre companies and theatre-makers. Yet 'copying' and 'imitation' are terms that are often associated with a lack of creativity or vision and can be used as a shorthand for parasitism, leeching off the ideas of others for one's own benefit. This chapter examines how Brecht set about rethinking the practice of copying in order to make it productive rather than merely reproductive.

Brecht's method, and the ideas that helped him develop and revise it, were novel: they offered fresh ways of engaging with and staging plays. Brecht saw the propagation of his method as one of his main aims on returning to Europe. He wanted his own productions and those of the Berliner Ensemble to act as the best possible advertisement for his new approach. Indeed, he dispatched his assistants to other theatres that showed an interest in the company's work in order to disseminate his rehearsal process. He also developed forms of documenting his work, discussed below, that set out how he applied dialectical analysis to a play in the context of a real production. He wanted other theatre companies to consult the documentation and produce their own work based on his dialectical principles. This invitation, both to imitate and innovate, already signals the constructive role Brecht ascribed to copying.

As noted in the previous chapter, Brecht did not want directors to come to his plays with a pre-formed concept that they would push through in order to create an original production. Instead, he hoped that they could substitute their own old methods for his new ones, apply them to the play that formed the basis of the documentation, and then take his method and apply it to different dramas.

Theatre documentation was in its infancy in the late 1940s, and so Brecht found himself in a curious position: there was little material in circulation either, on the one hand, to act as a pointer or, on the other, to inhibit new ideas. He thus had free rein to consider how a theatrical method might best be presented to his readership. The question he faced was how to communicate a sense of process rather than simply display the product to his readers. If his new form of documentation was to deal with more than just the final production, it would have to rely on notes taken during rehearsal as well in order to capture important moments of discovery. Brecht realized that he would have to dispense with the standard way of taking rehearsal notes – the faithful description of what took place – in order to include other elements that could account for the decisions taken.

The building blocks of documentation at the Berliner Ensemble: *Notate*

When Brecht returned to Europe, he had already developed theoretical approaches to staging dramatic material dialectically.

As artistic director of the Berliner Ensemble, he not only set about putting his ideas into practice, but also recording the process. The initial reason was purely pragmatic: that the achievements of any one day's rehearsal could be referred to and returned to. Yet Brecht did not only want rehearsal notes to describe events in the rehearsal room.

In German, the standard word for 'notes' is 'Notizen', yet from the Berliner Ensemble's first production onward, Brecht introduced the practice of assistants taking 'Notate', a word that also means 'notes'. However, as is often the case with Brecht, the term had a special meaning in the context of his theatre work. *Notate* are not just records of rehearsals, but writings that seek to get inside the process, to account for why a decision has been made or why it has been discarded. *Notate* combine description, analysis and reflection. Two assistants at the Berliner Ensemble recount that the submission of *Notate* to Brecht was initially a process in which he offered comments of his own and counter-suggestions.[1] The note-taking thus had an educational function, too: in compiling *Notate*, the assistants became sensitized to Brecht's criteria for successful performance and were able to develop a dialectical perspective. Once the assistants had understood the form and function of the *Notate*, they no longer submitted them to Brecht's scrutiny. And once the *Notate* were ready, they provided the critical basis for the following day's work.[2]

In addition, *Notate* were not usually taken by a single assistant, but by at least two. While one could say that having more than one person making notes ensured that more ground could be covered, that less was missed, there is also a point to be made regarding the very *status* of the observations and analyses. Brecht promoted collaboration as a way of involving more perspectives than just his own. By engaging several note-takers in the rehearsal process, he could gather several points of view on the reception of his work. Note-taking is not objective, and different people see different things and process them in their own way. Thus, Brecht was able to recognize the differences observed by the assistants and have them inform the creative process as a whole. *Notate* were not only a repository of record, but an active part of a feedback loop, too.

The way rehearsals were conducted also supported the taking of *Notate*. Brecht's inductive approach (see Chapter 6) laid bare the creative process because decisions were established in rehearsal through creative collaboration. We can see what happened when a different style of rehearsal was initiated at the Berliner Ensemble:

- Brecht suspended rehearsals for his own play, *Life of Galileo*, in March 1956 due to ill health; he died in August of that year. His one-time directing partner, Erich Engel, took over as director, and the show premiered in January 1957.
- Käthe Rülicke, an experienced assistant who had worked with the company since 1950, wrote that she found it virtually impossible to take *Notate* from Engel because he did not reveal the process by which he came to his theatrical solutions.[3] Engel preferred to direct like a more conventional director, issuing instructions to be carried out by the actors, and so this special form of note-taking had little to work with: it could only record what had happened because the director did not open up the creative process as Brecht had.

Of course, anyone taking notes can stand back from a decision and analyse it, regardless of how a director directs, but the point here is that Brecht's rehearsal process deliberately sought reflection and integrated the *Notate* into the overall development of a project. For this to work optimally, it helped to rehearse in dialogue with all concerned. *Notate* were not external to the process, but a part of it.

So what do *Notate* look like? For the following overview, I have made a selection from one of the most elaborate sets of *Notate*, those that accompanied Brecht's production of *Katzgraben* by Erwin

Strittmatter. This new play, whose title is the name of a fictitious farming village, is about agricultural reform in the years directly preceding the foundation of the German Democratic Republic in 1949, the state in which Brecht lived and worked up to his death. Käthe Rülicke was one of the assistants who compiled the *Notate* for this project.[4] She had already worked with the Berliner Ensemble for four years and was, by then, sensitive to the ways *Notate* were written there. Hers can thus be considered representative of the qualities Brecht wanted to see in a production's documentation. The following examples survey the different roles of the *Notate* at the company:

- The *Notate* here are almost exclusively impersonal, as is the case with almost every set made under Brecht. They mostly refer to the figures rather than to the actors. In this way, they could be used as assistance for other actors if roles were re-cast, something that was not unusual at the Berliner Ensemble because its shows could run for many seasons. The focus on the figure also grounds the note-taking in the fiction of the play rather than the abilities of the actor. The analysis looks at a figure's contradictions and its relationships with the world of the play without clouding this aspect with comments about execution. *Notate* are not so much concerned with the actors, but with the tasks with which they have been charged.
- There is an emphasis on process, of contextualizing the figures' behaviour in the specific conditions of a scene. We find, for example, 'up till now, the maids were completely helpless. Now [...] there is someone standing behind them, namely the Free German Youth [a mass organisation for young people, a part of the socialist party]. This helps Erna adopt a new *Haltung* [to her employer]'.[5] The *Notat* does not describe what the new *Haltung* is, but rather how it comes about.

- Instructions appear in general terms and are to be negotiated by
  the actors themselves. Much of *Katzgraben* is written in verse,
  something that pleased Brecht because verse usually denotes
  nobility, as when Shakespeare distinguishes between verse and
  prose in his plays. Brecht found it liberating for working-class
  figures to speak in verse, and Rülicke notes, 'speaking in verse
  should be fun, like the to-ing and fro-ing of a swing. [...]
  Naturally, naturalness should not be sacrificed to the verses'
  rhythms' (I ii 1, 8 April 1953).

- Discussions are noted and solutions offered. In one scene,
  for example, the team dwells on a detail concerning the two
  wealthiest figures in Katzgraben, Herr and Frau Großmann. The
  question is seemingly minor: should she light his cigar for him?
  The answer is that she should not, and the reasons given go far
  beyond the simple act itself: 'she fulfils her duties as a wife, that's
  what religion asks of her, but nothing more. She will not support
  vice. There's a difference between selling tobacco and smoking it
  yourself' (I iv 3, 6 March 1953). This gesture, that can be shown
  in a 'not – but' (she does not light his cigar, but lets her husband
  light it himself), points to social aspects of Frau Großmann's
  biography: (i) She is a Christian and acts on its precepts.
  Socialists do not believe in God, and so she is already placed
  in negative opposition to the more positive figures in the play.
  (ii) However, she uses religion as a weapon against her husband's
  implicit authority. She does not mechanically submit to his will
  and undertakes her own small act of defiance. (iii) That said,
  she is not yet a fully progressive figure. There is a contradiction
  between her business sense (selling tobacco to others) and her
  religious beliefs (reducing smoking in her own family) that
  renders her a hypocrite. The detail and its implications have been
  recorded as a way of analysing the complexity of the figure in her
  social context.

- *Notate* can help develop the *Fabel*. The scene that introduces the Großmann family was suggestively named 'the last days of the dinosaurs' (I iv 1, 5 May 1953) only on its fifth rehearsal. The title helps to give more specificity to the action: the figures are relics from the (capitalist) past, and the audience thus view them on the verge of extinction, so they must exhibit certain qualities that are clearly out of step with the social and political changes that are afoot.
- *Notate* also register problems and suggest solutions. The socialist hero of the play, Party Secretary Steinert, is defeated in the third act, before he and the village triumph over the old order in the fourth. However, Brecht found it difficult to deal with the scene. The record shows that the problem could not be surmounted, and the proffered solution was based in his own staging method: a new *Arrangement* to address the scene's contradictions afresh (see III ii 8, 7 March 1953).

The examples above offer only a snapshot of the many staging points in a complex rehearsal process. Yet they show how *Notate* can do more than just describe what is happening: they undertake interpretation, open up dialectical contradictions, and engage with social context. They do not represent a slavish attempt to describe the minute details of each session, but a careful consideration of crucial aspects of the process.

The Berliner Ensemble's *Notate* were never published in Brecht's lifetime and were mainly used internally by the company itself. Its productions could run for long periods and so new cast members and directors could refer back to them in order to understand both how decisions were reached and how improvements might be made over time. However, they also provided the raw material for a form of documentation Brecht introduced and that *was* made available for a wider constituency: the 'modelbook'.

Demystifying the theatrical process: 'Modelbooks'

The *Notate* reveal that the first stage of the documentation process was to engage fully with the business of staging plays dialectically. They continually move from the particular to the general, using specific details to illustrate the principles in question. Documentation is thus not so much about recording the intricacies of a rehearsal process, but exposing how it works. *Notate* alone set out the many discoveries of the rehearsals, yet Brecht needed a form that was more accessible and immediate to those not directly involved in the rehearsal of a particular play: wading through the twists and turns of a single scene's development over months may interest scholars, but theatre people want a more compressed and helpful account. To this end, Brecht arrived at the concept of the 'modelbook'. The very title immediately signals that the books were designed to serve as an aid by providing representative examples of practice; however, Brecht and his team had to find a suitable form.

In the late 1940s and early 1950s, affordable cine-cameras were all but unheard of, and so preserving performance on film as a record was not an option. However, Brecht's emphasis on *Arrangement* and *Haltung* called for a different kind of document. His collaborator Ruth Berlau came up with the idea of photographing performances extensively and compiling documentation by assembling the most significant images in sequence. The photos were mostly those of the whole stage, not close-ups of particular actors or gestures. The camera could thus follow the development of *Arrangements* and the various figures' *Haltungen* as any given scene progressed. Assistants at the Berliner Ensemble were charged with selecting the most significant photos from the thousands that were taken, that is, the ones showing the *changes* that took place on stage most clearly.

In a book documenting the company's first six productions, Brecht writes a note called 'Photographability as Criterion', a curious title, because, essentially, anything can be photographed. Brecht's point here is that photographs of *his* theatre have to satisfy certain criteria if they are to be of any use to a viewer. He criticizes both naturalistic and overly stylized productions because photos of them show either too much or too little: 'where there is disorder or arbitrariness, the basic process cannot come to the fore'.[6] He associated 'disorder' with naturalism because it reproduced the everyday in all its gestures and details, whether they were important or not; 'arbitrariness' denoted his understanding of abstract productions in which anything could stand in for anything else. Regardless of his prejudices, it is clear that photography was there to reproduce Brecht's theatre of showing. If socially significant details and contradictions could not be seen by the camera, they could not be seen by the audience.

'Modelbooks' were produced for every production of the Berliner Ensemble. The ones made for internal use sometimes only included photographs; others matched each photograph with a figure's lines or an extract from the dialogue in order to locate the picture in the flow of a scene. Here, 'modelbooks' were a point of reference for people already familiar with the work done at the company. Their manufacture also afforded new staff an opportunity to develop their eye for significant moments in a production. However, after Brecht's death, other theatres started to request these in-house 'books' in ever increasing numbers in order to learn about Brecht's method from the Berliner Ensemble.[7]

The best known examples of 'modelbooks' are those that appeared as commercial publications. Brecht documented his Swiss production of *Antigone* of 1948, the East German *Mother Courage* of 1949, and there was a special comparative edition that engaged with his American (1947) and East German (1956–1957) productions of *Life of Galileo*. In addition, the Berliner Ensemble published a series of smaller 'modelbooks' based on productions they had developed as professionals for use by amateur companies in the mid-1950s, and one on Brecht's play *Señora Carrar's Rifles*. The published 'modelbooks' develop the 'basic' form of those made for internal use at the company by offering three complementary components: sequential photographs of the production; the full text of the play in question; and a series of notes, setting out the issues at stake and/or explaining why decisions were taken. Introductory material and short essays explaining more general staging principles also appear.

The arrangement of the three sections differed between the different examples: in some, they appeared as three separate booklets contained in an elegant box. The idea was that each component could be consulted individually or in connection with the others: the reader could learn about a certain moment while comparing it with another in the photographic record of the production, for example. Elsewhere, practicality was key. This is best demonstrated in the 'modelbook' of *Hans Pfriem, or Boldness Pays Off*, which was aimed at amateur theatre groups. When this book is open, the right-hand page is in fact a double page folded in on itself. When folded, the page as it stands is blank, awaiting the amateur group's notes; unfolded, one finds photos and a commentary on directorial decisions. The text itself is on the corresponding left-hand page. Such a book presented itself as deliberately unfinished, awaiting, as it was, input on the blank pages from the troupe staging the play.

'Modelbooks' of whichever format were intended to offer insights into the theatrical process by shining a light into its workings. Readers could compare image with text and its explication. The following examples are taken from the 'modelbook' of *Mother Courage and her Children*:

- In the first scene, two members of an army happen upon Courage and try to recruit her son Eilif. Courage seeks to prevent this, and we read in the play: '*she pulls a knife*. Go on, you kidnap him, just try. I'll slit you open, trash. I'll teach you to make war with him'.[8]

One might imagine an infuriated Courage, resorting to violence to defend her son, yet the comments on her performance in the 'modelbook' tell a different story: 'Mother Courage shows no savagery in pulling a knife. She is merely showing how far she will go in defending her children. The actor must above all show that Mother Courage is familiar with such situations and knows how to handle them.'[9] The note offers a suggestion that appears to be at odds with the lines themselves, but justifies its stance plainly and clearly.

- The eleventh scene is one of the play's most famous: Courage's daughter saves the children of the city of Halle from advancing soldiers by banging a drum to wake them up. A note to the scene states, 'it is important to avoid clichéd heroism. Mute Kattrin has two fears: one for the City of Halle and one for herself'.[10] Here the advice pits the deed against its price: this is what Brecht would call a 'realistic detail', a way of anchoring the action in the reality of its context. Kattrin's actions have a purpose, but may be cut short; yet achieving her ends will seal her fate. The action is complex, yet Brecht breaks it down into its two contradictory pressures: Kattrin's fear of failure and her fear of success.

The 'modelbooks' were designed to provide theatre-makers, and those simply interested in theatre, with an insightful understanding of the work of Brecht and his team. The 'model' status of the books points to their role as examples to be copied. Yet Brecht's own agenda for the 'modelbooks' proved more controversial and threatened to undermine their potential usefulness.

Making use of the 'models'

Brecht returned from exile to find not only Germany but German theatre in ruins. He felt that the Nazis had debased the theatre and that he was in the perfect position to offer an alternative to the contrived, pompous productions that had graced German stages during the Third Reich. The first production he directed in Europe was his adaptation of *Antigone*. In the introduction to the show's 'modelbook', Brecht clearly states that the new text is not to be made freely available to theatres, but comes as part of 'a *binding* production model' (my emphasis).[11] On the back of the success of the East German production of *Mother Courage*, Brecht insisted that subsequent productions of the play staged elsewhere use the 'model' and banned a production in Dortmund in the same year for diverging too greatly from his instructions. In Wuppertal, the imposition of the 'model' caused provocative comments in the press, such as the headline 'Author Command – We Will Follow!'.[12] The phrase parodies a Nazi slogan ('Führer command – we will follow!') and maintains that Brecht has installed himself in post-war Germany as an artistic dictator. Later, Brecht tried to defend himself by maintaining that he 'turned to gentle intimidation', itself a deliberate and retrospectively playful oxymoron, in order to prevent a free-for-all on the part of directors approaching his plays.[13]

Brecht's initial heavy-handedness was the result of a desire to establish a new way of making theatre in the wake of the Nazi's deformation of culture. Such zeal, as has just been shown, was not well received, and the charge has been levelled on several occasions that Brecht wanted to stifle the creativity of others while creating a monopoly for his own.[14] Brecht was clearly doing himself no favours by insisting, as a condition for granting performance rights, that his models be followed – although he did rescind the imperative after a short while.[15]

Before the controversies of 1949, Brecht had written an introduction for the first 'modelbook', the *Antigone Model 1948*. This is thus an important essay because it is not reacting against a torrent of criticism. On the other hand, it may be viewed as a pre-emptive strike, given that this is the essay in which Brecht defined his staging approaches to *Antigone* as 'binding'. The essay's main points regarding the use of the model run as follows:

1. Brecht maintains that 'such a model will of course stand or fall according to the ease with which it can be imitated and varied'.[16] Here he states quite clearly that the model is something that works in two ways: it provides something that can be copied *and* something that can be altered. The question thus arises as to which elements fall into which categories.

2. He goes on to note that a model cannot affect an actor's performance in the form of the delivery of lines, gestures or movements. These he calls 'not exemplary so much as unparalleled' (167). He makes an important distinction here, because the model is clearly intended to have an exemplary character, too. The exemplary is thus more concerned with the shape of a production (*Arrangement* and the figures' *Haltungen* to each other), what can be 'read' from the 'modelbook's combination of text, image and commentary. In the second example from the *Mother Courage* model, above, the actor playing Kattrin would receive a framework for a performance, but has to negotiate its terms and produce a response that deals with the challenge of showing two kinds of fear.

3. Brecht makes the argument for collective creativity, something that challenges the notion of the individual's originality. He asks that the status of the original 'model' is not given too great an importance, as it is the task of the ensemble to make changes to it. However, this does not imply that the 'model' can simply be done away with: it is there as a starting point for further development.

4. Brecht then distinguishes between the ways in which an ensemble can deal with the *Arrangements* and the *Haltungen* in the 'modelbook': they can respond either 'slavishly' or 'masterfully'

(168). To Brecht, the masterful approach is about suffusing the exemplary blueprint with extra material, taken from reality. In this way, those using the model create new models themselves.

5. With specific reference to the *Antigone* production, Brecht notes that the results on show are themselves unfinished, due to the short rehearsal period, and that the shortcomings themselves 'cry out for improvement' (168). He thus directly solicits the readers' and theatre-maker's input.

6. He also notes that working with a 'model' is made all the more difficult because 'it contains much that is unintentional and provisional; this has to be located and eliminated' (170). Those using the model thus have to be discriminating and determine what elements fall into these two categories and what elements should be preserved and/or improved upon. The emphasis is on the active evaluation of what might or might not be useful.

7. He concludes that 'working with models need not be pursued with greater seriousness than is necessary for any kind of performance' (171). In equating the use of the model with other forms of rehearsal, Brecht emphasizes the amount of play and experiment involved in the process. The model has rules, which are to be obeyed, but actors are invited to approach them with strategies, tactics and virtuosity of their own.

In the light of Brecht's observations, the model is itself contradictory: it is at once exemplary *and* unique, and it is an ensemble's task to make the exemplary parts work for them while adding their own uniqueness through their unrepeatable performances. The exemplary nature of the model is communicated in its treatment of specific *Arrangements* and *Haltungen*, yet the underlying constant is the dialectical method of approaching staging. The model is thus an example of how the method can be applied to a particular play and how its principles can be understood in practice.

However, despite the dialogue Brecht sought to create between other ensembles and the 'models', it turned out that it was not easy to negotiate the line between adhering to dialectical staging principles and providing creative input. In 1950 Brecht noted that the model of his play *The Mother* was like a 'straitjacket' when it was used in the town of Schwerin because the team were not able to 'transfer humour and grace' from page to stage.[17] On the other hand, when Brecht, leading by his own example, made use of the same model with the Berliner Ensemble, he wrote: 'our more relaxed handling of the old model [...] seems successful'.[18] It appears that a productive use of the model had as a prerequisite a clear understanding of the principles involved its construction. Brecht's ideas were still new and not well known at the time, and so that which was self-evident to him (the movement from *Fabel* to *Arrangement*, to *Gestus* and *Haltung*) was still something of a mystery to those who either chose to adopt the model or had the model imposed upon them.

Brecht drew the conclusion: 'while meant to simplify matters, models are not simple to use'. This, Brecht went on, was because 'they are designed not to make thought unnecessary, but to provoke it; not to replace, but to compel artistic creation'.[19] This response, founded on the principle of activation, has more to do with Brecht's understanding of copying, than might initially be apparent.

Copying as productive activity

Copying might appear to be a simple process in which one observes the person or action to be copied and then reproduces it. This view is one that Brecht contests, especially in the field of art. Brecht maintains that copying 'is not the "easy option". It is not a shameful failure, but an art'.[20] Brecht's transformation of imitation into a creative practice takes two premises as its basis:

1. One-to-one copying is simply impossible because people are different from one another, and so the copy will never be exact.[21]
2. Imitation is never a wholesale, but a selective process.[22] There is much in an original that can be copied, and so the copier has to decide on the particular aspects that are to be copied and why.

Brecht elaborates on the consequences of these points in the 'Short Organon' when he contends that imitation is not only a physical, but a mental process as well (see Organon §54). Thought is essential to the act of copying because it gives it a rationale, as is clear from the following short poem:

> He who only imitates and had nothing to say
> On what he imitates is like
> A poor chimpanzee, who imitates his trainer's smoking
> And does not smoke while doing so.
> For never
> Will a thoughtless imitation
> Be a real imitation.[23]

Normally one might consider a 'real imitation' to be one in which the copy has the same appearance as the original, but Brecht begs to differ. One need only consider the work of great impersonators: while they might be able to approximate their appearances with the people they are imitating, their talent actually resides in an ability to reproduce mannerisms and, to use a Brecht's term, *Gestus*. Michael Sheen may not look that much like Tony Blair in the film *The Queen* (2006), but his performance garnered plaudits for the vocal inflections, the manner of the delivery and the gestures. In these he could draw attention to certain of Blair's attributes while dispensing with others. To Brecht, copying is more about studying the object to be imitated and making a series of choices in order to achieve certain ends.

In the case of the 'model', Brecht did not suggest that actors view the images of the production in question and place themselves in the same positions for no reason. He wanted them to ask *why* the actors stood where they did, what it told the audience about their relationships or their place in society, and then to find appropriate theatrical solutions based on the ideas that underpin the original. This is why Brecht could successfully re-use the 'model' of *The Mother* at the Berliner Ensemble; he 'copied' it by understanding its workings and making it anew.

The 'modelbook' of *Mother Courage* approvingly concludes its photographic documentation with a section entitled 'Variants' that display contrasting images from the Berlin and the Munich productions, both directed by Brecht. The Munich production 'copied' the Berlin 'model', yet the results of the copy betrayed both clear similarities and marked differences. The two sets of *Arrangements* and *Haltungen* are not commented upon in the 'modelbook' because they are the product of the same artistic process. The photos show that creative imitation of a 'model' can produce different results:

- At the end of *Mother Courage*, for example, Courage pulls her cart around in a circle. She has lost her three children, although she believes that one is still alive.
- In the Berlin production, Brecht's wife, Helene Weigel, looked down, lost in the manual labour, exhausted. In Munich, another great German actor, Therese Giehse, looked up with resolve and energy.
- Clearly, neither solution was singularly the 'right' one, but each was doing a different kind of work in response to the heading in the 'modelbook': 'Mother Courage learns nothing'.[24] In Weigel's case, she carries on as she did before; in Giehse's, she still has hope, even though the audience knows it is mistaken.

To Brecht, copying is a critical appropriation of the original. One has to know *why* one is copying, and in understanding the reason, one is selective and emphasizes certain qualities in order to say something specific. Copying starts by identifying features and then asks why they are as they are. When copying someone's *Gestus*, the copier may well ask why a confident man is so sure of himself and whether a confident woman would be confident for the same reasons. Merely reproducing the outward signs of confidence is not enough because the copier has not understood where they have come from. Is the confidence a product of the man's upbringing, his success, his talents? Is it for show or is it genuine? Is it a quality expected in a certain situation or does it surprise? Can the woman's confidence be accounted for in the same way as the man's? Copying is an art form, one based not only on close observation, but also on a series of decisions. Copying is a dialectical activity that is not only focused on surfaces, but on cause and effect.

This book has been conceived to offer exemplary instances of Brecht's central ideas and practices in the hope that readers who are interested in working through them can make use of them in rehearsal rooms, on stage or in any other location where performance might take place. Clearly, imitation is a part of that process, but imitation born of Brecht's own thoughts on the process as an art form: there is nothing mechanical about copying. Rather, copiers have to know why they are copying and what they intend to achieve. In doing so they are evaluating the original and making decisions. The final chapter offers two suggestions for how directors and actors might approach a play by Brecht and a play by a dramatist not writing in the Brechtian tradition. Both examples reflect an engagement with the ideas of the book, and in copying them represent a critical appropriation.

8

Using Brecht's Method

Applicability and approach

This chapter takes the theories and practices discussed in the previous seven and applies them to two very different plays: one written by Brecht, and one by a playwright with no acknowledged connection to Brecht. The aim is not only to show what a Brechtian approach to a Brechtian play can reveal, but also to ask what is to be gained by interrogating a play with no overtly social or political ambitions.

The reason Brecht gives for applying his own dialectical approaches to works written by others is set out in one of *Buying Brass*'s dialogues, in which the Philosopher advises the Actor not to wait for radical new plays:

> Even when [playwrights] make things up, […] it seems as though the incidents have been lifted from real life. All you ought to do is take the incidents themselves as seriously as possible, and the playwright's use of them as lightly as possible. You can partially ignore the playwright's interpretation, you can insert new elements; in short, you can use plays as raw material. (*Brass* 23)

Through the voice of another, Brecht suggests that his method can be applied to any play that satisfies his criteria for 'realism'. However, the play itself has to be treated critically, so that the events, the play's main achievement, take precedence over the playwright's opinions or biases (see Chapter 6). In short, Brecht wants to focus on any 'realistic' play's action in order to develop a dialectical *Fabel* and use it as a starting point for further practical work. He also mentions the practice of adaptation, of making strategic additions and cuts in order to support his interpretation. This was Brecht's practice when preparing dramas for performance at the Berliner Ensemble: he wrote and supervised a number of adaptations, perhaps most famously Shakespeare's *Coriolanus*.

However, Brecht, never one to set his ideas in stone, revised this position in an interview given in 1956, the year of his death. On the subject of stagecraft, Brecht opined, 'if I were putting [Shakespeare] on today, it is only small changes I would have to make in the production, changes of emphasis'.[1] Here he accepts that his method of analysing and staging other people's drama might indeed suffice without interfering with the fabric of the texts themselves, and I will be exploring this approach, rather than one based on adaptation, in this chapter.

I have chosen Brecht's *The Resistible Rise of Arturo Ui* (1941) and Patrick Marber's *Closer* (1997) for special attention. One might assume that Brecht's plays were written in such a way that they suggest clear links between his method and its realization on stage, but this is not the case, as the 'modelbooks' discussed in Chapter 7 already show. The dialectical method requires sensitivity to the social and political issues at stake and to the contradictions they bring about in the action of the figures on stage. In the case of one of his own plays, Brecht noted that the well-intentioned first production of *Mother Courage* (staged in Zurich in 1941 when he was in exile in the USA) encouraged the audience to pity the protagonist rather than to adopt a critical attitude to her failure so as to learn from her mistakes.[2] A more difficult test is, of course, set by playwrights who are not writing in the Brechtian tradition. What can a Brechtian interpretation achieve on stage, and why should one want to approach such plays with Brecht's method in any case? This chapter will address these questions when considering *Closer*.

The following discussions and analyses will also practice what the book so far has preached: to apply the dialectical method first and only then to propose suitable means of realizing its insights on stage. So, the starting point is interpreting dramatic material and identifying contradictions in the various figures and situations. Only then can suggestions be made as to how a production might highlight social details in a 'theatre of showing'.

Any play is, of course, a complex of issues and problems that need to be addressed, and it would require another book to apply Brecht's method to every episode in the plays under discussion. The following case studies are necessarily selective, but they focus on different aspects in each case in order to trace the movement from theory to practice.

The Resistible Rise of Arturo Ui: Identifying the problems of a potential production

As already noted, Brecht's plays neither implicitly nor explicitly provoke a Brechtian production: directors can take and have taken a great many approaches to staging them that have followed, resisted or ignored Brecht's ideas for a dialectical theatre. The examples of the 'modelbook' for *Mother Courage* in Chapter 7 offer sometimes-unexpected advice on how to avoid the traps of approaching the play in a more conventional manner. Productions of *Arturo Ui* have also produced results on stage that run contrary to Brecht's ideas.

In the play, Brecht re-tells the story of Hitler's rise to power as an allegory, replacing Hitler, other historical personalities and events with figures and situations taken from the underworld of Chicago in the 1930s. Hitler is now Arturo Ui, a down-at-heel gangster who teams up with a group of businessmen, the Trust, to boost sales of cauliflowers, of all things. The focus on this unexpected commodity and the gangster setting in general is a way of distancing the action from real historical incidents, of making the familiar strange.

The play itself opens with a prologue that sets the scene, outlines the main episodes and introduces the main figures. Almost every subsequent scene has a reference point in real events. Scene twelve, for example, involves Ui, his lieutenant Givola, and Ignatius and Betty Dullfeet. Ui and Givola, the figure who represents Hitler's Minister of

Propaganda, Joseph Goebbels, visit the Dullfeets in Chicago's Cicero district. Here Cicero stands for Austria and Dullfeet for Engelbert Dollfuß, the country's Chancellor until he was murdered by the Nazis in 1934. The assassination paved the way for the Nazi annexation of Austria in 1938. The scene shows how Ui exerts pressure on Dullfeet; the next scene depicts his funeral. The play concludes with a brief epilogue, delivered once Ui has taken over Cicero's cauliflower markets, warning that the conditions that brought Ui to power are still 'going strong'.[3]

The drama has been popular over the years, even since its premiere in 1958. The Berliner Ensemble staged the play in 1959, when it ran for over 500 performances in fourteen years, and again in 1995, in a production directed by Heiner Müller that, at the time of writing, is still in the repertoire and has been given over 385 times. *Arturo Ui* has proved to be a popular play in the English-speaking theatre, too. Yet there are, perhaps surprisingly, features of the text that threaten to undermine the principles of Brechtian theatre. Three major issues emerge:

- The focus on the central character.
  Of course, a role like Ui's, at the very heart of the play, has to be played by an exceptional lead, and Al Pacino, Antony Sher and John Turturro are among the great actors who have taken the part in English. Hitler himself was the charismatic centrepiece of the Nazi Party. The problem is, as the last line of the epilogue makes clear, that the play is not only about Ui's rise, but also the conditions under which it took place. As already noted, Brecht's is not a theatre of individual characters, but of figures informed by and in dialogue with their social contexts. A production team thus has to grapple with the tension between the show's protagonist and the situations that inform his actions.
- *Arturo Ui* is an allegory: its fictional scenes have a concrete relationship with real historical people, places and events. Here the problem lies with both the production team and the audience: allegories ask spectators to make connections between

fiction and reality, but that is also where their work can end. An audience may feel that it has 'understood' *Arturo Ui* because it has, say, connected scene twelve to Hitler's designs on Austria, yet the play is not a history lesson as such. The portrayal of Dullfeet, for example, is not terribly accurate: in the scene, he comes across as a cautious man, wary of Ui's violence and his ambitions. In fact, the historical Dollfuß was a militaristic autocrat himself, yet it served Brecht better, in the fictional world of *Arturo Ui*, to portray him in a different, contrastive light to Ui.

The play requires the audience to do more than just decode the allegory. Brecht wanted the scenes to function on their own merits and to reveal more than just historical details. He wrote it in verse and wanted the scenes to remind the audience of an Elizabethan history play. In a note, he asked for it to be played in what he termed 'the grand style' (353) as a way of focusing on the play itself, rather than on its connections with history. That said, it is still a challenge for a production team to foreground the action over the historical allegory.

- Doing justice to the play's *complete* title.
  The play charts Ui's rise from depressed hoodlum to mighty mafia boss. His upward trajectory is the product of powerful support and ruthless violence – most of those who try to oppose him are murdered. So what does the adjective 'resistible' mean in the title? Brecht suggests that history is never inevitable and that certain contexts need to be put in place for Ui to gain so much power and influence. A production of the play is thus charged with the task of not only showing Ui's journey and the conditions that permitted it, but also the opportunities for stopping it.

The following sections consider these problems as ones that can be resolved by observing Brechtian principles: identifying contradiction, defining the *Fabel*, incorporating the social dimension and emphasizing difference and not consistency in performance.

Relativizing the centrality of *Arturo Ui*

One of the ways to understand Ui's role in the drama as a whole is to think through what each scene's *Fabel* might look like. Once this has been done, it should become easier to identify Ui's role in events and the role played by other figures and external conditions. The table below sets out the action of the first seven scenes in relation to Ui only and interprets it as *Fabel*:

Events	*Fabel*
1. Five members of the Cauliflower Trust meet to discuss the poor state of the market. They reject Ui's offer to support their trade by intimidating shopkeepers. Instead, they hatch a plan to coerce support from an influential and well-respected politician, Dogsborough,[4] for a loan from the City.	The Trust are desperate, due to economic hardship. They are comfortable with morally dubious plans to compromise Dogsborough, but draw the line at the morally dubious use of violence.
2. Ui is not mentioned and does not appear in this scene, in which the Trust succeeds in getting Dogsborough involved in their scheme.	Dogsborough acts just as the Trust imagine.
3. Ui and his gang are deflated and short of funds. They discover that the respectable Dogsborough encouraged the City to give the Trust a loan while he was himself a member of the Trust. Ui detects an opportunity.	Business is not good for Ui and his gangsters, either. Ui is little different from the Trust in that he has fallen on hard times and is prepared to act illegally to further his own ends.

Events	*Fabel*
4. Ui threatens Dogsborough at home in his country house. Ui tries to blackmail Dogsborough with his inside information about the dubious loan. Dogsborough holds his nerve and Ui leaves empty handed. The City Council, however, has opened an investigation into the loan. Dogsborough turns to Ui.	Although he is compromised and exposed, Dogsborough is still able to defy Ui's allegations by trading on his own prestige. Ui lacks the power and credibility to expose Dogsborough by himself. The appearance of the City Councillors, however, changes the situation by involving a public authority, and so Dogsborough chooses to defend already illegal action with more of the same.
5. Ui appears for Dogsborough at the hearing in City Hall. A key witness, Sheet, has been found dead. Ui then declares that he has discovered who has embezzled the money: Sheet. Ui has another witness killed as he tries to enter the building. The Trust gets nervous about Ui's methods.	Ui and his gang exploit their opportunity and show how easily murder can be used for political gain.
6. Ui learns how to perform in public by taking a lesson from an actor.	Ui learns how to change his *Gestus* in the interests of furthering his ability to communicate with large masses of people.
7. Ui makes his pitch to the city's greengrocers and offers them his 'protection'. They turn it down, having experienced no intimidation as yet. News arrives that one of the grocer's warehouses is on fire. When the grocers accuse the gangsters of arson, they are threatened and withdraw their claims.	Ui's lesson in scene six is not wholly successful: his oratory does not convince the grocers and a change in their minds is only effected when they understand his ability to turn threat into violent action.

The table shows how Ui may well be the focus of the play, as the title suggests, yet the *Fabel* column shows that his rise is not merely the triumph of Ui's will. Scene seven clearly shows that Ui cannot impose his ideas on the greengrocers without the threat of violence and so the play is also an exploration of the use of force as well as Ui's personality. It is the figures' relationship to violence that defines the rise of the gangsters, and this insight can affect the staging as a whole, as shown in the following examples taken from the first half of the play:

- As gangsters, Ui and his lieutenants have no qualms about using violence to achieve their ends. The Trust, as evidenced in scene one, initially does. A Brechtian production can thus engineer a development of *Haltungen* over the course of the scenes. Violence is not a stable entity and implies contradictions of its own. Violence inspires terror not only in its victims, but, as its use becomes more widespread, in its *potential* victims, too. Those who wield force are not immune to suffering its use, and so the relationships among the gangsters can also be marked by suspicion and anxiety.

- Changes in *Haltung* with respect to violence need not only extend to the members of the Trust. Ui takes a risk in scene five by using murder as a political tool, and the scene itself can be played in contrasting ways. If Ui is assured of his success, then there will be little development in his *Haltung* and this will reinforce him as a consistent confident character and not as a changeable figure dependent on the given situation. On the other hand, the actor in the role of Ui can play with the contradiction of Ui's gambit: on the surface he is in control, yet to his gang and/or the audience, he is a bundle of nerves. Such a dialectical intervention exposes his dependency on having read the situation correctly, and he may well betray surprise rather than assurance when his criminality finally triumphs. After all, at this point in the play, the

City authorities are still the ones with the power (as seen in the way they, and not Ui, force Dogsborough's hand in the previous scene).

- Ui's individuality is further undermined in scene six, where he learns a completely new *Gestus*. The spectators view the construction of a personality before their very eyes, and the new gestures and intonations give the actor playing Ui great opportunities in the subsequent scenes to contrast the mannerisms exhibited before the scene with those deployed after. Ui can become profoundly 'unnatural' as he seeks to make use of the methods he has learned, but slips back into his old ways when his oratory fails or he encounters other problems. Ui is not an inspired individual who can bend situations to his own will, instead, he is an amalgam whose gestural repertoire alters in response to changes in a scene's situation. Ui oscillates between taking the initiative (as in scene seven when he believes his speeches will succeed in intimidating the grocers) and having to react by resorting to violence once again. This tension undermines Ui's autonomy.

The three strategies for dealing with Ui's centrality all stem from the starting point of identifying a workable *Fabel*. The *Fabel* looks beyond character and redefines it as figure, and all figures are in dialogue with their situation. In the above examples, the interpretation of the *Fabel* centres on the different social groups' use of and dependence on violence to secure power.

Avoiding the 'allegory trap'

The simple mapping of *Arturo Ui*'s scenes onto those of German history can give spectators the false impression that they have done the work required of them in making a fairly obvious set of connections between fiction and reality. A production of the play, however, can focus on the ways in which the play does not reflect history accurately because it is doing something else with the historical material. Rather than offering a seamless connection between fiction and reality, Brecht as dramatist takes history as a source and develops it into scenes that may have little to do with events as they really happened, but more with historical processes and their contradictions.

If the play is actually more about the nature of power than an illustration of historical episodes, then a focus on situation and not the characters can help to give the scenes a dynamism born of contradiction. This approach can be understood by investigating a specific scene for the forces that run through it and the way that the figures respond to them. Scene ten, for example, is pervaded by uncertainty: it twists and turns because Ui's power is not properly established and Dogsborough's last will and testament may contain unwelcome surprises for the gangsters. It runs like this:

1. Givola writes his own version of Dogsborough's will, one that recommends high office for Ui and his gang.
2. There is a split between Givola and Giri[5] because the latter seems to have been cosying up to the dying Dogsborough.
3. Giri protests that he is on Ui's side, but doubts now arise about another of Ui's lieutenants, Ernesto Roma.[6] Roma, in turn, criticizes Giri's place in the faked will.
4. Roma is suspicious of the gang's involvement with the Trust and defends the small greengrocers against the larger ones.
5. Giri and Givola declare that Roma's attacks on the Trust's lorries are alienating the Trust.
6. Ui tries to placate the bickering factions by assuring them that the cauliflower operation is working well. When this has little effect he makes a speech about how all his men should have faith in him.

7. The speech does not diffuse the tension and Giri exits with a veiled threat to Roma.
8. Ui reveals his closeness to Roma by confidentially sharing his plans to take over Cicero.
9. It turns out that these are not Ui's plans, but the Trust's, and Roma interprets the plans as a ruse to make use of Ui's muscle before the Trust dumps the gangsters. Ui is convinced by this interpretation and backs Roma against Giri and Givola. Roma leaves, contented.
10. Clark from the Trust arrives with Betty Dullfeet and Giri. They apply pressure and tell Ui that their problem is not with him, but Roma.
11. Ui stands by Roma.

In the next scene, Ui has Roma shot. The two scenes allude to the 'Night of the Long Knives', in which the Nazi Party purged the wing within its ranks that favoured working people (of which Röhm was a prominent representative) and retained in leading positions those people who were happy for the Nazis to ally themselves with big business. There is thus much in the scene that parallels historical events, yet a director could look more closely at the shifts in the relationships on stage and the interactions between situation and response as reflected in the performance of *Gestus* and *Haltung*.

The sections with Ui, Roma, Giri and Givola offer gestic potential for all four actors due to the social tensions that lead to Roma's liquidation in the following scene. It is fair to assume that the gangsters' social background is broadly similar: working-class men who have sought a better life not through honest hard work, but criminality. However, while Roma still betrays a connection to his roots through his support for the smaller greengrocers, Giri and Givola entertain aspirations to a more comfortable middle-class life, as reflected in their interest in the business world of the Trust. Ui, at this point of the play, has more in common with his roots and he thus initially supports Roma over the other two lieutenants. What is at stake here are political points of principle.

However, these points are also triangulated through the co-ordinates of the gang's power dynamics. Ui is indisputably the leader, and the other three seek his favour, yet Giri has been spending time with Dogsborough, and so he may merely be hedging his bets by paying lip service to Ui until the situation becomes clearer. The dynamic is one that might be defined by Ui, but Ui himself is described initially as '*indifferent*' and '*morose*' (180). He is not a tower of strength, but someone who is also affected by the state of uncertainty because old Dogsborough is still alive and thus threatens his ambitions.

The tensions between the different social agendas of the four characters and the gang's pecking order can be played out on stage to demonstrate the interplay of personal ambition and social status. Giri and Givola, for example, can display traits of manners employed by those of lower birth seeking to emulate the middle class, while Roma looks on in incredulity and with disdain. The entrance of Clark and Betty Dullfeet later in the scene offers further social material. Both figures represent the kind of 'classiness' and respectability to which Giri, who accompanies them, aspires, yet Ui can show a contradiction in the signs he offers the audience on meeting them. Gangsters of the 1930s still wore hats and Ui, out of deference for existing class division could doff his hat almost involuntarily as the bourgeois figures arrive. Such a gesture can indicate to the audience the contradiction between Ui's support for Roma and the assassination the gangsters carry out in the following scene. That is, despite what Ui says, he *is* in the thrall of upward social mobility, regardless of how much he might want to see himself as a friend of the workers. The audience thus has to negotiate the tension (or separation) between his words and gestures.

Playing the situation and not the character is a way of keeping the scene lively by highlighting its evolving dynamics: with each shift in the action, relationships change, and the changes have their roots in the social stakes of the play as a whole. The actors are invited to process the scene line by line and understand how their action affects their gestically informed *Haltung*. The social backgrounds of the figures enter the foreground of the scene, and social mechanisms emerge as formative factors.

When viewed like this, the complicated scene no longer merely reflects historical events, but gains a life of its own. The shifts in power and loyalty can tell an audience more about the nature of power and the social forces that shape it rather than about the 'Night of the Long Knives'.

Making Ui's rise 'resistible'

The body count in *Arturo Ui* is high. Anyone who stands in Ui's way usually ends up dead; violence and threats run through the scenes as a means of achieving the gangsters' ends. Resistance, when it does occur, is short-lived: in scene seven, the greengrocers are intimidated into agreeing to Ui's protection racket, and the same tricks are used in scene fifteen, when Ui takes over Cicero. How, then, can a production suggest that Ui's rise *is* 'resistible'?

The play itself offers no concrete suggestions because no-one sustains resistance for long, if at all. Resistance can be shown, however, in what is *not* said and *not* done, rather than what is. Consider scene nine, which is tellingly divided into two parts:

9a: A woman staggers out of a shot-up lorry. She pleads for help, openly blames Ui for the attack and asks why no-one will help her. She collapses against the sound of machine-gun fire nearby.
9b: Dogsborough is writing his will. He owns up to his acceptance of the activities of Ui's gang and confesses his knowledge of all the murders that brought Ui to a position of power. He concludes that his motivation was 'lust for gain, and fear of forfeiting your trust' (176).

The scene juxtaposes resistance and acquiescence. The woman dies for the stand she takes; Dogsborough guiltily acknowledges the role of his silence in Ui's rise. Both speeches have addressees who are not named in the script:

- The speeches can be delivered to on-stage audiences. In 9a, the actors can *show* the various reasons for not getting involved: they can pretend not to hear, gesture that they cannot do anything as mere individuals, or that they simply do not want to get involved, for example. The spectators can observe not only the desperate appeal, but its response on stage. By keeping these non-speaking players on stage for 9b, the production can also show that the people who let the woman down are the same people who gave Dogsborough their trust without asking any questions.
- The addressees could be represented by the audience, thus making the spectators complicit in the refusal to help the woman *and* in maintaining the stature of the old man. If this option is taken, the two parts can be performed in ways that play with the audience differently. The woman can appeal directly to the auditorium and virtually demand a response. Dogsborough, however, only mentions his addressee in his last line. Up until then, he conducts a conversation with himself, moving between the self ('I') and a self-stylization ('honest Dogsborough' – 176). The audience observes this from the outside and can note the irony of 'honest' because it is repeated three times. Dogsborough can lacerate himself, and the audience can sit comfortably until it is implicated in the final line: the 'fear of forfeiting *your* trust' (my emphasis). Directing that line out into the auditorium can have the effect of pointing a finger and showing that Dogsborough was never acting alone, but in a social context: his power was based on (the audience's) trust.

Other instances of resistance can take the form of the 'not – but'. In scene six (the hearing), one of the Trust's members reacts to the murder of the witness like this:

> BUTCHER, *to Ui*: More monkey business: Ui, it's all over
>   Between us if…
> UI: Yes? (155)

Butcher does *not* split with Ui, *but* remains in league with him. This can be shown in performance, as can other opportunities figures do not grasp to derail Ui. Scene thirteen is Dullfeet's funeral and it echoes I ii of *Richard III* when Richard woos Lady Anne, having killed her husband. The scene is alive with missed chances to act. The pastor delivering the oration off-stage does not mention how Dullfeet died, but passes over it; the Trust does not break with Ui over the murder, even though it disagrees with such methods, but continues to back him. Betty Dullfeet, however, does stand up to Ui and unpicks his arguments and rhetoric, thus appearing to offer a strategy to resist him. However, by scene fifteen, Betty has changed sides and speaks briefly in favour of Ui before the vote in Cicero, which he wins by intimidation. In this scene, Betty can also show that she does not refuse the hand of the Cauliflower Trust, but accepts it and that she does not decry Ui in public, but supports him.

Each 'not – but' points to an alternative form of action; it also allows the audience to consider why one option was chosen over the other. While these 'not – buts' exist in Brecht's script, they nonetheless need to be identified in rehearsal and clearly shown in performance. It would be simple to pass over all these examples and just let them 'happen'. Brechtian stagecraft, however, allows the moments to gain significance by performing the decision *not* to do something and to invite the audience to speculate on what might have been, had the figure acted differently.

The strategies suggested for a potential staging of *Arturo Ui* are interconnected: in order to contextualize Ui, to focus on the action of a scene rather than on its allegorical meaning, and to emphasize the possibility of change, a creative team can enact the Brechtian principles that have run through this book. These approaches to staging have been given different emphases in this chapter so far, and they show how flexibly they can be used to achieve a dialectical production of the play.

Closer: Why Brecht?

Closer by Patrick Marber was one of the big hits of 1997: it won major awards in the UK and the USA, including the Olivier for Best New Play, and was subsequently turned into a major feature film in 2004. The play follows the erotic entanglements of four characters: Dan, Alice, Larry and Anna. Its twelve scenes chart their complicated, intertwined love lives. Dan, for example, first meets Alice by chance while he is still with the never-seen Ruth; gets together with Alice; then meets Anna; cheats on Alice before breaking up with her to be with Anna; stays with Anna; leaves Anna on discovering she has had slept with Larry; goes back to Alice, who leaves Dan when he discovers she has slept with Larry; and is single again when Alice dies in a car accident. Similarly twisting accounts could be given for the other characters, too. It is only at the end of the play that we discover that Alice's real name is Jane; she has been playing a role all along.

To all appearances, *Closer* is a character-driven drama about the fickle nature of human desire. The play explores the characters' personal lives and their ways of dealing with physical attraction. In each scene, we learn more about the various emotional interactions and the ways that feeling tends to trump thinking in the characters' private lives. As the play's title suggests, *Closer* explores issues of human intimacy and the difficulties involved in achieving it. So, what would be the point of deploying Brecht's method and stagecraft with respect to a play like this?

In the section of Chapter 1, titled 'Making Theatre Politically', I noted that applying the dialectical method to characters and their actions can open up a politics that may be hidden or ignored by interpretations that see human beings as essentially unchanging and stuck in behaviours they are condemned to repeat *ad infinitum*. Brecht's theatre proposes that behaviour *is* linked to society, and so a production that employs his approaches can construct relationships between the two and suggest that the behaviour displayed could be different under different social conditions. That is, a Brechtian staging is concerned with revealing impermanence in the material offered by a playwright, suggesting that change is possible by connecting human action with the values and behaviours that exist beyond them. A Brechtian production of another dramatist's play is about subjecting material to analysis to see whether it yields insights into the interplay of individual and society.

The social contexts of 1990s Britain

A conventional production of *Closer* might be interested in the psychological lives of the characters and could ask ethical questions about the loves, lies and betrayals in the plot. The audience would see people on stage who reminded them of themselves – human beings with weaknesses, desires and aspirations. A Brechtian approach to staging *Closer*, on the other hand, wants to detect in rehearsal and signal in performance differences between what happens in the play and the experience of the audience, exposing what spectators might think they understand as something strange and worthy of investigation. The aim is to engineer *Verfremdung* and thus to confront the audience with dialectically posed problems that they are left to ponder. In addition, a dialectical portrayal of the fictional world also invites spectators to consider just how dialectical their own real world might be and how their feelings and actions may find themselves in dialogue with their social context and not divorced from it.

The figures on stage re-echo larger issues concerning their background, class and, as we will see in the case of *Closer*, the role of money: the production can propose a dynamic relationship between individual and society. In order to approach this task, the production team would need to research political and social issues that could inform a dialectical staging. In the case of *Closer*, these may include the following:

- The 1990s was a decade that inherited profound social changes brought about in the 1980s when Margaret Thatcher was prime minister. Her emphasis on the individual and the accumulation of personal wealth over social and communal concerns marks an important shift in values that is felt in *Closer*.
- Class difference tended to blur: the decline of the manufacturing base and the rise of service industries meant that traditional working-class occupations declined and the social bonds forged by them dissipated. Council tenants could also buy their homes, conferring upon them the property-owning privileges once reserved for the middle and upper classes.
- Political difference also tended to blur. The collapse of communism in Eastern Europe in the early 1990s made it more difficult for left-wing parties in the West to suggest concrete alternatives to an increasingly dominant globalized capitalism. Tony Blair's 'New Labour', which swept to victory in 1997, was considerably less radical than former incarnations of the party, and its approach to financial regulation (or the lack of it) tacitly licensed banks and other financial institutions to take the risks that led to the financial crises of 2007–2008.

This information can help inform basic elements concerning a Brechtian understanding of *Closer*:

- The characters in *Closer* are all a part of a broadly defined middle class in which a pride in or an obligation to one's roots defers to the middle-class ideals of individualism, self-serving autonomy and living for the moment. A production would thus look to revealing how *similar* the characters were despite their attempts to differentiate themselves as individuals. The use of shared gestures and modes of delivery can help establish such links and thus draw attention to the contradiction between individual and community.

- As will be shown below, the characters *do* have a history despite their attempts to efface it. Details of their backgrounds can thus be included in their performance to suggest that the past is not dead and actually plays a role in the present.

- The flattening of class distinctions repositions the characters not only as members of the middle class, but also as consumers. As Steven Miles notes, 'the study of consumerism is a broader and more reflexive enterprise than a concern for the relatively straightforward process of simply purchasing and consuming a good or service'.[7] Robert Bocock writes that consumerism 'has served to legitimate capitalism in the eyes of millions of ordinary people'.[8]

  In other times, ideology differentiated opposing political systems. Yet even if the clash of political systems has diminished, ideology persists as a glue that, perhaps less visibly, bonds individuals to the dominant conditions in society. The characters may thus betray little in the way of political affiliation, but are nonetheless committed consumers. One task of a dialectical production is thus to draw out the ideology of consumerism that runs through the play, but that is never overtly acknowledged.

In the following sections, I will consider ways in which ideology can be exposed and links forged between the characters' actions and broader social values.

Investigating the 'Micro-*Fabel*'

A conventional starting point for a Brechtian production would be the establishment of the play's *Fabel* in order to understand how the scenes progress and tell a larger story. Yet this approach is made difficult by a play like *Closer* because its episodes are variations on the themes of love and loss; there is no sense of development as such. In addition, in a play that revolves around a cast of four capricious lovers, there is little overt reference to their outward dealings with society. Most of the scenes are set in the private sphere, although social material can be excavated from the dialogues and used to add extra dimensions to the characters and their interactions with each other. Larry, for example, reveals in scene six that he is originally of working-class stock, which comes as a surprise to Anna (and the audience). We know him as a successful, apparently middle-class doctor, and so his whole performance is based on a social contradiction that seeks to hide the past and project a socially prestigious present. Anna, on the other hand, comes from a more privileged background: in scene five, Larry asks her whether her parents considered him to be 'beneath her'.[9]

Scene five is set in a gallery and scene seven in a lap-dancing club, and these public locations offer vistas into the world beyond the characters more clearly. The latter has a particular focus on the role of money in the late 1990s. Thus, rather than constructing an overarching *Fabel*, as one can for *Ui*, analysis starts at the level of the most revealing scenes themselves. An investigation of scene seven's action reveals interesting social dynamics that extend beyond the individual characters and can influence the performance of other scenes, too. A first task, then, is to establish what is happening and how it might be interpreted as a 'micro-*Fabel*'. As discussed in Chapter 4, a *Fabel* is a possible interpretation of the dramatic material, and here my interpretation focuses on issues concerning money and control:

An analysis of this kind confers a number of Brechtian 'virtues' on the performance of the scene:

Events	Fabel
Alice dances for Larry in a private room of a lap-dancing club.	The well-heeled can pay for privacy because it promises a more personal experience.
Larry asks whether he has to pay to talk to her. Alice replies he does not, but that she does accept tips.	The financial contract is established: it is not that each service has a tariff, but that the customer is expected to pay continuously for each service.
Larry and Alice talk. Larry asks whether he is hearing the truth from her. She replies that she is telling him the truth because that is what he wants to hear.	Even conversation is subject to the terms of the contract: everything spoken will be in the interests of generating more revenue.
Alice tells Larry that she is allowed to flirt with him in order to generate more money.	Alice is explicit about the contract; it does not need to be hidden.
She adds that customers are not allowed to touch the dancers. If they do, they will be removed by security, who are monitoring the dancing behind a two-way mirror.	The contract is not merely between the dancer and the customer, but between the business and the customer, and the business will ultimately ensure that the agreement is honoured, with violence if necessary.
Larry says he would like to touch her outside the club, to which she replies that she is not a prostitute. Larry retorts that he would not be paying.	Larry introduces a different kind of relationship into the conversation, one that Alice initially assumes to be an extension of the one in the club.

Events	Fabel
Larry and Alice engage in a conversation that is both playful and serious.	Larry attempts to subvert the financial contract by asking questions that try to get behind Alice's 'act'; Alice deflects them.
During the conversation, Alice tells Larry her real name, Jane, but he does not believe her as he 'knows' her as Alice. Larry pays her £500 for the truth, which Alice gives him by calling herself 'Jane', but Larry, understandably, does not believe her.	Larry believes that a large sum of money can buy the truth, yet he finds himself in a situation where the presence of money makes it all but impossible to determine the truth.
Larry reminds her that they met the previous year and demands a real conversation as he confesses his love for her.	Larry again tries to prise himself out of the financial contract into which he has entered by evoking 'the real'.
Larry offers to pay her to come home with him. He then asks whether she could see him as anything other than a cash machine.	He finds himself a prisoner of the monetized system that he is trying to circumvent.
Having spent all his money asking Alice for her real name, Larry asks her to lend him his cab fare home. Alice says that the dancers do not give but take the money in the club.	Alice enforces the rules of the club, as she has already been doing by responding playfully to his serious questions.
Larry discusses how the traffic in the strip club is not all one way: the strippers do not just take, but give something of themselves, too.	Larry, unable to wield any financial power, asserts himself intellectually.
Larry asks Alice to strip for him because it is all he can ask of her there.	All Larry has left is the service he has paid for.

- The 'micro-*Fabel*' is discontinuous and thus invites actors to view their figures not as organic wholes, but as collections of contradictory qualities. The actors are thus involved in a process in which they do not seek to preserve fixed 'characteristics', but discover new ones.
- Figures become sites of difference and not consistency, provoking the audience to account for the changes as the scene progresses.
- The emphasis on the situation, and not its protagonists, ascribes centrality to the conditions under which they act rather than to their own behaviour. The figures decide on a course of action, but only within the limited field of options offered by the situation itself.

The interpretation of the events in scene seven allows a director and the actors to establish the possible dialectics of the scene. These revolve around the tension between money and feelings. We learn that Larry is a frequent customer at the club and, having discovered that Alice dances there, wants to use the one-to-one contact afforded by the private room to initiate a relationship. He thus seeks to use money (purchasing time in the private room) to achieve intimacy (getting truth from Alice and offering her his feelings), yet he fails to understand that the means corrupt the end. So, an undialectical, character-based scene that could paint Larry as a poor, emotional dupe ignores the fact that Larry, initially at least, considers himself to have the upper hand because he is the one with the money. Indeed, he continues to resort to money as a solution throughout the scene, but finally concedes that he can only abide by money's rules. The scene can thus be played as a series of negotiations in which Larry rationally tries to realize his goals, but discovers that money has a logic of its own. In this reading, the scene depicts a painful initiation into the ways of the modern world, rather than one man's feelings and his attempts to communicate them.

Extending the reach

How then, might these insights into the dialectic of money and feelings influence other scenes? In a general sense, they may be used to inform the interactions between all the characters. Each character has a different relationship to money, and this difference can generate productive tensions between them. Larry, as a well-paid professional who had to apply himself to lengthy training in order to achieve personal wealth, has a different relationship to money than Anna, who was born into wealth. Alice and Dan present more material with which to work: Alice, for example, travels and travels light – she earns money only when she needs it, and her job as a stripper allows her to work whenever she pleases. She has no problems with the stigma of sex work: she tells Dan what she does in the first scene and is not fazed by Larry's appearance in the lap-dancing club. She thus represents a different attitude to money, as well, and her responses to it can also be brought out rather than passed over in performance. So, for Larry, money allows him to play the role of middle-class doctor and to purchase anything he requires to satisfy his desires; Anna may take money for granted; and Alice has a more functional relationship to it. Such different *Haltungen* can be performed in many situations, in, for example, the figures' relationships to the objects around them. Larry enters the gallery scene in a cashmere sweater, which would allow him to show off his expensive clothing in public. Alice, however, mistakes him for a waiter, which may bring out a gestic response from Larry. This could show how his faith in money's ability to generate prestige or kudos is often disappointed. Gifts play a role in the play, too, and their status can elicit a range of *Haltungen* from the figures that tell an audience about their differing social attitudes.

Money, as the scene in the lap-dancing club shows, is not independent of feelings: in a society where seemingly everything is buyable, relationships themselves can gain the characteristics of commodities, and this is a way that the dynamics identified in the lap-dancing club can be used to inform scenes that precede and succeed it. The changes of partner over the course of the twelve scenes reflect the impetuous desire for a new product, the equally swift onset of disenchantment, the upgrade to a better version or nostalgia for an earlier one.

The central theme of *Closer*, of how the characters can get 'closer' to each other, suggests that there are obstacles to the goal of intimacy. In a politicized reading, personal relationships themselves come under pressure from factors that exist outside of them. It is no coincidence that the altruism of the memorials in Postman's Park (referred to in scene one) is implicitly contrasted with the behaviour of the characters in 1997. A Brechtian production can propose that the four figures are not just fickle lovers, but fickle consumers, never fully satisfied with the product at hand and always seeking something more that eludes them. This, after all, is an essential element in the logic of consumerism: the acts of purchase and consumption should never dampen the desire for bigger, better or more. Capitalism would not survive if individuals were satisfied with what they consume; it thrives on purchase after purchase after purchase. By exposing the action on stage as dialectical, rather than simply portraying it as natural, a production can suggest that the serial dalliances are connected to wider issues in society and are not merely the result of an individual's whims.

But how can such analogies be constructed?

- In several scenes, liaisons are initiated, sustained or terminated with reference to the 'truth' of a character's declared feelings. Honesty becomes a surrogate currency. It is difficult to establish whether a figure is or is not being honest at these moments, and so the actors are not required to show whether they are telling the truth or lying about their feelings as such. Instead, the employment of honesty can be signalled, perhaps with a gesture, perhaps with a tone, that draws attention to its occurrence. In this way, the audience can note that 'honesty' is being used again and again, and can reach its own conclusions as to why.

- There is also a set of dialogues in the various scenes concerning satisfaction – or more precisely the frequency of orgasms – and this too becomes a bargaining position, a marker of 'relationship quality'. Here, the link between human beings and consumable objects is clearer, and actors can emphasize such sections to bring out the connection.

- The life cycles of the relationships repeat themselves throughout the play as the audience observes processes of birth, maturation and death. The repeated stages allow the actors to point to both similarities and differences in order to expose their different strategies in playing the same game.

In scenes one and two, for example, Dan tries to cheat on a current girlfriend with a new woman. In scene one he asks Alice out on a date, having just told her that he is in a relationship with the never-seen Ruth. In scene two, Dan is now with Alice, but he propositions Anna. If Dan is played as a consistent character, then he is something of a jack-the-lad: impulsive and self-centred. Yet if Dan is read as a Brechtian figure, an audience can examine how he has had to vary his behaviour to achieve the same end. Alice and Anna differ in terms of age and background: Alice is younger and has revealed that she has been a stripper; Anna is older and is of a socially higher class than Dan. Dan can thus show that although he is engaging in the same action, it is with different women, and so he needs to negotiate the social distinctions in different ways. Does Alice represent an 'easy catch' to Dan because she was a stripper? Does Anna represent a 'challenge' because she is socially superior? Each question locates Dan as a consumer, tired of the current girlfriend in search of something new and exciting.

If the private scenes are re-envisioned as a series of negotiations, actors can study the strategies adopted or the defences employed. Here, the characters are never 'innocent', which does not mean that they are always *consciously* game-playing. 'Innocence' is the quality of simply 'being oneself'. A naturalistic production considers actions normal or inevitable, a part of modern life, without questioning why modern life is lived in such a way. Yet if a dialectical production 'exhibits' the behaviour of its figures by drawing attention to their similarities and differences, it already considers the action 'strange' and worthy of inquiry.

A Brechtian production wants to exhibit the characters as figures, as people who are more than just psychological units; they are dialectical members of a contradictory society. Thus, no gesture is 'private': it points to something else, something that may indicate the role of social background or the presence of other factors that may influence behaviour. By turning gestures outward, the stage engages in the act of showing, of de-naturalizing actions and consciously offering them to the audience for their evaluation.

By the end of Marber's play, the characters on stage *appear* not to have altered, a sentiment made by Larry in the final scene: 'everyone learns, nobody changes'.[10] But the audience does not have to agree with this opinion, especially as it is delivered by the play's most jaded figure. The audience has the opportunity to stand back and observe the way the figures treat each other. If bargaining positions, strategies and defences are highlighted by the act of showing, and if these facets form a visual lexicon of different yet related gestures involved in this particular version of the mating game, then spectators can step back and start to make connections between the values of the figures and the values of the world beyond them.

A Brechtian production is thus not as interested in the joys and sufferings of the figures in themselves, than in the dynamics between them and where these behaviours might come from. Such a staging constructs a connection between individual and society, and proposes that the short-term, disposable nature of the relationships echoes the world of short-term, disposable goods. A contradiction emerges between a desire for intimacy and a dissatisfaction with permanence. There is also no reason why consumer culture cannot impinge upon set design, either, so that even the private realm of the home is pervaded by goods or televisions selling ever more products, or that the figures' historicized costumes change as often as their partners. The aim is to connect desire to the market and to propose that a different kind of world may produce a different kind of relationship.

The suggestions for Brechtian productions of *Arturo Ui* and *Closer* connect dialectical analysis with approaches to staging. These can be summarized as follows:

- Identifying a play's and/or a scene's *Fabel* and exploring how the figures function within it.
- Identifying a figure's contradictions and abandoning a consistent conception of 'character'.
- Bringing out these contradictions in both what is and is not performed (the 'not – but').
- Playing the situation and not the character.

The strategies present ways of thinking about practical stagecraft and can be used as starting points for inductive rehearsal (see Chapter 6). The method treats dramatic material in a way that views figures as changeable and situations as embodiments of contradictory social norms. By establishing these two basic principles, productions can show an audience the relationships between the two. They can invite spectators to look beyond 'character' and think more carefully about the active role society plays in shaping a figure's opinions and behaviour.

Epilogue

Working with Brecht

Brecht gives us a lot to think about. His critique of traditional theatre practice invites us to look behind the façade of representation and identify the factors that influence or have influenced the way that figures behave. In his theatre, dialogue and action are no longer 'innocent' – they do not simply 'happen' – because everything on stage is a part of a larger social and historical network of forces. Human desires encounter the norms of society and are exploited, accepted, tolerated, ignored or prohibited. Brecht also provides the theatre with the practical means to embody his theoretical speculations about the relationship between individual and society in the theatre. Consequently, Brecht has become a central figure in the theatre and performance studies.

The dialectical method and Brecht's innovative theatre practice can be combined and directed towards many classic and less well-known plays, and offer new insights and perspectives on cherished works from the repertoire. Brecht invites actors to break with ideas of characters as 'islands' of autonomous motivations and unchangeable characteristics, and proposes the 'figure' as a way of reconnecting characters with each other, their social contexts and the values they give rise to. He actively embraces the theatre not as a place in which reality is seamlessly reproduced, but where reality can be unpicked and displayed as a network of contradictory components. The theatre's inherent artifice is not passed over, but explicitly embraced in order to highlight artifice in the lives of the figures. Brecht thus heightens realistic signs on stage to expose that which often goes unspoken.

The discrepancy between what is seen on stage and what informs it has also proved productive for work that is not text based. Feminist theatre theorists and practitioners, for example, have looked to Brecht for ways of confronting and combating sexism in performance by revealing patriarchal structures and dramatizing the dialectic of oppression and liberation.[1] The performance of ethnicity and sexuality has also invoked the Brechtian tradition as a means of de-naturalizing racist and homophobic representation.[2] Brecht still offers a way of coupling theoretical with practical approaches so as to question ideological positions. By making representation contradictory and problematic, Brechtian performance can pose questions that strike at the heart of how an audience views and responds to material that runs through much mainstream film, television and, yes, theatre culture.

However, despite his achievements and their continued efficacy in contemporary theatre and performance, Brecht can perhaps also be easily dismissed today: he stood for a system and a politics that appears to have been discredited and rejected by history. Brecht bore the banner for a Marxist theatre founded on a dialectical approach to reality. Yet the German Democratic Republic, in which Brecht was artistic director of the Berliner Ensemble, collapsed in the wake of the fall of the Berlin Wall, and the socialist East, with the Soviet Union at its centre, is no more either. Even nominally communist China has embraced the free market in its own way. We now live in what has been termed a 'post-ideological society' in which the erasure of an obvious political alternative to capitalism has brought about the more resigned attitude that the world is indeed unchangeable because one system has thoroughly and globally triumphed over its only rival.

In such a political landscape, Brecht's might be written off as a theatre of its time: the hopes of the past must accept the sober realities of the present. Alternatively, in the light of recent history, Brecht can be defended all the more vigorously. In a world that *appears* to offer no alternatives to capitalism, Brecht invites theatre-makers to search for contradictions, to investigate what goes unmentioned and to draw attention to untold stories. Brecht allows us to challenge the view that 'there is no alternative' to contemporary capitalism by teasing out the *processes* it uses to establish such opinions.[3] He can help unpick what appears to be solid, reveal its component parts, and suggest that things could be different.

The 'not – but' is a useful device for opening up alternatives, but is merely one way of dialectically interrogating the present. The Brechtian focus on difference still offers theatre-makers a powerful means for pointing out and to social, political and ideological division, rather than representing all characters merely as variations of generic consumers under an all-encompassing capitalism. And the role money plays in the construction of social bonds and values also suggests itself as a productive object of inquiry in a contemporary Brechtian theatre.

The most powerful weapon Brecht offers to the theatre is the dialectic and, by extension, his dialectical method. It challenges audiences not to accept what they are shown, but to doubt and question. *Verfremdung* is central to this end because it presents the familiar in such a way that it is rendered strange and worthy of curiosity. Historicization questions whether values and behaviours are universal, and invites audiences to compare the way things were with the way things are in order to tease out differences and to account for them. The Brechtian arsenal is extensive and useful, yet as times have changed, practitioners have both recognized the significance of his work and made use of it as a starting point for their own forms of socially engaged theatre, too.

Working with Brecht beyond Brecht

The shift from antagonism between two competing economic systems to the new dominance of capitalism has also been accompanied by a shift in the way we think about what we can actually know about the world. The postmodern period, which emerged in the West in the 1970s, is notable for its introduction of an all-encompassing relativism into many areas of everyday life. Relativism acknowledges difference, but tends not to ascribe absolute values to such differences. So, whereas phenomena such as sexism or racism would traditionally characterize men or white people as innately 'superior' to women or other races, respectively, in a postmodernist environment, such binary oppositions are merely markers of difference, with neither side necessarily 'better' or 'worse' than the other. This change in attitudes is connected to the postmodern era's problems with establishing absolute values in a world that has become increasingly unknowable. Brecht's ideas on theatrical representation stem from a period in which knowledge appeared to be more stable and this is reflected in some of his theoretical claims.

In an essay of 1938, Brecht talks of the different forms at an artist's disposal that can 'put reality in the hands of people in such a way that it can be mastered'.[4] Here Brecht is connecting an accurate depiction of reality with the means of subjecting it to effective control. Elsewhere, he considers *Verfremdung*, making the familiar strange, another way of mastering reality,[5] because it reveals what is really happening at any given moment in a drama. He is saying that reality is complicated and that one requires special ways of approaching it if one is going to be able to change it. Dialectical analysis gets behind the surface of reality and suggests causal relations that can account for what appears as reality. Brecht introduces a more vigilant approach to understanding reality: not to take it at face value, but to ask questions about the conditions under which people behave as they do.

So far, so good. But there is also a problem of knowledge here, of what one can know about reality: how does one get into a privileged position and identify precisely what is causing the complex phenomena of every day life while also being a part of that life? The practice of inductive rehearsal with an ensemble (see Chapter 6) was one way of using collaborative methods to get at the nature of reality by bringing several differing perspectives to the problem. Objectivity – the ability to stand outside something and offer an accurate account of it – is a utopian aim because human beings (especially given the dialectical understanding of human identity) are always implicated in the systems they seek to represent. Does a man see the world in the same way as a woman, a poor person in the same way as a rich person, an Italian in the same way as a Japanese? Different experiences affect our view of the world, something that denies any individual a 'master perspective' and thus absolute knowledge.

The subjective element suggests that while we can try to approach reality with a view to understanding it, the limitations of our own minds and senses prevent a universal analysis or understanding. Brecht acknowledges that reality is something with which we have to engage in order to understand it – the *Fabel*, after all, is only an *interpretation* of events, an *attempt* to get behind the surfaces we encounter every day. Interpretation means deploying ideas about reality, and these ideas cannot be objective; they will be subject to our place in history and society. This is not to say that representation should be given up as a lost cause; more that its strategies might not be able to deliver Brecht's 'mastery'.

Dialectical performance is able to ask questions, make accepted behaviours questionable and open them up to further scrutiny, and so Brecht can remain a potent theatrical force even if we forsake his claim to 'mastery'. Brecht's is a sceptical method that asks us to question the things we think we know and open them up for further interrogation. Instability and contradiction still form the basis of Brechtian work, but it may be the case that certain aspects of his stagecraft need to be rethought.

The biggest problem for a contemporary reception of Brecht's ideas is the establishment of the *Fabel*, the interpreted version of reality that informs the representation of the drama. It is not so much that this task is futile – the examples from Chapters 6 and 8 show that the exercise is still tenable and can produce insights into the action. It is more that the *Fabel*, as an interpretation, suffers from the limited perspective of any director's or ensemble's subjectivity. In 'post-Brechtian' theatre, where Brecht's ideas are rethought and re-evaluated, the *Fabel* gives way to more suggestive forms of performance. 'Suggestive' here contrasts with 'definitive'. Such an approach sets out contradictions without interpreting them further; larger questions regarding the meaning of the contradictory material are passed on for the audience to process. Without the master narrative of a *Fabel*, the questions can beg responses from the audience because there is little or no interpretive help offered from the stage.

One might, for example, imagine two different productions of *Arturo Ui* as a way of grasping the distinction between the definitive and the suggestive. In Chapter 8, the suggestions for analysis and staging the play read Ui and his gangsters negatively. Ui is the focus of criticism and the production aims to unmask the dynamics and the strategies of fascism in order to prevent a repeat in the present. However, a critical production of that kind necessarily places fascism at a remove: a rational, reasonable audience watches the unfolding *Fabel* and gains insights into the processes through which fascism can gain a foothold and build an empire. This is a viable way of understanding the play, but it does have its blind spots.

What such a production does not do is account for *why* so many people were drawn to fascism over time – in *Ui* the small people are almost exclusively threatened with violence to give their support to Ui. However, it is clear that the Nazis used more than just force – they also appealed to large swathes of the populace and convinced them how right Nazism was for them, even before intimidation became endemic. An alternative *Ui* may, then, not be that interested in simply marking Ui negatively and signs of resistance positively. Instead, it may position

Ui as an attractive figure. This does not mean that such a production acts as a recruiter for the far right. Rather, the Brechtian proclivity for contradiction and *Verfremdung* can be re-functioned, so that the darker aspects of Ui might throw a more appealing Ui into relief. This is no longer a production that makes use of rational distance, but one that exploits emotional experience as a way of manufacturing contradiction. Spectators can thus feel proximity *and* repulsion towards Ui as the two qualities oscillate throughout the production. However, in order for such an approach to work, Ui has to be able to connect with the audience, not stand at a distance for cool contemplation. As a result, Ui is no longer purely the bogeyman, but instead a more relativized figure. His popular appeal is not dismissed, but actively encouraged in performance, but only for it to find its points of contradiction, when the audience is snapped back into a more critical position.

A dialectical theatre can still exist without its *Fabel*, despite the key position Brecht ascribed to it. Dialectics is about articulating contradiction, yet in an intellectual landscape hostile to objectivity, theatre-makers may find themselves presented with the task of identifying rather than accounting for contradictions. In doing this, they do not seek to resolve contradictions, but to keep them 'open' for the audience to decide how to deal with them.

By definition, contradictions are evidence of difference. Brecht's idea of *Haltung* thus remains a useful way of showing contrastive behaviours, and *Gestus* still constructs a connection between individual and society. The precision that is associated with Brecht's theatre also remains useful because it draws attention to the work on stage as deliberate and thus worthy of an audience's interest – the material being presented may be suggestive, but it is not fanciful. The lack of interpretive aid for the audience can shift a theatre-maker's focus from representation to presentation.

Contemporary theatre has some notable directors and groups who push forward the Brechtian tradition in working with certain Brechtian ideas and putting them through the prism of postmodernism. The American director Robert Wilson, for example, may be considered a post-Brechtian director. That is, even though his work was never consciously informed by Brecht's theories,[6] his engagement with Brecht's plays since 1998 (and other playwrights' before that) has shown how appropriate his methods can be for a dialectical theatre:

- Wilson invokes a radical 'separation of the elements' in that voice, body, set and lighting all pull in different directions as autonomous sign-systems. Consequently, the *spectator* has to negotiate their interplay in order to approach his productions' meanings. The contradictions that Wilson identifies threaten to overwhelm the stage because they refuse to explain themselves and throw down a gauntlet to the audience.
- Wilson uses repetition and slowness to insist on the importance of the moments he selects for special attention. The specificity of the performance draws attention to each detail.
- Wilson radicalizes a term Brecht used to describe his play *Fear and Misery of the Third Reich*, a montage of different scenes taken from everyday life under the Nazis. Brecht called his play a 'table of gestures'.[7] That is, beneath the realistic surface of the scenes lay a connected repertoire of gestures, both offensive and defensive, brought about by the oppression of the Nazi regime. Wilson's theatre is full of stylized gestures that develop a physicalized language of their own, and so meaning emerges by recognizing patterns and observing difference. The abstract nature of the movements tears them away from concrete reference points in everyday life and focuses attention on their communication with themselves and each other. Such an approach gives the audience an interpretive freedom: they are charged with the task of translating the gestures into their understanding of the piece as a whole.

Wilson's theatre shows how certain post-Brechtian practices push Brecht's understanding of stylization (see Chapter 4) far beyond his own understanding of it. Brecht, as we have seen, tends to 'heighten' the realistic sign in his theatre: he offers recognizable signs of human behaviour, but makes them stand out. Wilson has no difficulty in deploying radical stylization and then inviting the audience to relate them back to reality.

The Swiss director Christoph Marthaler also keeps performance material uninterpreted despite maintaining its specificity:

- Marthaler's productions often concern social matters yet they rarely comment on these matters, but present material to the audience. One show, for example, dealt, among other things, with the demise of the national airline Swissair in 2002. Several scenes featured business people in various situations and ended with one sitting or being sat in a chair that crashed through a Styrofoam wall. Each executive knew that the chair meant unemployment, yet there was never any sense of resistance as the colleagues performed a litany of clichés regarding how sorry they were. Each time the 'ejection' took place, there was a slight difference in the process that led to it, but it was never clear why it had happened or why the executives behaved as they did. However, the director was clear in presenting an action that was recognizable.
- Elsewhere, Marthaler, himself an accomplished musician, makes use of songs as suggestive material for his work. In the above scenes, for example, the departure of each executive was accompanied by a beautifully sung German folk song, 'If I were a Little Bird'. The song is one of longing, that if the singer were a bird, he or she would fly to his or her beloved. On first hearing the song, one could understand it as an ironic lament for the recently ejected colleague, suggesting that the last thing the colleagues would do would be to follow the hapless executive.

Yet, as the song was repeated after each of the other departures, one might start to wonder just why the song was being sung. Was it a ritual, a compulsion? Was it a joke whose staleness its singers could not appreciate? Was it a moment of harmonious beauty in the face of corporate brutality done to one of their number? The melody, the lyrics and the delivery failed to guarantee any of these interpretations.

Theatre-makers of the past few decades have found ways to offer contradiction to an audience without interpreting it on stage and instead passing that work over to the audience.

Another implication of the emphasis on presentation over representation is that the audience is involved in a more sensuous experience of dialectical theatre. Because interpretation takes place in the auditorium rather than on the stage, the audience is not so busy decoding information; instead it *experiences* it. This shift acknowledges that the rational mind is not the only factor involved in making decisions. Desires can dissuade us from doing the 'sensible' thing and lead us into making different decisions. A Brechtian theatre that consciously engages both the mind and the feelings is concerned with enabling experiences, not for their own sake, but in order to examine those feelings, too. Contradiction and *Verfremdung* thus still play an important role in engineering moments of distance in which spectators can reflect and evaluate what they have previously experienced.

The movement away from the centrality of the *Fabel* marks an important shift in the reception of Brecht's theatre practice in some quarters today. Theatre-makers do not presume to 'have all the answers' while nonetheless retaining central elements of Brecht's dialectical method. In effect, they have reformulated Brecht's theatre for the more uncertain conditions of contemporary life.

Brecht's theories and practice represent a seismic shift in thinking about theatre and what it can achieve. His dramatization of the dialectic, the focus on difference, the social responsibility of art, and the new vocabulary he developed and deployed all offer fertile ground for practitioners today. An 'orthodox' Brechtian production can achieve a great deal, especially in the theatres of the English-speaking countries, where it has the power to challenge the 'standard fare' of naturalist or stylistically realist productions that still dominate the stage. Its ability to open up apparently closed ideas and bring out unspoken contradictions for the audience demonstrates the enduring attractiveness of Brecht's theatre. Brecht is not only of historical interest, but can throw a productive spanner into the works of conventional dramatic theatre. His concepts of *Fabel*, *Gestus* and *Haltung* may inspire many a director to rethink the Greeks, Shakespeare or the Naturalists, among others. And the usefulness of his approach and the questions he asks is more than apparent in the way that it has been further developed by a generation of more experimental theatre-makers.

Notes

Introduction

1   Alice Jones, 'Edinburgh 2013: The Events – David Greig's Play Drawn on Anders Breivik's Norway Killings', *The Independent*, 6 August 2013.

2   Tim Auld, '*Public Enemy*, at the Young Vic', *The Telegraph*, 18 May 2013.

3   Michael Patterson, 'Brecht's Legacy', in Peter Thomson and Glendyr Sacks (eds.), *The Cambridge Companion to Brecht*, first edition (Cambridge: CUP, 1994), pp. 273–287, here p. 276.

4   Michael Billington, 'When Did "Brechtian" Become Such a Dirty Word?', *The Guardian*, 20 October 2009.

5   Margaret Eddershaw, *Performing Brecht: Forty Years of British Performances* (London: Routledge, 1996), p. 5.

6   John Rouse, *Brecht and the West German Theatre: The Practice and Politics of Interpretation* (Ann Arbor: UMI Research Press, 1989), p. 83.

7   See Martin Esslin, *Brecht: A Choice of Evils* (London: Eyre and Spottiswoode, 1959).

8   Michael Billington, 'B is for Brecht', *The Guardian*, 21 December 2011.

Chapter 1

1   See *BFA* 23: pp. 106–420. Even more is to be found in notes to specific productions with the Berliner Ensemble in *BFA* 24, and the majority of *BFA* 25 contains Brecht's extensive reflective commentaries on his productions of *Antigone*, *Mother Courage* and *Katzgraben* (the name of the rural village where the play is set). For comparison: between 1926 and 1933, the seven-year period between Brecht's exposure to Marxism and the start of exile, Brecht wrote about 470 pages of theory in the standard edition (see *BFA* 21: pp. 119–588). For a key to this and other abbreviations, see the Bibliography.

2   Brecht, 'Two Essay Fragments on Unprofessional Acting', *BoT*
     pp. 206–11, here p. 210.

3   N. J. Schweitzer and Michael J. Saks, 'The *CSI* Effect: Popular Fiction
     about Forensic Science Affects the Public's Expectations about Real
     Forensic Science', *Jurimetrics*, 47 (2007), pp. 357–364, here p. 363.

4   W. Stuart McDowell, '*Verfremdung* … be damned! Putting an End to
     the Myth of Brechtian Acting', *Communications from the International
     Brecht Society*, 38 (2009), pp. 158–168, here p. 159.

5   See, for example, Regine Lutz, *Schauspieler – der schönste Beruf.
     Einblicke in die Theaterarbeit* (Munich: Langen Müller, 1993), p. 84.

6   See, for example, Benno Besson, 'Die Praxis des Berliner Ensembles',
     in Christa Neubert-Herwig (ed.), *Benno Besson. Jahre mit Brecht*
     (Willisau: Theaterkultur, 1990), p. 29.

7   Brecht, 'Does Use of the Model Restrict Artisic Freedom?', *BoP*, p. 239.

8   Brecht, journal entry for 13 November 1949, *Journals*, p. 424.

9   See Brecht, journal entry for 7 February 1954, *Journals*, p. 457.

10   See Brecht, '[Vom epischen zum dialektischen Theater]', *BFA* 23:
     p. 299.

11   Brecht, '[Über die eigene Arbeit]', *BFA* 22: p. 447. *BFA* 25: p. 386.
     Translations from the German, unless otherwise acknowledged, are
     mine.

12   Brecht, journal entry for 18 August 1948, *Journals*, p. 392.
     NB The *Messingkauf* has been retranslated in 2014 as *Buying Brass* for
     reasons that will become apparent in Chapter 2. I will be using the new
     title in the rest of this book.

13   John J. White, *Bertolt Brecht's Dramatic Theory* (Rochester, NY:
     Camden House, 2004), p. 255.

14   See *BFA* 22: pp. 695–869.

15   See *BoT*, pp. 255–8.

16   John Fuegi, *Bertolt Brecht. Chaos According to Plan* (Cambridge: CUP,
     1987), p. 132.

17   Brecht, 'Short Organon for the Theatre', in *BoT*, pp. 229–55, here p. 229.
     Because the essay is organized by paragraph and for ease of reference,
     all subsequent references to this essay appear as 'Organon', followed by
     the paragraph symbol (§) and paragraph number.

18 Anon., 'Zur *Winterschlacht*', undated, Bertolt Brecht Archive 940/13.

19 Brecht, 'Appendices to the "Short Organon"', *BoT*, pp. 255–8, here p. 257.

20 Brecht, '[Hamlets Zögern als Vernunft]', *BFA* 22: p. 611.

21 See Käthe Rülicke-Weiler, *Die Dramaturgie Brechts. Theater als Mittel der Veränderung* (Berlin: Henschel, 1966), p. 221; Manfred Wekwerth, 'Berliner Ensemble 1968. Oder: was blieb von Brecht?', *Theater heute*, 1 (1968), pp. 16–19; and Werner Hecht, *Aufsätze über Brecht* (Berlin: Henschel, 1970), p. 81.

Chapter 2

1 See John J. White, *Bertolt Brecht's Dramatic Theory* (Rochester, NY: Camden House, 2004), pp. 257, 258 and 261.

2 This role is common in German theatre and is now creeping into Britain and the US. It has a variety of meanings, depending on where one works. Dramaturgs, among other things, read copious numbers of plays to help inform a theatre's repertoire; work with scripts, developing new ones and revising older ones; provide contextual information and research for productions; contribute to approaches to staging; can form teams with directors in order to advise on the literary aspects of the texts on stage; and write and/or select material for theatre programmes.

3 Brecht, *Buying Brass*, in *BoP*, pp. 11–125, here p. 11. All subsequent references appear as *Brass*, followed by a page number.

4 Brecht, 'Appendices to the "Short Organon"', *BoT*, pp. 255–8, here p. 256.

5 White, *Bertolt Brecht's Dramatic Theory*, pp. 240–241.

6 Brecht, 'Der Wettkampf des Homer und Hesiod', *BFA* 22: p. 847.

Chapter 3

1 Brecht, *Stories of Mr. Keuner*, translated by Martin Chalmers (San Francisco: City Lights, 2001), p. 20.

2   See Charles Horton Cooley, *Human Nature and the Social Order*
     (New York: Transaction, 1983), originally published 1902.

3   See Francis Fukuyama, *The End of History and the Last Man*, new
     edition (London: Penguin, 1993).

4   Rülicke's book, referenced in Chapter 1, was written after she married
     Fritz Weiler, hence the double-barrelled surname. She was unmarried
     when she worked with Brecht at the Berliner Ensemble, and I have thus
     preserved her maiden name here and elsewhere.

5   Käthe Rülicke, 'Zu den Figuren: 1–32. Probe', Bertolt Brecht Archive
     2071/17.

6   Brecht, 'Short Description of a New Technique of Acting That Produces
     a *Verfremdung* Effect', *BoT*, pp. 184–96, here p. 185.

7   See See Regine Lutz, *Schauspieler – der schönste Beruf. Einblicke in
     die Theaterarbei*t (Munich: Langen Müller, 1993), p. 120; or Hilmar
     Thate, with Kerstin Retemeyer, *Neulich, als ich noch Kind war:
     Autobiografie – Versuch eines Zeitgenossen* (Bergisch Gladbach:
     Gustav Lübbe, 2006), p. 142.

8   Harris, in David Smith, 'Don't Rush to Judge Winnie Mandela, says
     Naomie Harris', *The Guardian*, 21 November 2013.

9   Brecht, 'Short Description of a New Technique', *BoT*, p. 185.

10   Bruce McConachie, *Theatre and Mind* (Basingstoke: Palgrave, 2013),
     p. 15.

11   Jon Ronson repeats a chilling anecdote on psychopaths and empathy in
     The Psychopath Test. A Journey through the Madness Industry (London:
     Picador, 2011), pp. 10–11: '[a psychologist] showed [a psychopath] a
     picture of a frightened face and asked him to identify the emotion. He
     said he didn't know what the emotion was but it was the face people
     pulled just before he killed them'.

12   See Brecht, 'Über die Theatralik des Faschismus', *BFA* 22: pp. 561–569.

13   Brecht, 'Stanislavsky Studies [3]', *BoT*, p. 280.

14   Brecht, 'Stanislavsky Studies [3]', p. 280.

15   See the rehearsal notes for *Mr Puntila and his Man Matti* of 1949
     (Anon, 'Puntila VII. Stellprobe 17. 9. […]', undated, p. 1, Berliner
     Ensemble Archive File 2) and for *Life of Galileo* (B.K. Tragelehn,
     'Notate', undated, n.p., Berliner Ensemble Archive File 23).

16 Brecht, 'Über das politische Bewusstsein unseres Publikums', *BFA* 22: p. 663.

17 Brecht, 'Notes on the Opera *Rise and Fall of the City of Mahagonny*', *BoT*, pp. 61–71, here p. 65.

18 Hans Bunge, 'Tagebuch einer Inszenierung: Bertolt Brecht inszeniert *Der kaukasische Kreidekreis*', undated, Bertolt Brecht Archive 944/104.

19 See Brecht to Konrad Schrader, 14 March 1953, *BFA* 30: p. 120.

20 See Palitzsch, 'Finnische Erzählungen', in Berliner Ensemble/Helene Weigel (eds.), *Theaterarbeit*, pp. 29–31, here p. 29. The following quotation is on the same page.

21 Anon., '*Puntila* VII. Bild, Stellprobe 17. 9. […]', undated, p. 2, here p. 2, Berliner Ensemble Archive File 2.

22 Anon., 'The Universal Declaration of Human Rights', http://www.un.org/en/documents/udhr/, undated, accessed 25 June 2013.

23 Brecht, 'Episches Theater, Entfremdung', *BFA* 22: p. 211. Readers of German will note that Brecht has not yet settled on the term 'Verfremdung' here and still uses 'Entfremdung', 'alienation', in the title, although his meaning is still that of 'making the familiar strange'.

24 Brecht, journal entry of 11 December 1940, *Journals*, p. 118. I have opted for my own translation over Willett's here.

25 See Brecht, '*Verfremdung* Effects in Chinese Acting', *BoT*, p. 156.

26 See, for example, Carolyn S. Vacca, *A Reform Against Nature: Woman Suffrage and the Rethinking of American Citizenship, 1840–1920* (New York: Peter Lang, 2004).

Chapter 4

1 Brecht, journal entry for 9 May 1942, *Journals*, p. 229.

2 Brecht, 'Zweck des Theaterspielens', *Theater der Zeit*, 10 (2004), pp. 34–36, here p. 34.

3 The new edition of *Brecht on Theatre* translates *Fabel* as 'plot'. I argue that the two are separate concepts.

4 Brecht, 'Additional Appendices to the "Short Organon"', *BoT*, pp. 258–62, here p. 258. I have substituted *Fabel* for 'plot'.

5   Carl Weber, 'The Actor and Brecht, or: The Truth is Concrete', *Brecht Yearbook*, 13 (1984), pp. 63–74, here p. 71.

6   Rülicke, '*Leben des Galilei*. Bemerkungen zum Schlußszene', *Sinn und Form*, Zweites Sonderheft Bertolt Brecht (1957), pp. 269–321, here p. 319.

7   Brecht, in '*Leben des Galilei*.Bemerkungen zum Schlußszene', *Sinn und Form*, Zweites Sonderheft Bertolt Brecht (1957), p. 282.

8   Heinz Kahlau, 'Notate *Winterschlacht*', undated, pp. 35, here p. 8, Berliner Ensemble Archive File 18.

9   Egon Monk, 'Mittwoch, 26. Oktober 1949 BB EE und Assistenten V.', undated, pp. 6, here p. 3, Berliner Ensemble Archive File 2.

10 Brecht, 'Additional Appendices to the "Short Organon"'.

11 Brecht, 'About our Stagings', *BoT*, p. 274. Again, I have substituted '*Fabel*' for 'plot'.

12 Brecht, 'The Plot', *BoT*, p. 275, as is the following quotation.

13 Heinz Kahlau, 'Notate *Winterschlacht*', p. 5.

14 Anon., 'Puntila VIII. Bild, Stellprobe 23. 9. BB und Assistenten. P/K', undated, n.p., Berliner Ensemble Archive File 2.

15 Brecht, 'Elementarregeln für Schauspieler', *BFA* 23: p. 185.

16 Brecht, 'Über die Auswahl der Züge', *BFA* 22: p. 688.

17 See Brecht, 'Über einen Typus moderner Schauspielerin', *BFA* 21: p. 214.

18 Meg Mumford, 'Gestic Masks and Brecht's Theater: A Testimony to the Contradictions and Parameters of a Realist Aesthetic', *Brecht Yearbook*, 26 (2001), pp. 143–171, here pp. 144 and 145, respectively.

19 Brecht, 'Die Verschiedenheit um der Verschiedenheit willen dargestellt', *BFA* 22: p. 688.

20 Brecht, 'Showing has to be Shown', in John Willett and Ralf Mannheim (eds.), with the co-operation of Erich Fried, Brecht, *Poems 1913–1956* (London: Methuen, 1976), p. 341. I have substituted '*Haltung/en*' for 'attitude/s'.

21 Benno Besson, 'Drei Gespräche mit André Müller', in André Müller (ed.), *Der Regisseur Benno Besson* (Berlin: Henschel, 1967), p. 20.

22 See Brecht, '[Die Auswahl der einzelnen Elemente]', *BFA* 22: p. 253.

23 See Hans Bunge, 'Tagebuch einer Inszenierung: Bertolt Brecht führt Regie bei seinem Stück *Der kaukasische Kreidekreis*', Bertolt Brecht Archive 945/68–69.

24 Brecht, 'Anmerkungen zur *Mutter* [1938]', *BFA* 24: p. 155.

25 Brecht, quoted in Kahlau, '*Winterschlacht* Notate', p. 25.

26 See Brecht, journal entry for 26 November 1948, *Journals*, p. 404. Brecht uses the word 'Haltung' and thus Willett translates the word as 'attitude', yet 'stance' is more accurate in this context.

27 Brecht, journal entry for 30 March 1947, *Journals* p. 366.

28 Lee Strasberg, *At the Actors Studio: Tape-Recorded Sessions*, Robert H. Hethmon (ed.) (New York: Viking, 1965), p. 387.

29 Brecht, '[Kennzeichen und Symbole]', *BFA* 22: p. 263.

30 Steve Giles, *Bertolt Brecht and Critical Theory. Marxism, Modernity and the 'Threepenny Lawsuit'* (Berne et al.: Peter Lang, 1997), p. 176.

Chapter 5

1 See Brecht to Hans Curjel, 7 February 1948, in *Letters*, p. 444; and Brecht, 'Does Use of the Model Restrict Artistic Freedom?', *BoP*, p. 241.

2 John Rouse, 'Brecht and the Contradictory Actor', *Theatre Journal*, 36:1 (1984), pp. 25–42, here p. 26.

3 Brecht, 'Über die Bezeichnung "restlose Verwandlung"', *BFA* 22: pp. 178–179.

4 'Regine Lutz', in Joachim Lang and Jürgen Hillesheim (eds.), *'Denken heißt verändern…': Erinnerungen an Brecht* (Augsburg: Maro, 1997), p. 79.

5 See Brecht, journal entry for 7 February 1954, *Journals*, pp. 457–458.

6 See Manfred Wekwerth, *Schriften. Arbeit mit Brecht*, second, revised and expanded edition (Berlin: Henschel, 1975), p. 201.

7 See the two flyers in Neubert-Herwig (ed.), *Benno Besson. Jahre mit Brecht* (Willisau: Theaterkultur, 1990), pp. 114 and 116.

8 See Brecht, 'What Makes an Actor', *BoT*, p. 271.

9   See Hans Bunge, 'Tagebuch einer Inszenierung: Bertolt Brecht führt
    Regie bei seinem Stück *Der kaukasische Kreidekreis*', Akademie der
    Künste, Hans Bunge Archive, File 1145, pp. 238–239.

10 B. K. Tragelehn, entry for 16 December 1955, 'Notate', undated, n.p.
    Berliner Ensemble Archive File 23.

11 Brecht, journal entry for 8 December 1940, *Journals*, p. 115. The
    translation here is mine, not Willett's.

12 Brecht, journal entry for 11 July 1943, *Journals*, p. 284.

13 Angelika Hurwicz, 'Brechts Arbeit mit dem Schauspieler', in Hubert
    Witt (ed.), *Erinnerungen an Brecht* (Leipzig: Reclam, 1964), pp.
    172–175, here p. 172.

14 Käthe Reichel, in Christa Neubert-Herwig, 'Wir waren damals wirklich
    Mitarbeiter', in Neubert-Herwig (ed.), *Benno Besson. Theater spielen
    in acht Ländern. Texte – Dokumente – Gespräche* (Berlin: Alexander,
    1998), pp. 33–36, here p. 33.

15 Wekwerth, *Schriften*, p. 111.

16 Brecht, in Anon., 'Über die Arbeit am Berliner Ensemble', in Werner
    Hecht (ed.), *Brecht im Gespräch. Diskussionen und Dialoge* (Berlin:
    Henschel, 1979), pp, 154–174, here p. 159.

17 Brecht, 'The Street Scene', *BoT*, pp. 176–83, here p. 176.

18 Brecht, 'The Street Scene', *BoT*, p. 177.

19 See Angelika Hurwicz, in Bärbel Jaksch, 'Angelika Hurwicz im
    Gespräch', *Brecht Yearbook*, 22 (1997), pp. 155–167, here p. 162.

20 See Brecht, 'Short Description of a New Technique of Acting That
    Produces a *Verfremdung* Effect', *BoT*, pp. 184–96, here p. 186.

21 The text, translated by Edith and Warner Oland, is available
    here: August, Strindberg, *Miss Julie*, http://www.gutenberg.org/
    files/8499/8499-8.txt (accessed 23 July 2013).

22 Craig Kinzer and Mary Poole, 'Brecht and the Actor', *Communications
    from the International Brecht Society*, 20: 1 and 2 (1991), pp. 79–84, here
    p. 82.

23 Bella Merlin, *The Complete Stanislavsky Toolkit* (London: Nick Hern,
    2007), p. 75.

24   I have replaced the official translation ('character') with 'figure' for clarity.

25   Brecht, *Couragemodell 1949*, BFA 25: p. 228.

26   See Brecht, 'The Street Scene' and 'Some of the Things That Can be Learnt from Stanislavsky', *BoT*, pp. 176–83, here p. 180 and pp. 277–9, here p. 278, respectively.

27   Brecht, 'Foreword [to the *Antigone Model 1948*]', *BoP*, pp. 165–71, here p. 169.

28   Brecht, '*Courage Model 1949*', *BoP*, pp. 183–222, here p. 190.

29   Anon, entry for 16 March 1950, *Der Hofmeister*, undated, n.p., Berliner Ensemble Archive File 4.

30   It is registered in the rehearsals of *Mr Puntila and his Man Matti* in 1951 (see Berliner Ensemble Archive File 2) and of Synge's *The Playboy of the Western World* in 1956 (see Berliner Ensemble Archive File 22), for example.

31   Brecht, 'Will man Schweres bewältigen, muß man es sich leicht machen', *BFA* 23: pp. 168–169.

32   See Brecht, 'Will man Schweres bewältigen, muß man es sich leicht machen', p. 169.

33   What is often overlooked, or indeed omitted when the table is reprinted, is Brecht's crucial footnote to the table: 'this table does not present absolute antitheses, but merely shifts of accent' (*BoT* 65).

34   Brecht, 'Short Description of a New Technique of Acting that Produces a *Verfremdung* Effect', *BoT*, pp. 184–96, here p. 194.

35   Brecht, 'Short Description of a New Technique of Acting that Produces a *Verfremdung* Effect', p. 194.

36   Bruce McConachie, *Theatre and Mind* (Basingstoke: Palgrave, 2013), p. 18.

37   Brecht, quoted in Käthe Rülicke, '[*Notate* for rehearsal on 28 December 1955]', Bertolt Brecht Archive 2071/157.

38   Käthe Rülicke to Helene Weigel, 28 January 1955, in Weigel, '*Wir sind zu berühmt, um überall hinzugehen.*' *Briefwechsel 1935–1971*, Stefan Mahlke (ed.) (Berlin: Theater der Zeit, 2000), p. 71.

Chapter 6

1   As with earlier examples, I have substituted *Fabel* for 'plot'.

2   See Brecht, 'On Rehearsing', *BoT*, pp. 50–1, here p. 50.

3   Brecht, '[Originale Auffassungen zu Brechtstücken]', *BFA* 23: p. 127.

4   See Brecht, 'On the Gradual Approach to the Study and Construction of the Figure', *BoT*, pp. 198–200, here p. 199.

5   William Hughes, Jonathan Lavery and Katheryn Doran, *Critical Thinking: An Introduction to the Basic Skills*, sixth edition (London: Broadview Press, 2010), p. 203.

6   Brecht, 'The Attitude of the Rehearsal Director (in the Inductive Process)', *BoT*, pp. 212–13, here p. 212. All subsequent references to the essay are taken from this source.

7   Brecht, 'On Rehearsing', *BoT*, pp. 50–1, here p. 50.

8   Brecht, 'Foreword [to the *Antigone Model 1948*]', *BoP*, pp. 165–71, here p. 167.

9   See Brecht, 'Über den Bühnenbau der nichtaristotelischen Dramatik', *BFA* 22: p. 234.

10 See Hans Bunge, 'Tagebuch einer Inszenierung: Bertolt Brecht führt Regie bei seinem Stück *Der kaukasische Kreidekreis*', undated, Bertolt Brecht Archive 944/19.

11 Berlau, in Hans Bunge, *Brechts Lai-Tu. Erinnerungen und Notate von Ruth Berlau* (Darmstadt: Luchterhand, 1985), p. 288.

12 See, for example, W. Stuart McDowell, '*Verfremdung*... be damned! Putting an End to the Myth of Brechtian Acting', *Communications from the International Brecht Society*, 38 (2009), pp. 158–168, here p. 160.

13 Brecht, quoted in Anon., 'Probe *Zerbrochener Krug* 3. 1. 52', undated, p. 6, here p. 3, Berliner Ensemble Archive File 7.

14 Brecht, quoted in B.K. Tragelehn, entry for 15 December 1955, 'Notate', undated, n.p., Berliner Ensemble Archive File 23.

15 Anon., '*Puntila* – Stellprobe – 1. Bild, 19. 9. 49', undated, n.p., Berliner Ensemble Archive File 2.

16 See Anon., '*Der Hofmeister* – 14a', undated, n.p., Berliner Ensemble Archive File 4.

17 Reichel, reported in Monika Buschey, *Wege zu Brecht. Wie Katharina Thalbach, Benno Besson, Sabine Thalbach, Regine Lutz, Manfred Wekwerth, Käthe Rülicke, Egon Monk und Barbara Brecht-Schall zum Berliner Ensemble fanden* (Berlin: Dittrich, 2007), p. 66.

18 Angelika Hurwicz, in Renate Seydel, ... *gelebt für alle Zeiten: Schauspieler über sich und andere* (Berlin: Henschel, 1975), p. 334; and Egon Monk, *Regie Egon Monk. Von 'Puntila' zu den Bertinis. Erinnerungen* (Berlin: Transit, 2007), p. 57

19 Carl Weber, unpublished interview with the author, 28 May 2010.

20 Lutz, in Holger Teschke, ' "Bei Brecht gab's immer was zu lernen". Regine Lutz im Gespräch mit Holger Teschke', *Dreigroschenheft*, 1 (2009), pp. 5–7, here p. 7.

21 See, for example, Angelika Hurwicz, in Seydel, ... *gelebt für alle Zeiten*, pp. 333–334.

22 See, for example, Carl Weber, 'Brecht as Director', *The Drama Review*, 12: 1 (1967), pp. 101–107, here p. 103.

23 See, for example, Bunge, 'Tagebuch einer Inszenierung', Bertolt Brecht Archive 944/15, for Brecht's critique of his own play *The Caucasian Chalk Circle*: Brecht criticizes 'the author' for being 'sloppy' in some of his formulations and stage directions.

24 Brecht, 'The Zero Point', *BoT*, p. 162.

25 Brecht, 'Abnehmen des Tons', *BFA* 23: p. 174.

26 See Anon., 'Phases of a Stage Direction', *BoP*, pp. 230–2, for a schematic, fifteen-point list of elements that comprised the production process at the Berliner Ensemble.

27 Brecht, '[Die Auswahl der einzelnen Elemente]', *BFA* 22: p. 253.

28 Brecht, 'Schwierigkeiten, denen Burians Konzeption in Berlin begegnet', *BFA* 24: 449.

29 See, for example, Carl Weber, 'Notate [on *Katzgraben* – the name of a village]', Bertolt Brecht Archive 551/19.

30 Anon., '2. Szene – Vorschläge, um den Monolog aufzumachen', undated, Bertolt Brecht Archive 940/11.

31 See, Anon., '*Der Zerbrochene* [sic] *Krug*', undated, pp. 3, Berliner Ensemble Archive File 7.

32 Anon., 'Probe *Zerbrochener Krug* 2. 1. 52', undated, pp. 4, here p. 2,
    Berliner Ensemble Archive File 7.

33 Anon., 'Kleist-Aufsätze. Bemerkungen Brechts', undated, pp. 2, here
    p. 1, Berliner Ensemble Archive File 7.

34 See Anon., 'Probe: *Zerbrochener Krug* 31. 12. 51', undated, pp. 5, here
    p. 4, Berliner Ensemble Archive File 7.

Chapter 7

1 Peter Palitzsch, unpublished interview with John Rouse, 7 June 1988,
   p. II–2–3; and Hans Bunge, unpublished interview with Rouse, 18 May
   1988, p. III–9.

2 See Monk, *Regie Egon Monk* (Berlin: Transit, 2007), p. 87.

3 See Käthe Rülicke, 'Kleine Notate zur Probe von Engel', undated,
   Bertolt Brecht Archive 2071/16.

4 They are not, however, to be confused with the published *Katzgraben-
   Notate* (*BFA* 25: pp. 399–490, some of which also appear in *BoP*): Rülicke
   prepared her documentation for use in the Berliner Ensemble only.

5 Käthe Rülicke, entry for scene I ii 1, 23 March 1953, '[Untitled
   documentation of *Katzgraben*]', undated, n.p., Berliner Ensemble
   Archive File 13. All subsequent references appear as a scene number
   and rehearsal date in the text.

6 Brecht, 'Photographability as Criterion', *BoP*, p. 237.

7 Statistics compiled by the Berliner Ensemble show that in the years
   from 1964–1967, for example, the company sent the 'modelbooks' of
   23 different productions to 165 theatres. 63 remained in East Germany,
   29 went over the border to West Germany, and 73 were sent further
   afield to Europe and beyond, to Cuba, Argentina, the USA, Turkey,
   Ceylon (as was), Israel, and Egypt. See: Anon., 'Berliner Ensemble –
   Modellbücher-Ausleihe', undated, n.p, Berliner Ensemble Archive File
   'Modellbücher: Archiv-Statistik'.

8 Brecht, *Mother Courage and her Children*, in Brecht, *Collected Plays*,
   John Willett and Ralph Mannheim (eds.), vol. 5 (London: Methuen,
   1995), pp. 107–186, here p. 114.

9   Brecht, *Courage Model 1949*, BoP, pp. 181–222, here p. 199.

10   Brecht, *Couragemodell 1949*, BFA 25: p. 231.

11   Brecht, 'Foreword [to the *Antigone Model 1948*]', BoP, pp. 165–71, here p. 167.

12   See the editorial apparatus to the *Couragemodell 1949*, in BFA 25: p. 523.

13   Brecht, 'Einwände gegen die Benutzung von Modellen', BFA 25: p. 393.

14   See, for example, James K. Lyon, 'Brecht in Postwar Germany: Dissident Conformist, Cultural Icon, Literary Dictator', in James K. Lyon and Hans-Peter Breuer (eds.), *Brecht Unbound: Presented at the International Bertolt Brecht Symposium held at the University of Delaware February 1992* (Newark: University of Delaware Press, 1995), pp. 76–88, here pp. 84–85.

15   See Klaus-Detlef Müller, 'Brechts Theatermodelle: Historische Begründung und Konzept', in Jean-Marie Valentin and Theo Buck (eds.), *Bertolt Brecht. Actes du Colloque franco-allemand tenu en Sorbonne* […] (Bern et al.: Peter Lang, 1990), pp. 315–332, here p. 319.

16   Brecht, 'Foreword [to the *Antigone Model 1948*]', BoP, pp. 165–71, here p. 167. All subsequent page numbers in this section refer to this source.

17   Brecht, journal entry for 2 April 1950, *Journals*, p. 426.

18   Brecht, journal entry for 10 January 1951, *Journals*, p. 432.

19   Brecht, 'Creative Evaluation of Models', BoP, pp. 246–7, here. p. 247.

20   Brecht, 'Does Use of the Model Restrict Artistic Freedom?', BoP, pp. 238–42, here. p. 240.

21   See Brecht, 'Creative Evaluation of Models', BoP, pp. 246–7, here. p. 246.

22   See Brecht, 'The Street Scene', BoT, pp. 176–83, here p. 178.

23   Brecht, 'Der nur Nachahmende', BFA 15: p. 166. There is no translation of this important verse in the standard 'Poems' volume. I have thus taken the translation from the following uncredited source: Anon., 'The Theatre of the Future III – Shanzhai & the Interactive Paradigm', 20 September 2012, http://brechtinchongqing.wordpress.com (accessed 1 February 2014).

24   Brecht, *Courage Modell 1949*, BoP, pp. 181–222, here p. 220.

Chapter 8

1   Brecht quoted in Ronald Hayman, 'A Last Interview with Brecht',
    London Magazine, 3:11 (1956), pp. 47–52, here p. 50.

2   See Brecht, *Courage Model 1949, BoP*, pp. 181–222, here p. 221.

3   Brecht, *The Resistible Rise of Arturo Ui*, in Brecht, *Collected Plays*, John
    Willett and Ralph Mannheim (ed.), vol. 6 (London: Methuen, 1994),
    pp. 113–211, here p. 211. All subsequent references to the play appear
    as bracketed page numbers in the main text.

4   In *Arturo Ui*, Dogsborough is the allegorical depiction of the German
    president, Hindenburg. Hindenburg, as the nation's most senior
    political figure, represented the last obstacle to total Nazi dictatorship
    due to his constitutional position and his popularity among large
    swathes of the German populace. Theoretically, he had the power to
    remove Hitler from office (although this conservative politician was
    also the one who appointed Hitler to office in the first place). However,
    this prospect became increasingly unlikely: Hindenburg was already an
    old man when he made Hitler Chancellor in 1933 and died at the age
    of 86 in 1934. The threat he posed to Hitler was thus short-lived, and
    Hitler then set about manipulating his last will and testament to 'show'
    how he favoured the Nazis in general and Hitler in particular.

5   Giri is based on Hermann Göring, the high-ranking Nazi who was
    involved in an ongoing power struggle with Goebbels throughout the
    Third Reich.

6   Ernst Röhm was the head of Hitler's paramilitary storm-troopers, the
    SA.

7   Steven Miles, *Consumerism – as a Way of Life* (London: Sage, 1998),
    p. 4.

8   Robert Bocock, *Consumption* (London: Routledge, 1993), p. 2.

9   Patrick Marber, *Closer*, Daniel Rosenthal (ed.) (London: Methuen,
    2007), p. 47.

10 Marber, *Closer*, p. 110.

Epilogue

1   See, for example, Elin Diamond, *Unmaking Mimesis: Essays on Feminism and Theater* (London: Routledge, 1997).

2   See, for example, Katrin Sieg, *Ethnic Drag: Performing Race, Nation, Sexuality in West Germany* (Ann Arbor: University of Michigan Press, 2002). It is worth noting that both Sieg and Diamond propose building on Brecht's work and not merely accepting it 'as is'.

3   See, for example, Mark Fisher, *Capitalist Realism. Is There Really No Alternative?* (Winchester: O Books, 2009) for a book that takes issue with the narrative that contemporary capitalism is the only choice for the modern world.

4   Brecht, 'The Popular and the Realistic', *BoT*, pp. 200–6, here p. 202.

5   See Brecht, 'Der V-Effekt', *BFA* 22: p. 217.

6   See Wilson, in Holger Teschke, 'Mit dem Körper hören, mit dem Körper sprechen', *Spiel-Zeit* supplement of *Der Tagesspiegel*, February 1998, n.p.

7   Brecht, journal entry for 15 August 1938, *Journals*, p. 13, my translation.

Bibliography
(including list of abbreviations)

Works by Brecht

Brecht on Performance: Buying Brass and Modelbooks, ed. by Tom Kuhn,
   Steve Giles and Marc Silberman (London: Bloomsbury, 2014). Appears
   as *BoP*.

Brecht on Theatre, Third Edition, ed. by Marc Silberman, Steve Giles and
   Tom Kuhn (London: Bloomsbury, 2014). Appears as *BoT*.

Buying Brass in *BoP*, pp. 11–125. Appears as *Brass*, followed by a page
   number.

Große kommentierte Berliner und Frankfurter Ausgabe, ed. by Werner
   Hecht, Jan Knopf, Werner Mittenzwei and Klaus-Detlef Müller (Berlin
   and Frankfurt/Main: Aufbau and Suhrkamp, 1988–2000) [= Complete
   Works in German]. Appears as *BFA*, followed by volume and page
   numbers.

Journals 1934–1955, ed. by John Willett (London: Methuen, 1993). Appears
   as *Journals*.

Letters 1913–1956, ed. by John Willett (London: Methuen, 1990). Appears
   as *Letters*.

Mother Courage and Her Children, in Brecht, *Collected Plays*, ed. by
   John Willett and Ralph Mannheim, vol. 5 (London: Methuen, 1995),
   pp. 107–186.

Poems 1913–1956, ed. by John Willett and Ralf Mannheim with the
   co-operation of Erich Fried (London: Methuen, 1976).

'Short Organon for the Theatre', in *BoT*, pp. 229–55. Appears as 'Organon',
   followed by paragraph number.

Stories of Mr. Keuner, trans. by Martin Chalmers (San Francisco: City
   Lights, 2001).

The Resistible Rise of Arturo Ui, in Brecht, *Collected Plays*, ed. by John Willett
   and Ralph Mannheim, vol. 6 (London: Methuen, 1994), pp. 113–211.

'Zweck des Theaterspielens', *Theater der Zeit*, 10 (2004), pp. 34–36.

Other works

Anon. 'The Theatre of the Future III – Shanzhai & the Interactive Paradigm', 20 September 2012, http://brechtinchongqing.wordpress.com

———. 'The Universal Declaration of Human Rights', undated, http://www .un.org/en/documents/udhr

———. 'Über die Arbeit am Berliner Ensemble', in Werner Hecht (ed.), *Brecht im Gespräch.Diskussionen und Dialoge* (Berlin: Henschel, 1979), pp. 154–174.

Auld, Tim, '*Public Enemy*, at the Young Vic', *The Telegraph*, 18 May 2013.

Berliner Ensemble/Helene Weigel (eds), *Theaterarbeit. 6 Aufführungen des Berliner Ensembles* (Dresden: Dresdner Verlag, 1952).

Billington, Michael, 'B is for Brecht', *The Guardian*, 21 December 2011.

———., 'When Did "Brechtian" Become Such a Dirty Word?', *The Guardian*, 20 October 2009.

Bocock, Robert, *Consumption* (London: Routledge, 1993).

Bunge, Hans, *Brechts Lai-Tu. Erinnerungen und Notate von Ruth Berlau* (Darmstadt: Luchterhand, 1985).

Buschey, Monika, *Wege zu Brecht. Wie Katharina Thalbach, Benno Besson, Sabine Thalbach, Regine Lutz, Manfred Wekwerth, Käthe Rülicke, Egon Monk und Barbara Brecht-Schall zum Berliner Ensemble fanden* (Berlin: Dittrich, 2007).

Cooley, Charles Horton, *Human Nature and the Social Order* (New York: Transaction, 1983).

Diamond, Elin, *Unmaking Mimesis: Essays on Feminism and Theater* (London: Routledge, 1997).

Eddershaw, Margaret, *Performing Brecht: Forty Years of British Performances* (London: Routledge, 1996).

Esslin, Martin, *Brecht: A Choice of Evils* (London: Eyre and Spottiswoode, 1959).

Fisher, Mark, *Capitalist Realism. Is There Really No Alternative?* (Winchester: O Books, 2009).

Fuegi, John, *Bertolt Brecht. Chaos According to Plan* (Cambridge: CUP, 1987).

Fukuyama, Francis, *The End of History and the Last Man*, new edition (London: Penguin, 1993).

Giles, Steve, *Bertolt Brecht and Critical Theory. Marxism, Modernity and the 'Threepenny Lawsuit'* (Berne et al.: Peter Lang, 1997).

Hayman, Ronald, 'A Last Interview with Brecht', *London Magazine*, 3: 11 (1956), pp. 47–52.

Hecht, Werner, *Aufsätze über Brecht* (Berlin: Henschel, 1970).

Hughes, William, Lavery, Jonathan and Doran, Katheryn, *Critical Thinking: An Introduction to the Basic Skills*, sixth edition (London: Broadview Press, 2010).

Hurwicz, Angelika, 'Brechts Arbeit mit dem Schauspieler', in Hubert Witt (ed.), *Erinnerungen an Brecht* (Leipzig: Reclam, 1964), pp. 172–175.

Jaksch, Bärbel, 'Angelika Hurwicz im Gespräch', *Brecht Yearbook*, 22 (1997), pp. 155–167.

Jones, Alice, 'Edinburgh 2013: The Events – David Greig's Play Drawn on Anders Breivik's Norway Killings', *The Independent*, 6 August 2013.

Kinzer, Craig and Poole, Mary, 'Brecht and the Actor', *Communications from the International Brecht Society*, 20: 1 and 2 (1991), pp. 79–84.

Lang, Joachim and Hillesheim, Jürgen (eds.), '*Denken heißt verändern...*': *Erinnerungen an Brecht* (Augsburg: Maro, 1997).

Lutz, Regine, *Schauspieler – der schönste Beruf. Einblicke in die Theaterarbeit* (Munich: Langen Müller, 1993).

Lyon, James K., 'Brecht in Postwar Germany: Dissident Conformist, Cultural Icon, Literary Dictator', in James K. Lyon and Hans-Peter Breuer (eds.), *Brecht Unbound: Presented at the International Bertolt Brecht Symposium held at the University of Delaware February 1992* (Newark: University of Delaware Press, 1995), pp. 76–88.

Marber, Patrick, *Closer*, ed. by Daniel Rosenthal (London: Methuen, 2007).

McConachie, Bruce, *Theatre and Mind* (Basingstoke: Palgrave, 2013).

McDowell, W. Stuart, '*Verfremdung* ... be damned! Putting an End to the Myth of Brechtian Acting', *Communications from the International Brecht Society*, 38 (2009), pp. 158–168.

Merlin, Bella, *The Complete Stanislavsky Toolkit* (London: Nick Hern, 2007).

Miles, Steven, *Consumerism – as a Way of Life* (London: Sage, 1998).

Monk, Egon, *Regie Egon Monk. Von 'Puntila' zu den Bertinis. Erinnerungen* (Berlin: Transit, 2007).

Müller, André (ed.), *Der Regisseur Benno Besson* (Berlin: Henschel, 1967).

Müller, Klaus-Detlef, 'Brechts Theatermodelle: Historische Begründung und Konzept', in Jean-Marie Valentin and Theo Buck (eds), *Bertolt Brecht. Actes du Colloque franco-allemand tenu en Sorbonne* [...] (Bern et al.: Peter Lang, 1990), pp. 315–332.

Mumford, Meg, 'Gestic Masks and Brecht's Theater: A Testimony to the Contradictions and Parameters of a Realist Aesthetic', *Brecht Yearbook*, 26 (2001), pp. 143–171.

Neubert-Herwig, Christa (ed.), *Benno Besson. Jahre mit Brecht* (Willisau: Theaterkultur, 1990).

———, *Benno Besson. Theater spielen in acht Ländern. Texte – Dokumente – Gespräche* (Berlin: Alexander, 1998).

Patterson, Michael, 'Brecht's Legacy', in Peter Thomson and Glendyr Sacks (eds), *The Cambridge Companion to Brecht*, first edition (Cambridge: CUP, 1994), pp. 273–287.

Ronson, Jon, *The Psychopath Test. A Journey through the Madness Industry* (London: Picador, 2011).

Rouse, John, 'Brecht and the Contradictory Actor', *Theatre Journal*, 36: 1 (1984), pp. 25–42.

———, *Brecht and the West German Theatre: The Practice and Politics of Interpretation* (Ann Arbor: UMI Research Press, 1989).

Rülicke, Käthe, '*Leben des Galilei*. Bemerkungen zum Schlußszene', *Sinn und Form*, Zweites Sonderheft Bertolt Brecht (1957), pp. 269–321.

Rülicke-Weiler, Käthe, *Die Dramaturgie Brechts. Theater als Mittel der Veränderung* (Berlin: Henschel, 1966).

Schweitzer, N.J. and Saks, Michael J., 'The *CSI* Effect: Popular Fiction about Forensic Science Affects the Public's Expectations about Real Forensic Science', *Jurimetrics*, 47 (2007), pp. 357–364.

Seydel, Renate, *... gelebt für alle Zeiten: Schauspieler über sich und andere* (Berlin: Henschel, 1975).

Sieg, Katrin, *Ethnic Drag: Performing Race, Nation, Sexuality in West Germany* (Ann Arbor: University of Michigan Press, 2002).

Smith, David, 'Don't Rush to Judge Winnie Mandela, says Naomie Harris', *The Guardian*, 21 November 2013.

Strasberg, Lee, *At the Actors Studio: Tape-Recorded Sessions*, ed. by Robert
 H. Hethmon (New York: Viking, 1965).

Strindberg, August, *Miss Julie*, tr. by Edith and Warner Oland: http://www
 .gutenberg.org/files/8499/8499-8.txt

Teschke, Holger, '"Bei Brecht gab's immer was zu lernen". Regine Lutz im
 Gespräch mit Holger Teschke', *Dreigroschenheft*, 1 (2009), pp. 5–7.

———, 'Mit dem Körper hören, mit dem Körper sprechen', *Spiel-Zeit
 supplement of Der Tagesspiegel*, February 1998, n.p.

Thate, Hilmar with Kerstin Retemeyer, *Neulich, als ich noch Kind war:
 Autobiografie – Versuch eines Zeitgenossen* (Bergisch Gladbach : Gustav
 Lübbe, 2006).

Vacca, Carolyn S., *A Reform Against Nature: Woman Suffrage and the
 Rethinking of American Citizenship, 1840–1920* (New York: Peter Lang,
 2004).

Weber, Carl, 'Brecht as Director', *The Drama Review*, 12: 1 (1967), pp.
 101–107.

———, 'The Actor and Brecht, or: The Truth is Concrete', *Brecht Yearbook*,
 13 (1984), pp. 63–74.

Weigel, Helene, '*Wir sind zu berühmt, um überall hinzugehen.' Briefwechsel
 1935–1971*, ed. by Stefan Mahlke (Berlin: Theater der Zeit, 2000).

Wekwerth, Manfred, 'Berliner Ensemble 1968. Oder: Was blieb von Brecht?',
 Theater heute, 1 (1968), pp. 16–19.

———, *Schriften.Arbeit mit Brecht*, second, revised and expanded edition
 (Berlin: Henschel, 1975).

White, John J., *Bertolt Brecht's Dramatic Theory* (Rochester, NY: Camden
 House, 2004).

Works by Brecht: List of Abbreviations

BFA: *Große kommentierte Berliner und Frankfurter Ausgabe*, ed. by Werner Hecht, Jan Knopf, Werner Mittenzwei and Klaus-Detlef Müller (Berlin and Frankfurt/Main: Aufbau and Suhrkamp, 1988-2000) [= Complete Works in German]. References take the form of a volume number, followed by page numbers.

BoP: *Brecht on Performance: Buying Brass and Modelbooks*, ed. by Tom Kuhn, Steve Giles and Marc Silberman (London: Bloomsbury, 2014).

BoT: *Brecht on Theatre*, third edition, ed. by Marc Silberman, Steve Giles and Tom Kuhn (London: Bloomsbury, 2014)

Brass: *Buying Brass* in BoP, pp. 11–125.

Journals: *Journals 1934–1955*, ed. by John Willett (London: Methuen, 1993).

Letters: *Letters 1913–1956*, ed. by John Willett (London: Methuen, 1990).

Organon: 'Short Organon for the Theatre', in BoT, pp. 229–55.

Index

26212209R00142

Printed in Great Britain
by Amazon